Words From a Friend
A Daily Guide to a Purposeful Life
Copyright 2016 Marty Keary

Editor: Ruth Beach
Cover Photograph: Jeff Foley
Cover Design and Layout: Stacie Gerrity

Printed in the United States of America

Sunny Day Publishing, LLC
Akron, Ohio 44333
www.sunnydaypublishing.com

ISBN 978-0-9903823-8-6
Library of Congress Control Number: 2016955690

To my new friend Molly — Thank You for all you do !

Words From a Friend

A Daily Guide to a Purposeful Life

Much Love —
Marty

Marty Keary

SUNNY DAY®
PUBLISHING, LLC
a health education company ™

NOTE TO THE READER

This heart-full guide was written over the course of an entire year. The book is filled with candor, humor, and also with pain and joy. A real life. A real man.

With each passing day and page, Marty's generous spirit shines bright as he shares his insights with us. In addition to this, each day Marty challenges us to do something in order to activate our own hearts. This "Call to Action" or "CTA," found at the end of each entry, is an invitation for each of us to become active, versus passive participants in our own lives.

It is our hope that as you read these words, they will resonate with your spirit and inspire you to live a purposeful life, too.

The Sunny Day Publishing Team

Introduction

I am just like you. No different. No higher and no lower. I am just a guy who heard the truth and listened.

It's easy to think that wisdom only comes from sages, doctors, holier-than-thou authorities, and people we consider to be professionals. I am none of these. I am just like you.

When I really started to tune in to the wisdom that has been spoken since time began, it sounded true, but at first I wondered how this wisdom would ever fit into the world I had already created. I was afraid my friends, family, and most of the world would think of me as some weird holy roller. But the more I read and the more I listened, the more my newfound wisdom just became a part of me.

I realized that what I thought was the truth, in many areas of my life, was the result of lies of the ego. Lies I'd told myself, beliefs, and paths of others that I'd followed instead of my own, and a lack of grounding in who I really am. Lies that had left me anxiety-ridden, fearful, and with low self-esteem, hoping to fit in.

Yes, I've known all of these feelings, just like you.

What we all must do, my friends, is awaken. It's not about religion, although truth can be found there. It's not about adopting someone else's manifesto as your own. It's about waking up to your own true nature—your goodness and eternal life force.

You are so much more than you think you are. You are amazing and the truth shines its light on you. The more you exercise your own true power, the more it will grow. Your life will expand in amazing ways and problems will present opportunities to use more of your power. Kindness and generosity will become your calling card when you live each day in the marvel of the present moment instead of in the mistakes of the past and the worry of an unknown future. This is the gold within you: inner peace and strength that you've never known.

I am only able to write these words every day because I've tested their truth in every area of my life. And every area has improved immensely because of it. My guidance for my family is sound. My marriage is the best it's ever been and I am truly grateful for all I have. These are no longer just thoughts I practice. They are the real me. The me that I uncovered through this wisdom.

So, I am happy to share my most important credential: I'm just like you. You too can—and must—shed the heavy coat of all the inessentials you've worn for so long. Strip them away one by one. Use the truth as your filter and discard the stuff that never worked for you anyway.

It is my sincere wish that these words from a friend will open your eyes and be a catalyst for your awakening. Waking one another other up from the false nature of the ego and sharing our light every day will indeed change the world. It will most certainly change your life, as it did mine.

Have a great day!

Dedication

First, I dedicate this book to the higher source that brings these words through me, rather than from me. Thank you, Spirit, for writing the right words for those who need to hear them. May they bring healing to all.

Second, I dedicate this book to my closest tribe; my beautiful wife Jan, for her love and support of all our dreams; my children, for giving me the flame inside to write this book. It is my every desire that you know and live your best lives through the lens of love and truth. I pray that these words will help guide you on your own amazing journey. To my loving parents, grandparents and amazing sisters, who have always shown and known the power of love. For this I am truly blessed. And to my beloved family at The Old Daley Inn and Focusmaster Fitness; thank you for helping our dreams come true. I hope we're doing the same for you.

And of course, I dedicate this book to my closest friends and journey mates, Jim Pettit, Gene Coletti, and Tom Blake. You three have been and always will be my best friends and my mentors. You've given me some of the very best memories any man could ask for: laughter, struggle, growth, and new adventures in life. I thank all three of you for the constant inspiration for the subjects I write about and keeping me grounded in what's truly great about life. You guys are the best of the best and I couldn't imagine traveling this journey with anyone else as my best friends.

And finally, I dedicate this book to everyone who has touched my life in any way. Our every encounter has been meant to be, so I thank you for your particular brush stroke in my life's portrait. I hope these words bring value to your life as my personal thanks to you.

May God bless you all with a journey of love, peace, prosperity, growth, and light.

JANUARY 1

The Roles We Assume

We as humans have many roles we play each day. We are fathers, mothers, bosses, employees, friends, confidants, mentors, students, and teachers. Each of us able to give only what we know.

Training for our various roles in life starts at an early age. We learn how we will deal with conflict and adversity by our role models. This can be very good or the cause of most of our suffering.

When you become brave enough to admit that you are 100% responsible for your own results in life, you will be well equipped for positive change in *all* your roles. It is only through the inward journey that we begin to recreate ourselves and our life's course. We choose to begin anew. This ability is the most powerful gift we have—the gift of change and renewal. In other words, when you know better, you do better: a.k.a., growth.

Think for a second about your role as a partner. Are most of your thoughts, reactions, and responses familiar to you? Perhaps the lines you use and the overreactions you are known for simply come from one or both of your parents? I know mine were. I overreacted to everything based on the vibe and tone I felt when any negative news came my way. It's what I witnessed and soaked up as part of who I thought myself to be. I took on the energy of another to fulfill my own roles, never giving a second thought as to another possible response to the very same issue. I just fell right into my usual anxious role. Then I would usually react rather than mindfully respond. I assure you, the outcomes from each are very different indeed. Mindfulness and the wisdom of looking at the same issue from a higher perspective is what brings better results. Every time.

We unwittingly inherit our judgments, roles, and the way we communicate our life's message from our family, our friends, and the people we interact with on a daily basis. Almost 100% of the time, we simply react to life through the prism of these inherited, conditioned beliefs and roles. Most often these are just someone else's handed-down perceptions. What I hope to do in this book is to lead you back to your true self; your authentic spiritual self. The role you were born to play! Underneath all the conditioning, pain, suffering, anger, shame, guilt and fear, lies the real you. It is my hope that these words will lead you to self-discovery and an amazing new journey. A journey filled with love and light; the awakening of your true role in life. You are meant to thrive, grow, and expand. Let this book be the passageway to your unique expression of the energy of unconditional love. That's who you really are anyway.

CTA: What roles do you play each day? Examine them for truth and begin to let go of those that no longer serve you or others.

Have a great day!

JANUARY 2

Taking Responsibility for Our Approach in Our Roles

We have a great responsibility in the roles we play. The goal in all our roles must be solution-oriented rather than blame-, judgment-, and domination-oriented. The one thing that has been 100% true in my life is that there is always a solution grounded in love that works better than the ego's rendition. The ego will always argue for the fist, when an open hand and understanding brings the possibility for new growth for all involved.

Love penetrates and gets to the heart of the matter, because we all feel good in the solution. We stay connected instead of divided. We find common ground instead of taking sides. We play a role that is worthy of all rather than just based on inherited reactions and the methods we've seen demonstrated by others.

So often we assume a new authority role at the workplace, still using old information to lead from. We mix some of the same old us with what we think others want from us. We move up on the outside without ever looking inside and improving upon old methods from outdated models.

My friends, it is incumbent upon all of us to effectively grow on the inside in order to blossom to new and lasting heights on the outside. If you don't, you can expect to stay pretty stagnant. Your thinking must be for the benefit of all and your heart must have a say in all your roles. Love, integrity, good character, forgiveness, apology, kindness, generosity of spirit, and the understanding that we are all in different places in our lives—these are what bring truth into the mix. Only the energy of love in all these forms can truly break through life's toughest problems and daily dramas. Staying in old roles without ever questioning their validity in your current life leads only to mediocrity, surface relationships, and no new growth.

We see this shifting in today's society in many areas. The old models are becoming outdated and we realize their short and long term ineffectiveness from our own growth and loving expansion.

CTA: How can you shift the roles you struggle with to higher ground today? Lead with a new approach. Use your light. I promise, you will get better at it.

Have a great day!

JANUARY 3

Your Unique Awakening

The journey to awakening is an amazing one indeed. It is very personal. Yet there will be many similarities when we begin to break out of the cocoon of the ego into our true selves. Our new decisions are what will be similar. The effects of the growth we choose, as a result, will be the personal part. You will certainly know where you have grown and this process will lead to your inner freedom and peace. When we break the chains of outdated, ego-centric constructs and paradigms (beliefs), we will see ourselves exchanging the old thoughts about ourselves—who we really are and our true purpose of connectedness—for a higher path grounded in Universal truth.

We decide to choose love as our lens to view everything. When the ego has its internal or, worse yet, external reactions, we decide instead to now give space and ask a very crucial question: "what would love say about this same issue?" I guarantee that the plan forward from the truth of love will be quite a different voice indeed, one you can trust to disseminate the same information constructively instead of with ire, judgment, and blame. These are the hammers that defeat the soul of another. We've all been nailed by those. Sometimes we unwittingly nail others in life without realizing how we've affected them. The hammer is fine, but the damage is done. We do this to each other every day, never questioning our methods. Your methods should seem very familiar to you. You've learned them. It is time to learn and live from higher realms and role models.

So today, whatever role you are called to, pack your bag with truth before you unpack your response. Give space to every usual reactionary desire and know full well that there are always two choices as to the path your role can take in every interaction. Make sure it's one you'll want to be remembered for by those you say you love. Oh, and give the same to those you don't even know or necessarily like. They are in the soup too, just like you. Choosing to give love in all your roles keeps you and the vibe around you at its highest level. From here, all goodness enters your life. That's the truth.

CTA: Awakening happens one right-minded decision at a time. Love must be in every one.

Have a great day!

JANUARY 4

The Ego

So I've been talking about the ego and now I'll explain what it is. I'm not talking about someone who has an arrogant, big head about himself, although that too is an outward reflection of the ego. The ego is our false self, the one that is created by our lower energies, our individual negative conditioning, habits we've inherited that don't serve us, and what the outer world tells us to be true.

We are all aware of our personal egos. In most cases we try to hide them from being seen, but in other cases, we let the ego loose on a regular basis. This is when we get ourselves in trouble and feel guilty and ashamed in the aftermath. The contrast between the true self and the ego are very easy to detect when we practice self-awareness and embark on a journey of stripping away these lower energies to increasingly reveal our inner light. The more you practice this stripping away, the better your life becomes.

So simple a concept but so hard to do. I assure you it's worth it. Here are a few examples of the polar opposites of the upper and lower energies. Our true self or spirit vs. our false self or ego. Ego demands we compete, spirit says to collaborate. Ego demands anger and revenge while spirit says forgive and move forward. Ego says *it's them* when spirit says *look inside and see the truth*. Ego says *why them and not me?* Spirit *says you are enough and you have everything it takes to succeed*. Ego says to hate when spirit says to love. Ego says your past defines you when spirit says you are born anew each day and can go forth in confidence and courage. Ego says destroy when spirit says create. You get the picture.

It seems so easy and yet the ego gets the best of all of us from time to time. And yes, some more than others. We need to recognize that none of us is exempt from this earthly truth and that the only way to change is through our personal journey—taking responsibility for what we let out into the world, our relationships, and what we do each day. We need to make the shift from an ego-dominated world to one that lives from the heart. It's the only way we will survive the long haul. We need to tame our ego and let out our true nature more and more in each interaction with our family, friends, and even strangers. What you will find when you do this is more and more of what you are seeking, coming right through your door. Always give what you want in return. Give only the light and that's what you'll get, in many beautiful forms and symbols.

CTA: Begin to listen more deeply, my friend. Begin to decipher which voice is up front and what it wants you to think, say, and do. Your spirit is the more subtle voice and guides, it does not demand. You know which one that is. Know both, but act on only the one.

Have a great day!

JANUARY 5

Letting Go of the Past

If anything in the past keeps you stuck there, you must let go of it in order to live a full, happy, and expanding life. We all have things in our past that we'd rather forget or wish we didn't have to go through, but these things came as either a call to change or a lesson to be learned.

When we hold on to negative experiences for too long, we rob ourselves of the joys and positives we have in our present. Failure or loss in your past does not dictate your present or future unless *you* let it! We've all been hurt, felt loss, had rough relationships, etc. The key to a great life lies in your hands when you decide to let go of the ghosts of the past. If you've lost someone and you have trouble getting over it after years of sadness, guilt, anger, shame, or whatever emotion you find yourself stuck in, please remember that the loved one who is now free would want only for you to be happy and at peace. They too want you to let go so you can enjoy all the joy and beauty your earthly experience has to offer while you are here.

As the famous saying goes, "The past is the wake of the boat. It is left behind and does not power the boat forward." Letting go is a spiritual practice that you need to be mindful of every day. Practicing this art will give you tremendous power to heal yourself and stay in a state of well-being. Letting go of all the little distractions that try to grab our ego's attention every day is a great place to start. Let these distractions blow through you instead of hit you like a brick wall.

Deciding not to hold onto or even control a situation leaves you free to make great decisions and choices in the present. The past and its demands to be in your present all the time is simply an illusion. Negatives we find ourselves constantly clinging to as our compass for the present will only keep us off course and off purpose. It's an old record that you need to discard so that you may be free. Free to create a whole new positive life for yourself and those around you. Forgive yourself for holding on to disappointment, failure, or loss.

You are spirit in a frame of bones and flesh. Inside in our truest form, we are all free. We can be free while we are still here, giving the best of ourselves and showing others the way. Get yourself out of the past and move forward in confidence that your past is gone. Today is a new sheet of paper on which to write your chosen future. It's done only one way, one choice at a time. Choose to be free. Declare that your past is gone and your destiny will be determined by present moment awareness and choice-making. Make the consistent choice to give only the good stuff. You'll be amazed at the result and the legacy you will leave.

CTA: Practice letting go of everything that usually annoys you. Realize you have the choice. Go get it!

Have a great day!

JANUARY 6

Getting Rid of Your Inner Critic

We *all* have an inner critic. You know this voice. It's the one that tells us we're not good enough, or too old, too fat, too skinny, not good looking enough, less than, and even less than less than. These are the despicable lies we tell ourselves each and every day and it's simply not true. You've heard the old saying, "tell a lie long enough and it becomes the truth." Well I am here to tell you that if you speak against yourself in these ways you are simply sabotaging yourself and your chances to live a full and happy life. These are all the tall tales of the ego and they cripple those who decide to believe them.

You need to break your agreement with these lies one at a time. These are lies that most likely started from outside ourselves in our youth, possibly caused by someone who told us we were this or that. Or we looked into the mirror one day and believed the inner critic and held onto the lie for our entire lives to this point.

My friend, this inner critic is a persistent liar who plays both judge and jury. This darker nature we all possess must simply become like rocks on either side of the stream. When we hit these rocks of the ego, we know it's time to get back into the middle of the stream instead of using these rocks to hammer ourselves or someone else. Use the dark side to find your light. Never again should you believe that you are less than anyone else. Ever. In addition, we are also above no one else either! That's another lie we tell ourselves.

The truth is that we all have amazing potential, no matter what our current circumstances are. I assure you, you are much more than you think or know. If you are like most, you have fallen prey to the inner critic and need to break free of the life-sucking lies in your head. We've all gotten lost along the way and the only way to break free of the inner critic is to break our attachment to it. Recognize through present-moment awareness that these are just old stories we decide to keep telling. And I know, to you they've been true. The critic will point out evidence to you that they are true. If this is the case, you need to recognize that you have been attracting these circumstances

14

into your life *because* you believe the lies! You're looking through the lens of the liar. You create your life based on the beliefs you hold about yourself and the outside world. This is your life pattern. You wonder why you keep going through the same drama with the same people? It's because you need to change. Change the recording you tell yourself and what you will start to see is positive change in your life.

I'm sure that you too are sick of the same old patterns you've seen in your life. If it's low energy, destructive behavior, or self-sabotage, today is your day to begin spinning a new record. A record of the good stuff you have to offer. Loving yourself is the first step in this pattern change. This can be difficult if you've believed the lies about yourself. The truth is that the authentic, loving person who is stuck behind this low-energy facade is the real you. The more you let it be your new truth, the greater your life will become. It does take time, but time is what we have been given. It's never too late and you're never too old to know your true self.

Remember, self-awareness, not self-loathing, is the key. Become the witness to your patterns of thought and action and you can start to see your pattern and how it affects you and your life. The critic is a liar. This needs to become your mantra every time you slide into your negative thinking patterns. You are greatness waiting to wake up from a kind of sleep. You've been asleep to the loving truth of who you really are. Say goodbye to the liar. Challenge the lies at every turn. Tell yourself the opposite when the lies come forth and begin to untie those knots you've held onto for far too long. You are awesome and you were created to shine. Anything less is just a lie.

CTA: What are some of the lies you've been telling yourself? Examine them, shine the light of truth on them, expose them and let go of them.

Have a great day!

JANUARY 7

Letting Go of Anger

No doubt this will be a popular subject, as it is a big one for so many of us.

The only time I've seen the use of anger in a positive sense is in response to injustice, when anger is used as a trigger to help right a wrong or bring truth to a lie. And even in these cases, once we feel the anger, we must not stay in that state to move toward a solution. In fact, that would only serve to expand the problem.

We need to shift ourselves when the alarm bell of anger strikes. It's our cue to move to a higher level of energy.

Practice self-mastery and *choose* to be calm, assertive, and right-minded. This means that whatever offense has gotten you ticked off, you should first give it some space before an overreaction occurs, then move to understanding that another's opinion, bad manners, low energy, bad action, or bad attitude is *their* garbage, not yours. We instantly give our power away when we choose anger over higher awareness.

As the saying goes, a solution to a problem cannot be found at the level of the problem. In other words, the low energy of anger rarely solves a problem. Short-term maybe, but as a long-term practice, it poisons you. It poisons your body; it poisons your mind, relationships, families, and this planet.

Many have been raised in a household with an angry parent—always yelling, controlling, mean, etc. As much as we loathed this behavior, it was soaked up as energy within us and we were conditioned to add this negative aspect to our ego's backpack of low energy.

Once again, this comes back to change for you, choosing to take a new path and leaving behind the ghosts of the past. This is the process of stripping away the dark to reveal your light. This happens one choice at a time.

So today, when that familiar sidekick of yours called Anger wants to have a say in any part of your day, you need to respond internally with, *I don't need you anymore. I can choose to calmly solve this issue from a higher perspective* and let it go.

Let go of this hot coal of pain in your hand. You've been carrying it way too long. Have a day filled with light instead!

CTA: What is the hottest coal of pain you've been carrying? Make the courageous decision to begin its release today.

Have a great day!

JANUARY 8

Letting Go of Fearful Thoughts

Yesterday I had the privilege of paying it forward for an awesome friend who spends a lot of time creating in the wrong direction. I know all about this anxiety-ridden path that sucks the life out of us.

When I say creating in the wrong direction, I'm talking about the innate ability to create positive or negative scenarios, or stories in our heads, that have no real basis in truth.

When we as humans begin to believe in and give truth to these stories, we will either be creating positive or negative mind-states. For example, as parents we often create the worst possible stories in our heads about the what-ifs, and we allow ourselves to carry this anxiety as our first line of belief. 99.9% of the time, we are simply lying to ourselves. The same goes for our close relationships, friendships, working relationships, and our outlook and everyday perceptions. We tend to believe everything we think.

If you find yourself constantly creating untrue scenarios in your head, they will spill over into every area of your life and will create everyday experiences that are viewed through lying eyes.

I explained to my dear friend that I know the face of this liar in our head and that we all create this way as part of the human experience. We are all individual creators of our experience here and it begins in our thoughts and beliefs.

This is *very* important: You get to choose how you create by the thoughts you believe to be true. If you consistently believe in, and take action on, your every anxious thought, you will be living in, and reacting to, a nervous mind-state as your normal mode.

Here's some more truth: You can decide to give up and let go of this life-sucking, anxiety-ridden pattern. You can choose *not* to believe the stories you create by calling them out, one at a time, examining them under the microscope of truth, and then taking conscious action, which most times will be no action at all.

CTA: How can you challenge your untrue scenarios? It's all about looking down on them from a higher perspective. Most are not worthy of your attention.

Have a great day!

JANUARY 9

Your Theater of Worry

My friend always believes that if she can't get a hold of her husband and child, they are most certainly lying in a ditch and she must stay vigilant in her constant contact or she will not have control over her life. Sound familiar? It does to me. I also used to create like this. This is the art of creation. It's just using your creative gift in the wrong direction.

The cure? Trust is the cure. Faith is the cure. Belief in a higher power that protects you and your loved ones is the cure. You have the gift of faith, but you choose to believe your worst-case scenario instead.

I told my friend that it is in faith that we are able to say the magic words, "I choose trust" when that scary liar comes a-callin'. When the liar starts spinning its usual frightening tales of death, destruction, or failure, choose the magic words, "I will choose trust instead of you," and then *stop* the expansion of "the story."

The more you practice this faith-filled magic phrase, the better you will get at letting go of your scary script. You know your scary scenario-maker very well, I'm sure. I was great at creating these scripts until I realized how they were affecting my health, well-being, energy, relationships, and my life in general.

Letting go of the horror shows you create and replacing them with faith-filled trust will be your door to the truth. You might ask, "yeah, but what about the times when I was right?" My friends, we will all experience loss, challenge, pain, and suffering, but how we approach life, despite these inevitable, soul-stretching experiences, is our choice. My advice is to always believe you are not alone—not in the physical and certainly not in the spiritual. Trust in the very creative force that loved you into existence and give up trying to control everything. That's not your job! Your job is to love it all and trust it all. Give your worries away to your higher power and start creating in the other direction.

I also told my friend that people who suffer from continual anxious thought are extremely creative. They just haven't learned that they have the power to create in their favor instead of in opposition. Choosing and replacing crappy thoughts with faith-filled, positive ones is where you want to steer your mind ship.

So today, my fellow creators, begin the new journey forward as a student of the positive. When your lying director wants you to write another horror story, give that director his walking papers! Hire the truth as your director. Question and examine each of these scripts for 100% truth. If it is not 100% true, then the opposite is not only possible, but it is where your mind will find peace.

Inner peace is the gold we seek. You own this power. Give it to yourself as a gift of real living. What you're doing now is just believing in an old, worn-out script. *Let this go.* It's life through a pair of lying glasses. If you have difficulty with doing this on your own, there are many who specialize in helping you get past this insidious liar. Seek and ye shall find. Hope this helps. It changed my life.

CTA: Practice saying, "I choose to trust instead." A steady dose of this mindset will bring you to a much better place.

Have a great day!

JANUARY 10

Empty Your Cup

I read a book in my thirties called *Zen in the Martial Arts* by Joe Hyams. I was into Jeet Kune Do, Bruce Lee's martial art, and I read anything that had Bruce's name attached to it. Joe Hyams was a student of Bruce Lee and an author of many celebrity biographies in the sixties and seventies. Joe was already a fifth-degree black belt when he started training with Bruce.

On their first meeting, Bruce told Joe that the most important lesson he would ever teach must happen before beginning any training. He said, "Joe, I want you to completely empty your cup." Joe had no idea what he was talking about. Bruce explained to Joe that he was aware that Joe already had extensive training in karate and that his cup was full of preconceived knowledge, expertise, and confidence. This meant that his cup needed to be emptied of all of this in order to learn a completely new way. For Joe this was going to be tough! His body already knew all the moves. His mind had knowledge that was second nature to him and that's all he knew!

But in order for Joe to learn a completely new approach, he had to set aside all preconceptions and, especially, judgments. Bruce was actually teaching an ancient philosophy in asking Joe to empty his cup so that it could be refilled with the truth of Bruce's art.

This was a lesson to me as well. We must all empty our cup in order to move to a new way of thinking, approaching life, and being. We have to let go of much of what we were taught as kids or by those around us. If the info you've been given is average, so will be your path.

All success, whether personal or professional, comes from a deeper place than most of us know. It's the place where all success lies. Finding this place is the true journey and can seem ethereal or nonexistent to most but I assure you it is real and the energy that comes from this place is already familiar to you. It is your true self. This is the one that may only whisper to you now, but can become your one-stop shop for personal fulfillment and success. If you become an inner success, your outer success is a given. Dare to take this journey and see yourself and the world outside you change for the better. I'm not speaking from a holier-than-thou, religious position. I am speaking from a simple truth. You are a powerful being who can accomplish anything you wish and your spirit knows the way. Always. Exploring, seeking, and learning this will unlock your best self and you'll start to see doors opening that you never dreamed possible. Dare to dream, my friend! It's what we are here for. Your heart, your spirit, your higher awareness, or whatever you call it, is the best and fastest way to a great and amazing life. So today, empty your cup and fill it with new intel. Remember, garbage in, garbage out! Great, positive info in, your best self out! Go get it!

CTA: Visualize emptying your cup of all preconceived beliefs and egoic absolutes. Stay open to all possibilities instead of just a few. There are no limits my friend.

Have a great day!

JANUARY 11

Forgiving Yourself: Letting go of guilt, shame, and your past

Guilt and shame are useless emotions for the person of power. These two guns of your ego shoot both ways. Sometimes we shoot them at others in an effort to control them. Most often, we shoot ourselves and leave the bullets within us for a lifetime.

Forgiving yourself is the first order of business, so we can release our need and desire to use these guns.

Why do we carry burdens of the past that continue to pop up at will and make us suffer for them all over again? Unfortunately it is because we feel we've done something so ugly that we need to punish ourselves over and over again.

Your decision to hold on to this backpack of burdens is the very thing that is holding you back. Holding you back from being all God created you to be. Holding you back from expressing your best and highest self and holding you back from giving and receiving unconditional love from yourself and those around you.

Guilt and shame are just a couple more examples of the lower energies of your ego or false self. Just recognizing and accepting this truth will give you power to move past your past and into the present moment, where your true power to change lies.

Each day is like the gift of a brand new life. You need to finally take off your backpack of woes, forgive yourself for carrying it for *way* too long and move forward with a new vision of yourself and your life!

You know you are always forgiven from above, you know your family and friends who have crossed over and now watch over you would tell you to forgive and move on! So now, finally, it's your turn to help yourself! *Let it go!*

CTA: Visualize putting down your backpack of burdens. What must you let go of? That's your spiritual work my friend.

Have a great day!

JANUARY 12

Giving Up What No Longer Belongs

Have faith that your new life is certain to be better without the backpack and ego guns, because that fact is *assured*!

Hear me now and plug this into your success software: anytime you choose to let go of more and more of your ego and its low-energy demands, you become more light. Literally and figuratively. More light = better life experience. It's a simple choice that only takes practice. It is the most powerful of all practices. Let go of the dark and let in *your* light.

Today begins your new, forgiven, and forgiving life. Shifting your mindset to forgive quickly, not being offended, not holding grudges or spreading gossip, getting rid of judgment of others and yourself, spreading as much of your light as possible—this is your new path; your new path of greatness. Get started!

CTA: Visualize your new path and make it what you want to see. You can't create what you don't visualize. Don't let others give you this vision. You are the captain!

Have a great day!

JANUARY 13

Permission to Move Forward

When we have gone through or are currently going through a life struggle, like a divorce, breakup, or death of a loved one, we tend to get stuck in a negative emotional state for a period of time. Grieving or sadness is completely normal during these times and it is important to let these emotions out and express our feelings. If we don't go through this process, we bottle up these feelings and it affects all we do with the constant undertone of negative repression. We haven't internally or externally resolved and accepted what has happened.

If we are not able to process our emotions properly, we get stuck. Stuck in a pattern of low energy which, left unchecked, can lead to anxiety, depression, and an unfulfilled life.

We need to always move forward no matter what the circumstance. If it's a lost loved one, he or she would want you to be happy and live a full life until you see each other again. And I assure you, you will. If it's a divorce or breakup that cannot be mended, you need to accept this first and foremost and then decide to move forward.

Some people will stay stuck in low energy until they are told by someone outside themselves to get moving. For some reason, we need permission to move forward. It is so very helpful to have a close friend or even a professional healer of some sort help us through this, but ultimately, we need to be brave and give ourselves the permission to move forward.

There will inevitably be some bumps in the first stretch of road, but with your mind set on forward motion only, you will absolutely find your way and you will succeed. You need to be your own best friend during these times and treat yourself well. "What if' and "woe is me" has no place in forward motion. Only solution-oriented thinking and plenty of self-caring and love. If you are blessed to have close friends and confidants, lean on them during the tough moments but always declare to them and yourself that "I will rise from this and live my life!" It is your duty to do just that!

CTA: Who around you can help you in your forward journey? Find the most loving and compassionate in your circle and seek some wisdom. Be still and listen for the cues from within. It's all coming for you. Let it in.

Have a great day!

JANUARY 14

Rise

You are unlimited! You have this one life that is blessed by God and he wants you to be strong; to heal and rise to a higher level of understanding and victory—understanding yourself and victory of overcoming a big life change. It is there for your growth, not for your demise. This is the thought of a person of power. "I will grow from this experience. I will not wither and die. I have the same energy as my creator and anything is possible."

These are your mantras for times such as this.

Hear me now my friends who find yourselves stuck: *you have permission to move forward!* Anyone who loves you will tell you the same. Pick yourself up today and declare, "I start my upward climb today!" You will have help along the way. But *you* be your own champion. Be determined to blow through tough moments! The light you seek in your life is *you*. Rise up and take command. Move forward with strident determination and figure out the details as you go.

Today your new life calls you! Answer that call with faith and power.

CTA: What is your new life calling you to do? If it makes you feel good and full of light, follow it.

Have a great day!

JANUARY 15

The Mirror

Want to know what state of energy you are in? Notice the effect, or lack of effect, you are having on the people and the world around you. Are you feeling great much of the time? Or are you on more of a roller coaster of negative and positive, feeling less than in control?

You draw to yourself just what you give as your predominant field of energy. Your job is to become a great steward of what you emit. Your job is to live in your own favor; on your own behalf, so to speak. Discard the energies that have produced only scary, angry, jealous, judgmental reflections in your mirror and the mirrors of those around you. So many of us are still asleep to our true power and potential. We live at half-throttle at best, or in park or reverse at worst. You always have the choice to live in high gear; high, peaceful, loving, prosperous gear. The key to unlocking your high gear is all about how much attention you give to your daily practice of living and giving your very best.

Your very best energy that you have within you today will improve more and more, like anything else you give your attention to regularly. Your focus, your intentions, and what you give away as your life's message is your magnet to more; the abundance of all good things, opportunities, and beautiful relationships. Just be sure to give away exactly what you want to see in your own life; in your own mirror. It's a simple concept that just takes time and practice to master. No other practice in your life will glean as much for you as this one. It's the worthy path.

So today, look in the mirror. Give thanks for that beautiful reflection you see. Bless that reflection, for you are looking at spiritual royalty. That person you see is capable of anything. Give your very best love to that reflection every day. Speak in its favor, celebrate its victories and let go of old reflections. Smile constantly and tell that reflection that it's all possible. Because it is.

CTA: Look in the mirror. Give thanks for that beautiful reflection you see.

Have a great day!

JANUARY 16

Keep Your Mirror Clean

A quick way to remember how your energy affects your life and the lives of those around you is to picture the world as a massive mirror, reflecting back to you all your perceptions and actions. What you give is what you get.

Life is all in your approach to it. You have basically two choices when you get out of bed in the morning as to how your day will go: positive or negative. If we do not decide or intend to have a positive day, filled with harmonious dealings, giving our best self away and being productive, we fall prey to whatever comes our way. We will suck in the negative thoughts, actions, and perceptions of another and they will usually become our own.

If you decide to have a positive day, keeping your mirror clean, you will see the following looking back at you: Smiles; because you are smiling, laughter; because you are creating it, harmony; because you are giving it, and love; because you've decided to share it. This is what your mirror should be reflecting back to you. If it's not, you've got some Windex-ing to do.

Deciding to be a positive force in the world brings all good things to you like a magnet. When you're determined and committed to this practice, it just becomes your way. Remember, there is no *way* to happiness. Happiness *is* the way.

Leading with a happy demeanor and approach will open doors, lower the defenses in others so clear communication and cooperation can take place, and smooth out any rough edges in your day.

The world is a mirror, my friends. If you don't like what you see in it, you owe it to yourself and others to look deeper into it and wipe anything off of it that does not allow you to see your true reflection.

CTA: Today, begin the day with intention: "I will shine my light today. It is my choice in every moment and I choose to give my best self today. I will start this day determined and I will end it satisfied with what I gave."

Have a great day!

JANUARY 17

The Power of Sleep

We all know how important it is to get a great night's sleep, but did you also know that sleep is a spiritual practice?

Sleep is actually letting go. As in the letting go you always hear as the best way to move forward in life. Let go and let God, or Just let it go. I know most of you understand the meaning of this, and we do our best to do this, but yes, it can be *very* challenging.

Sleep offers us this innate miracle every day. Releasing all the pent-up mix of energies you've absorbed during your day is why sleep is *so* important. Sleep allows us to escape and be free for a bit. Leave the confines of the body. And if your daily practice is sound, you are better able to leave the confines of your mind for a time as well. Meditation is also able to do this for you and I highly recommend it.

We need to realize that the natural power of the altered state of sleep can be harnessed and used as a very powerful tool during your waking hours as well. In fact, in order to fully awaken to all your natural powers and gifts, the moment-to-moment practice of letting go and staying free is an absolute requirement. One you will love, once you set forth with determined, spiritual will and faith. You must trust that every single time you intentionally let go of some drama, struggle or whim of your ego, you have just blazed another fifty feet of a new life's path; the very path to your total freedom, the path of giving and receiving the very best life has to offer.

Living in the present moment, as an intentional practice for the rest of your life, coupled with truthful self-awareness and improvement, is the way in. Letting go of your troubled past and the old energies that helped to create it is the next step in this daily practice. This is the most challenging part for most, because we've added on so many unnecessary layers of self-judgment, jealousies, dramas, and negativity to ourselves, that we've let them become a large part of our identities. This, my friends, is your wake-up call. You are not these layers you've added. They can be removed one at a time with intentional, loving forgiveness and letting go of your habit of holding onto them. That's all they are now, just a bad habit that never serves you or anyone around you. When you wake up to this truth, change is at your door. Let it in and never look back. Look forward to only what you truly desire from here forward. *Prove* the very opposite of what your ego tells you is true. Constantly challenge the liar in your head that tells you that you are less than, or more than, anyone else. Release these habits as you release the daily tensions of the day during sleep.

Constantly give loving kindness, acceptance and non-judgment as your daily, awakened practice, and you'll be in the very energy that naturally releases negative layers during your day. This vibration you emit while in this giving mode is like a steady stream of absorbing the good and naturally releasing the negative. Be present. Give your best in the present. From here, your future takes care of itself. This is the path you are blazing now to a beautiful, fulfilling life.

So today, stay in the flow of giving and receiving the very best. The flow of Unconditional Love is always available to us. We must release the blockage to our sun within. From the sleep of the negative you must awaken. When you do this, your life will be an amazing dream come true. You can do it. It's just practice. Own your life, my friends!

CTA: Are you on your desired path? Write down what you want it all to look like. Keep this list where you see it every day and move on it all in small great ways. This will all add up over time and evidence of it will begin to be shown. Keep going.

Have a great day!

JANUARY 18

Awakening

I believe that we are in the time of awakening, despite the horrors of this world.

I believe we are finally becoming aware of the ego as the true enemy, and the only way to win this battle is for all of us to awaken. Maybe I'm an idealist, but I know it is our true destiny to live peacefully with each other here in the physical world.

The ego is the crazy bastard in the room and it needs to be exposed for its real agenda in our current world. You see the results of the ego's antics every night on the Evening (bad) News. Every horror story you see and even the ways they're sold to us are part of the agenda of the ego world. Politics is the high-stakes poker of the ego. It's the biggest ego game on the planet. Divide and conquer, hate, our side, their side, intolerance, and all-out war. All are games of the ego. It all starts in the micro, like your home, and then projects itself outward to the macro, or the world as a whole. You get it? This is why what you give as your personal energy matters so much. What are you personally contributing to the overall energy? It matters. You are 100% responsible for what you contribute. Make sure it's your best.

I believe we must have needed the ego during our formative years as a species. God makes no mistakes. But now I believe the shift in consciousness is in full swing and the need for such a negative teacher is coming to a close. A heart-centered planet is the goal. Always has been.

The contrast that the ego has supplied to us has shaped us and taught us the rules of nature and how to survive in the physical world. This negative force got carried away within man and for most, it became us. We forgot who we really are. This is the old, worn-out paradigm of this place we temporarily inhabit.

CTA: Notice the negative ego force around you. Is there something, or someone, that contributes to it disproportionally in your life? Make the shift, make the changes. Do it all with loving kindness.

Have a great day!

JANUARY 19

Releasing the Old Paradigm

The ego and the wars it causes, both in our personal worlds as well as the world as a whole, is outdated. It is no longer necessary as the signpost for the opposite of truth. Not if we do our jobs, awaken, and spread truth; real truth. Not man's truth that's fed to us and keeps us asleep, but inner truth. Truth that we are indeed all connected at the level of the soul and that we buried ourselves in the lies of the ego and its horrible agenda. Love is the opposite of ego. It's the only true cure for what ails you and this planet. Spreading it is the antibiotic to the infection.

Your job is to awaken, my friends. Stop living a mediocre or less-than-your-full-potential life. The very energy of life is, in fact, pure positive potential. Tapping into this stream of endless possibilities will only come to you in small spurts, unless and until you consciously choose to work with it, learn it, uncover it within you, and adopt a consistent, higher way forward.

The stripping away of your ego and its many ugly faces will be your vehicle to awaken your true power. It is the road less traveled, but it's the only worthwhile road to take. The other road is needless suffering.

So today, start opening your eyes and your mind. Learn, grow, and be steadfast on your new path. It always happens one awakened choice at a time. Never give up and never give in.

CTA: You can best help yourself and humanity by choosing kindness over ego. Do your very best.

Have a great day!

JANUARY 20

The Power of Taking 100% Responsibility for Your Life

This is probably the most important lesson to learn if you want to know your true power and have a life of greatness. But most choose the opposite.

Take 100% responsibility for your thought life first, then for your actions based on those thoughts, and finally, the results of those actions, or non-actions. This is where you get to know what a powerful, personal, creating machine you are.

Your life is *always* created by this very process. Once we know this, we can do better and thus create better.

When we choose to go the opposite road of blaming others for our misfortunes, we have left our power. We have decided to continue on a path of a victim. There is nothing you want on this road my friends, nothing. No character, no integrity, no positive change, and certainly no true success.

The mistakes of the past are gone and there's no changing those outcomes. However, right now, in this present moment, you can choose to rise. Rise above the negative voice that tells you that it's everyone else's fault. That is the voice of the liar in your head, known as your ego.

The only thing blaming others will ever get you is stagnation and a low-level life. You will continue to have the same type of experiences returning to your doorstep because you choose not to learn the lesson you are being given.

God gives us many opportunities every day to get it right, but it is our choice and our job to take them. Growth is what we are here for and it is always attained through taking 100% responsibility.

Remember, it always begins with changing our perception and thinking for ourselves on a higher level. Higher thoughts, like "I am not a victim, I am a victor," are the new pattern you must choose. Other power thoughts are, "I can overcome any obstacle and will learn from each challenge," "I will never give up on creating a better life for myself, and my only true job is me," and "I will always get up and I will always move forward with this new knowing."

From this place, truth enters the room and your power to rise above any challenge is found. If you are at the center of a seemingly negative occurrence, there's a lesson to be learned and a diamond of wisdom, just for you, in the bag of negativity you've been handed.

CTA: Is there a diamond in your bag of negativity? I assure you there is. Start removing the unnecessary today.

Have a great day!

JANUARY 21

The Great Way

Making positive changes in you is always the goal. This is literally a job for life. But it's the job that gets you all you need and desire. Taking the high road to success starts with personal responsibility.

Everyone knows and admires someone with this personal compass. When we are truthful with ourselves and we take responsibility for our part, we have chosen to grow and we have displayed true character, which everyone recognizes.

Admitting mistakes, taking our lumps, apologizing, and forgiving ourselves for falling short will be part of the path to success. It is never weakness to admit you've made a mistake and take responsibility for it. It is, in fact, true power on display. Know this and adopt it as a core principle for your life. Truth will always set you free and it will keep you free-flowing with great energy and great outcomes. Always.

Better results or a shift to a higher life pattern of goodness flowing into your life, instead of drama and negativity, always begins and ends with you and your thoughts, actions, and choices.

Continue to make only the choices that serve you rather than sink you. Common sense and positive self-talk go hand in hand in making good choices. Always demand the best choices from yourself and for yourself. Keep your eye on the prize and move forward, determined to rise and do better. Your whole future depends on the choices in every moment. Always remember that you are the master creator of positive or negative in your life.

We *all* make mistakes, each and every day. It's how we learn and grow. Weed your gardens, friends, and seed your life with self-awareness and truth. You'll always know greatness on this road.

CTA: Make the life-giving choice to take 100% responsibility for your thoughts, perceptions, speech, and actions. At the end of the day, give yourself a loving critique and move forward with the information you gathered and the lessons you learned.

Have a great day!

JANUARY 22

Self-Talk: Becoming the captain of your ship

Have you ever examined your daily mantras? We all have a pattern of beliefs that channel themselves as our thoughts. If you're not being the vigilant witness behind your thoughts, you are on a life ship with no captain at the wheel.

From the time of our birth, we are handed a slew of perspectives, prejudices, and beliefs that are not our own. If we are not mindful, we will live a life through another's perspective instead of choosing our own.

How you talk to yourself in your mind must become priority one. Do you consistently put yourself last in line? Do you constantly doubt your ability to succeed in any area of your life? Is your self-talk riddled with self-judgment, judgment of others, and less-than-kind thoughts on a regular basis? Then *you* are not the captain of your ship. You've handed over the wheel to the whim of your conditioned mind. You'll never change. You can expect to stay in a very shallow harbor, stuck in the sand, with no steady wind to guide you to new destinations.

It's time to grab the wheel.

Beginning to infuse new thoughts and beliefs into your mind will be the turning point to a new destination. Even a one-degree shift in your course will take you new places; places you never thought possible for yourself.

What positive influences are you diligently pursuing in your everyday life? If you just live and think the same way every day, guess what you can expect?

Your mind is like a map, my friends. It delivers new, improved results when you decide to chart a new course with new coordinates. Without new information and a new map to look at on a regular basis, how could you ever expect new and brighter destinations? You simply must grab a new map.

Becoming a seeker of wisdom and true knowledge will put you firmly back at your wheel, maybe for the first time in your life. But that's ok. We all begin to awaken at our own time.

CTA: Choose this moment as your time.

Have a great day!

JANUARY 23

Feeding Yourself

My recommendation, especially if you enjoy these daily entries and wisdom one-liners they contain? Get to the bookstore, or go online and type in "self-improvement" or "self-development." There's a slew of great authors and teachers of the wisdom I write about every day.

You will begin to download the truth as part of your daily diet and before long; your self-talk will begin to shift. You'll find yourself questioning old, worn-out ideas, thoughts, and beliefs. You'll finally shine the light of truth on your destructive, habitual thoughts. You will dismantle the thick walls you thought were there to protect you but in fact were just holding you hostage. You are unshackling your chains. You have found the key that was always there.

So today, do not waste another minute of this gift called the human experience. You are here to live! To explore! To find joy and beauty in all areas of your life! The only way to live with the treasured inner peace and happiness that you've always longed for is to uncover it! It's under all the lies, misperceptions, and ugly self-talk that you have endured to this point. Make the choice of positive change today. You only have to live one day at a time. Make each day a victory for yourself. You are the captain.

CTA: Start a search for more books like this one that can help you continue on your new chosen path. Good stuff in means good stuff out.

Have a great day!

JANUARY 24

Character

It's said that character is how you behave when no one is watching.

Do you ever contemplate this person you've created? Do you ever spend time sculpting and improving the character you play on the stage of life?

We become what we *believe* ourselves to be, my friends. You are a spirit on an amazing trip to the physical. If you are not working on the character you play in this human adventure, you're missing out on living the role of a lifetime—the role you were born to play.

Character, your character, is very unique indeed. With all the billions of souls on this planet, *you* are unlike any other. You are like a snowflake— similar to the others, yet singularly beautiful, with unique talents and gifts to give, a unique laugh and sense of humor, unique style and sense of purpose, and, of course, a unique perspective on life itself.

Life itself shapes our character. The dark times are when your true character shows itself. These dark times show your strengths, your weaknesses, your heart, your commitment, and your capacity to love.

Life itself can be the beautiful master sculptor, or it can seem like it's got it out for you. Developing your character *on purpose* is how you learn to become the sculptor, instead of remaining a rudderless victim of seemingly random circumstance. Life brings to us just what our character is offering to life. Once again, the very reflection of what you put in front of the Universal mirror. A shady character always produces a chaotic life, while a great character, grounded in principle and truth, always produces a beautiful reflection.

This a why it is *so* important to keep sculpting, to keep growing, and to keep doing what works, while constantly releasing those lower elements that have never worked and never produced what you truly desire.

CTA: Are you the sculptor of your own life? Pick up the chisel today and never put it down.

Have a great day!

JANUARY 25

Essential Elements

What are the elements of a great character? You know them. They are the ones you admire in others but don't always believe that you possess.

You do possess them. The very best elements that bring all goodness into your life are actually those of the real you; the eternal you. This is the voice of all positive change within you. This voice whispers to you. It's not the loud, angry, jealous, fearful voice that you've allowed to create much of your character to this point. It's the more subtle voice of truth that you don't always choose to hear. It is in making higher choices that we learn to become the master sculptor.

Integrity, honesty, generosity, empathy, cooperation, non-judgment, acceptance, kindness, collaboration, gratitude, persistence, positive attitude, great work ethic, keeping promises, forgiveness, moving forward, helping others move forward, wanting the very best for yourself, your family, friends, and total strangers. Giving love as your calling card and gifting others along your life's path. These are the elements to nurture. These are the gifts to give. This you is the one to constantly focus on and develop. Use these elements as your daily guidance system and your character, and your life, will be amazing. *Guaranteed*!

You are the master sculptor of your life. Never take this job for granted. Pick up the chisel of truth and begin the new process of chipping off the unnecessary to reveal the true character you came here to be. Be amazing! It's just a better choice.

CTA: Contemplate your character. Be brave enough to admit you've fallen short in some areas. Look inside and say *yes* to that subtle voice that calls you to rise higher.

Have a great day!

JANUARY 26

It's All in Your Approach

No matter what you do in life, your approach is everything.

Whether it's a simple phone call, conversation, job interview, difficult interaction or exciting new chapter of life, be sure you're putting your very best out front. First impressions are *always* about your approach.

The key is to have your heart open, your guard down, and a giant, confident smile on your face. This assures others that no matter how small or big the situation is, you come in peace and desire the best outcome for everyone involved.

Always bring your confident self when you leave your home for the day. Keep your eye on the prize and approach every interaction in your day with a happy countenance. This approach opens all doors, brings down defenses, and spreads your good will.

Always have your giving nature as your leading energy. You will attract back to yourself the very best opportunities, which will compound and multiply as you continue this open, trusting approach. If you go into any situation with your ego in the lead, including suspicion, anger, resentment, jealousy, fakery, or nervous energy, your outcome will often be less than successful.

Leading life in these lower energies will always attract the very same back to you. Is this what you really want? Always make sure you go into any life situation asking yourself the question, "What outcome do I want from this interaction?" If I am correct, you're not looking for a feud, a struggle, a loss, or bad energy, right? Then do not bring yours to the party!

In the unusual case that your great energy approach doesn't seem to penetrate another's negative attitude, always remember to keep yourself in that great state, wish the other a better day, outwardly or silently, and move on! It's not your job to change others. Your job is always just you. Everyone you touch will benefit from your approach. And the tough situations will be so much better than they would have been.

CTA: Today, pack your bags with your best self and then unpack them everywhere you go.

Have a great day!

JANUARY 27

Your Vibe

Everyone has a vibe, an energy. We can all feel each other's energy and we usually describe it as a mood. But we all have a pretty regular field of energy that emanates from us. This energy field is something that is compiled of our thought patterns, our actions, and our attitude toward life.

If I asked you to describe the high-energy, positive people in your life, I'm sure you could come up with a quick list. In contrast, we all have a list of the lower-energy people around us. The questions we all need to ask are these: where do I fall in the spectrum of energy? What is my pattern of thoughts, attitude, and actions? Do I live intentionally or just let my mood dictate my life?

The truth is this is one area of life that we have control over. And it happens to be the area that attracts great people, things and circumstances, or just the opposite. Constant complaining, for example, only attracts more things to complain about. Conversely, gratitude always attracts more things to be grateful for. It's pretty simple—good stuff out brings good stuff in. It's called the Law of Attraction. In sure you've heard of it.

The thing to remember about this law is that you attract what you are, not just the thoughts you think. If you want a steady stream of joy, happiness, and success, you must become and radiate these as part of your vibe. It must be real, and real is just practice perfected. You can shift and shape your vibe every day by practicing what you want to see entering your life. If you see or work with a curmudgeon every day, notice the people and circumstances they attract. It's probably pretty dim or chaotic at best.

On the other hand, that happy-go-lucky character that seems to love life and lives it to the fullest has many great experiences, friends, and opportunities. This all comes from their vibe.

The good news for the curmudgeon is that they, too, have the capacity to raise their vibe and their life to new heights. It starts with the willingness to change and uncover their true inner self. It may not be easy at first, but once they begin to see the awesome results appear, it becomes easier and a much more fulfilling path.

How would your friends describe your vibe? Maybe you're hanging with a low-energy group. If this is the case, they may not understand your new path. In any case, raising your vibe intentionally and consistently will raise your life experience to a whole new level. And there are no limits as to how high you can go. Start your new path today and seek out some of the info that will help you along. Digest it, ponder it, and make it your new thought pattern. You can either soar with the eagles or stay with the crows. The choice is always yours. Go after it today and build your new life on a solid foundation of truth.

CTA: Notice your vibe today. Is it one that elevates yourself and others? You raise it by giving your best.

Have a great day!

JANUARY 28

A Noisy Mind Knows No Peace

In today's lightning-paced world, multitasking seems to be a must. We work while listening to the radio or with the TV on in the background or even hold conversations while reading our emails.

We all do it, but does it really serve us? Usually, what we find at the end of a long day of this attention-grabbing, high-speed world is a very noisy, stressed-out mind and body. This is the norm in our society and it leaves us drained of vital energy and the will to practice any presence or peace.

Creating a peaceful mind and using this peace to guide your day and your life is a treasure worth seeking. Practicing the art of a peaceful, present self is the gold we seek. Devoting twenty minutes of silence each day will go a long way towards training your mind to be calm and quiet. Once you get a few months under your belt, you will begin to notice yourself becoming mentally sharper and easier in the way you approach challenges, including challenging people.

Calm energy in the face of chaos is the only way to make truly sound, heart-centered choices and decisions. If we go through life like a rat trap waiting to spring, we will make snap judgments, decisions, and choices that will not serve us and most likely will hurt us. You created your noisy mind by not realizing the life-giving importance of calmness. Your mind can be, and most likely has become, like a cage of monkeys that cannot be controlled by your outer will. Calmness, therefore, must be practiced like any other energy. And boy is it worth it! I often use Cesar Millan, The Dog Whisperer, as a perfect example of someone who understands that calm energy can calm even the most irate pit bull.

This is also true of people. You cannot know calm, right-minded thought and energy by using chaotic, hurried, or nervous energy. Just doesn't work. This twenty minutes of calm will create a new space for you to know within yourself. This will become the space you are able to go to in times of challenge or when you're in the midst of negative, harried energy from others.

It's so easy just to take on the nervous energy from some of our three-alarm friends or co-workers. If you are not mindful and have your own, still place to draw upon, you will live a roller coaster existence at best. No one really wants that. You are your job first. If you learn to have a calm, steady, and confident energy that is grounded in truth, you will then have the ability to shift others to that energy instead of your getting sucked into their vortex of chaos. You, in fact, become a healer for others.

You must become a seeker and practitioner of all your higher energies in order to live a full and prosperous life and it's a totally inside job. This road can be a lonely one at first, but remember that true treasure is found on this path and the peace and happiness you deserve is only found by your willingness and dedication to becoming your best self.

CTA: Today, practice calmness and present-moment awareness. Whatever tasks are at hand, choose to do them one at a time, giving total presence to each. Turn off any background noise and distraction. Listen.

Have a great day!

JANUARY 29

You Matter

The world needs you to change. It needs all of us to change. What we see happening around us is the microcosm of a world of cluttered minds and sleeping souls.

When we as individuals have no foundation in the truth of who we are and where we come from, we are left to drift in the world of the ego. This is the world of separation. We feel separate from each other and separate from a God we are taught to fear. No wonder the world is in chaos.

The highest and fastest form of energy we as humans know is thought. Yes, thoughts are energy. They themselves produce the outward circumstances of your life. Think about it—once you have a thought, it produces a feeling in your body. We then speak, act, and literally *become* the voice of that thought. Often we give no witness to the thought to see if it's even true. This is when we get ourselves in trouble and usually it bears negative fruit in our lives and the lives of those around us. This is why you matter so much to the whole.

When we finally decide to wake up and become conscious of our thought life, we will begin to intentionally produce better results by thinking better thoughts. Always remember that you have a choice. Purposely choosing to create positive thoughts and scenarios in your mind and acting on them will produce a whole new life experience for you.

Even if your whole life up to this point has been filled with negativity, violence, drama, and broken hearts, you can choose to begin again. A new path forward! How exciting! It's like starting the new story of you. *You* write this one on purpose. You allow only loving, kind, and positive people into your new story. You burn the old book, except for the love and the lessons learned, and you move forward, now with a new foundation of truth to build upon! You are spirit in human form. You possess the power within you to accomplish anything! You develop this power every day that you decide to give it away. As you. Your new energy. Intentionally positive and generous. The new you is amazing! You can start being amazing right this minute.

You, my friend, matter more than you'll ever know! But nevertheless, you must begin to act from a sense of duty. Duty to yourself as well as the whole you are connected to.

This duty only requires two things of you. First, love yourself 110%. You are a spiritual traveler with amazing inner powers. That's all you act from. Believe in your abilities and talents and exercise them every day. Perfect them and sell your creativity in all you do. The world is waiting.

And second, constantly raise your positive vibration by giving. Never let your inner thief steal from you or others again. Starve your ego and give this world what it really needs—the gift of your soul; your true self. Break out of the limiting cocoon of the ego and fly with your new wings.

The more positive energy we all choose to give, the better the world will become. Darkness cannot survive in the light. You must choose to be your light self as much as possible. No amount of man-made solutions will ever cure what we are all looking for. Peace, love, light, harmony, joy, cooperation, and understanding only happen when the majority of us begin to shine our collective inner light. Just tipping the scales in this direction changes everything. You matter.

CTA: Today, begin the shift. Now you know the best thing you can possibly do for mankind and this planet is to personally decide to rise. Just rise.

Have a great day!

JANUARY 30

Asking Yourself the Right Questions

As dual-natured beings, we humans get caught up each and every day in the struggle of the ego and its dark shadow over our true nature. This is the entry point to asking yourself the right questions.

Our ego, or false self, wants us to believe we are separate and singular. It wants us to compete with each other to get to supposed higher places in life. Our ego demands that we find fault and blame with ourselves and the world. This is our lower, conditioned, human side. This voice lives to judge and condemn in order to raise ourselves in some self-centered or socially accepted way. This needs to become the *old* way of the world. Its time is coming to a close in order to make way for the era of the heart.

When we begin to awaken, asking the right questions of ourselves and others will become much more frequent and in the present moment.

When the ego is in the room, we feel tense, angry, competitive, aggravated, annoyed, or judgmental toward ourselves or others. This is when we must ask the right questions. Here are a few to ponder.

Ask yourself:

1) Am I adding to this negative vortex, or can I instead express my voice and energy of peace, compromise, or positive solution?

2) What do I want the end result of this interaction to be? Forward movement, collaboration, or continuation of some underlying secret war?

3) Are the thoughts in my head serving me? Am I misperceiving the situation like so many times before, or do I have it 100% right? Chances are, 100% is not usually the case.

4) Will my thoughts create positivity or negativity in this situation? Should I even give this thought the light of day? So many times the answer is no. You must become aware of who is giving you the thought. Ego or spirit? One feels good for the whole and the other will just feed the ego in the moment, usually to the detriment to the whole.

5) Is this thought conducive to my new goals and dreams, or is it an old, worn-out story I used to tell? One of defeat, depression, loss, or lack? *Stop*

telling these stories. They sink you. They never serve you. Complaining, gossip, and half-truths live here.

6) Is this thought going to lead to giving, or is it somehow going to rob my spirit or someone else's?

7) Am I part of the problem or part of a higher, openhearted solution? How can I serve instead of starve?

CTA: Answer these most important questions and move forward with the answers from within.

Have a great day!

JANUARY 31

Questions to Release

Yesterday's CTA questions are but a few questions of an awakening mindset. The ego has its own list of questions. They sound something like this:

1) Who does she think she is? The nerve of her, thinking she's better than me.

2) Don't you think they should know how lazy and unorganized he is? He's probably not a good person. I should tell others. I'm sure he's a loser.

3) I could never do that. They are so much better than I am. Am I even smart enough to realize this silly dream?

4) What could I possibly offer? I'm worthless. I'm ugly, I'm too old. I'm too shy. I'm too good for that. I'm too fat, too skinny, too dumb, too slow, too (fill in your own lie here).

So, you're beginning to see the importance of questioning your thoughts. Becoming the silent witness behind your thoughts is the door to wisdom itself.

You must become your own best friend and know the truth of how incredible you really are.

Everyone has a purpose. You'll never find yours if you don't start asking the right questions and questioning the wrong ones.

When you begin to shift into the higher gear of being a beneficial presence to yourself and the world, your purpose will show up on your doorstep. It's there; hidden under all the pain and anguish you've unwittingly buried it in. Time to shovel out the old stories and untruths.

Know that you are of the highest order of all that is in the Universe! Accept this as absolute and begin treating yourself and others as such. The word Namaste must be forefront in your new life. It simply means, "I honor the spirit in you that is also in me." From this one phrase your whole life can transform. It's always from the inside out that we rise or fall. Asking yourself the right questions in every moment will be your steady rudder through the ocean of life.

CTA: Begin the big dig. Cast out doubt. Cast out fear. Cast out the lies you've become.

Have a great day!

FEBRUARY 1

The Power of Examining Your Thoughts

Our thought life is a tool of true power. Where do thoughts even come from? Do you ever examine your thoughts, or do you usually just speak and act on them automatically? All these questions are life questions. Life questions should be asked by you consistently.

Learning to examine your thoughts seems like a lot of work, and it can be in the beginning, but this is the entry point to life changing-awareness and growth. It will be your path to an amazing, meaningful life.

They say that we as humans have between 60,000 and 90,000 thoughts per day. Most of them are the same as yesterday, just in slightly different scenarios.

Most people never give much attention to their personal thought process and how it affects their lives. Our thoughts are usually a conglomeration of our upbringing, social and relational conditioning, and the type of people we surround ourselves with.

We take these thoughts on as our own and for the majority, we tend to keep these thoughts and their consequences with us as our life pattern, never questioning their validity or absolute truth. This is why most lives never change. Our thoughts keep us stuck at certain life levels. Higher thought = better life and gives meaning to it all.

All positive life change begins in our thought life. We must become seekers of higher knowledge and wisdom and then apply these new thoughts and principles to our everyday lives. I promise you, you will see everything differently.

Our outlook on life is what directs our journey and attracts to us things and experiences in that particular level of energy and vibration. Low energy and consistent negative thoughts and attitudes bring a pretty negative life experience. We see the results around us every day.

Conversely, a great thought life and higher attitudes will attract to you a great life experience, including all your goals and dreams manifested into reality.

Seems so simple, right? It can be, but if you've been in the negative outlook camp for most of your life, or somewhere in between, it will take practice, will, hard work, openness to new ideas and concepts, non-judgment for your past actions and leaving judgment behind all together.

CTA: Begin to become the silent witness behind your thoughts, always examining them for truth. This is the real you.

Have a great day!

FEBRUARY 2

Becoming Your Divine Nature

It will take perseverance and faith, a whole new kind of faith in yourself and in that pure positive energy of love that created you. Love for yourself and everyone else. Wanting the best for yourself and feeling completely deserving of it, because you are, and wanting the best for everyone else.

You'll need to create a new vision for your life, one that includes big, exciting things, new directions, and creativity. You'll need and want to tap into your sea of enthusiasm and be intentionally consistent in it.

All of this must be included as, and in, your new, higher thought life.

You'll need to become an astute student of your own ego and all the lies, misperceptions and half-truths it tells you and leads you to act upon. You need to know the truth so you can easily detect the lies you used to believe. Part of your everyday life will begin dispelling and releasing these old lies and lower energy thoughts. It will be like taking off a heavy, old, wet winter coat; one that you used to feel comfortable in. Getting comfortable in low energy is just a life-sucking trap. Never get comfortable there.

You'll need to give up competition with everyone, in your mind, speech, and actions. You'll be adopting collaborative energy in its place, where you truly wish others the best and bring the best out of others, on purpose.

You'll need to give up anger, envy, martyrdom, and complaining. You'll need to give up hatred, gossip, and retribution. You'll need to become a quick apologizer when your ego takes you over temporarily, and you'll need to be a quick forgiver for those caught in their own mind storm of the ego. All of these will need to be left behind and discarded as the unnecessary. Doing this will uncover your true self and your real power. From this place you can do anything.

CTA: Start becoming the lie detector of your life and learn more about your true power. Make the higher decision each day to guard and intentionally guide your thought life. When you crash on the rocky shores of the flow, apologize, forgive, free your energy and your mind, and you'll be right back in the middle of the river. This is the sweet spot of life. You'll never know it until you decide you must know it. From there, your new, brighter, happier and more fulfilling journey has begun. Go get it! It's your true inheritance.

Have a great day!

FEBRUARY 3

The Formula

More and more of us are becoming aware of ourselves. We are beginning to finally take notice of how our thoughts, emotions, and actions create our lives. We are becoming aware that we are each 100% responsible for our personal energy field, which creates our personal reality.

Getting to know how you've created your life to this point is the doorway to understanding the key to the rest of your life. You've always held it. It's you. Get to know *you.*

Understand that we all create our lives using the same formula, the *same* exact formula. The difference is that some know how to work *with* the formula in a certain way. Learn the formula. It's an easy one to understand, but not always easy to practice.

If you make the rest of your life about sticking to the formula, you cannot get it wrong. Your life will expand like you've never dreamed and happiness will become your daily blessing.

The Formula: 1) Your thoughts, your spoken words based upon those thoughts. 2) Then the actions or inactions you take based upon those thoughts and words. 3) Your inner beliefs affect all of the above. This is where you are either expanding or you are contracting from life. It's all in what you believe is possible for you. This is what you need to look at. Be brave and non-judgmental when you go inside. Be willing to admit where you limit yourself because of fear, anxiety, self-doubt, anger, resentment, self-loathing, and all the other lies. And that's what stops you, every time. Lies. Time to grab your life back!

You have this power to mold the formula in every minute of your life. Taking command of this power is the key you've always held. Your mind can be and must be opened to new possibilities for you. This is the only path of upward motion. Rising above your old, outdated beliefs of what's possible for you is first priority. Facing the liar, one victory at a time, is how you shed this voice that betrays you and all the rest of us.

CTA: Begin to follow your own version of this formula. Then become it.

Have a great day!

FEBRUARY 4

Old Beliefs

I once believed that I could not speak in front of a crowd. I once believed that I had to do what my dad did because I went to college for it. I once believed I was only capable of a certain potential in life. I once believed I was separate from you and from my higher power. I once believed almost everything I was told about myself from others. Sound like you? I didn't know, just like you.

Now that I know, I just follow the right formula. It's all about love. Love yourself! Love everyone in your life, even if you don't always like them. They are there for your higher good, even if they are in your life temporarily. You may be there to teach them something important to their journey, or learn something from them for your journey. If you look back, you'll know this to be true.

So, love is the main ingredient of the formula. Love has many seasonings to choose from and when they are the only seasonings you choose to think about, talk about, dream upon, achieve upon, create your life upon, give to yourself and give away freely to others, as much as possible, then you will have become the master creator of your own life. It's always as simple as a choice of what to give.

Most of us are sloppy creators at best. We keep forgetting to use the right formula for what we desire in our lives, so we end up with a mixed bag of experiences; many of them ugly and totally unnecessary. We tend to use the wrong formula to try and better our lives, but we all know the price we pay when we use the wrong formula.

Peace, harmony, prosperity, great relationships, self-love, generosity, wealth, health, and happiness are what we all say we want. It's simple my friends, just give that. Give what you need and give what you want to see show up in your life, leaving out the unnecessary that is your ego. Let love be your constant calling card wherever you go. Become known for it. Aren't you drawn to people who are light and loving? Let love be your magnet, for it is what draws all goodness into your life. The opposite is also true.

Use the darkness just to guide you back to the light. With your diligence and determination, your dark energies will become just a reminder to guide you back, like hitting a rock on the shore of the river. The rock should not be picked up and somehow used to steer the boat back! It's just an ugly reminder to let you know you're off course. Get it?

Don't become your reactions of the ego, just use it as your cue to take a breath and create a higher way forward. You give your best instead. Your ego is just a distraction that takes your focus from what is truly important and meaningful in your life. Never give it your power.

It will absolutely take lots of practice! It's not always easy. But love is the truth of who you really are. The part of you that is eternal. Living from your eternal nature of love is the key to unlock and live an amazing life. By shedding the need or desire to use your dark energy as a means in life, you will reveal you; the real you, the one that can be or do anything. You're in there. Let yourself out.

So today, start tweaking your formula. Use only the right seasonings. You know when it's right and you know when it's wrong. You *feel* it. Feel low? You're on the rocks. Look inside and see why. Whatever it is, solve it in a loving way. Give some space between your old reaction to a situation and your new response to it. If it's an apology needed, give it. If it's forgiveness, give it. Keep your mind and energy free of these viruses. They are not part of the formula.

CTA: Always choose the main ingredient first. Choose love.

Have a great day!

FEBRUARY 5

Re-entering the Flow

Feeling good and radiating goodness outward is known as being in the Flow. The Flow is also known as the energy of unconditional love.

When we are in the flow, we feel good about ourselves. We feel powerful. Able to take on the world and let the little stuff go. We are easy-going, we are harmonious with those around us, and we are living more in the blessing of the present moment.

When we are out of the flow, we all know that feeling, and the results of that field of energy. We are impatient, short, less than agreeable. Our minds are in a skirmish and, more often than not, out spills our thoughts, right into our actions and speech. We have entered the realm of our lower self, the ego. In this place, arguments, rivalries, jealousies and wars on many different fronts are the norm. In today's world, it is truly known as normal, but it is definitely not natural.

Our true nature is our spirit. When we are in the flow, we are viewing ourselves and our lives through this natural lens. And boy does it all look good from this place. Your job is simply to get back to your original nature. This means the daily shedding of the unnecessary.

Allowing anger, hatred, violence, revenge, fear, worry, anxiety, and depression to enter your day is what I mean by the unnecessary. Shedding these lower energies will automatically reveal more and more of your true nature; your light. This is the real thing, folks. It's not wishful thinking or sticking your head in the sand to hide from reality. It is simply uncovering your natural ability to live life in a higher zone of knowing and understanding. Your so-called problems will become opportunities to rise higher, or they will disappear from your radar. You will no longer attract the negativity that your ego finds so delicious, because you are no longer emitting this energy. Your circle of friends becomes that of a higher quality and energy. Your closest relationships become closer and deep-rooted. Your prosperity and wealth expand because *you* have expanded. You've expanded your conscious awareness of your higher self and its treasure. This treasure you will never lose once you know it. It changes everything.

Let's continue this one tomorrow.

CTA: Notice those areas of your life that are creating a lower energy, bringing you down, or making you anxious. Be aware as those feelings come on. Enter the flow.

Have a great day!

FEBRUARY 6

The Flow *continued*

The practice of re-entering the Flow is the learned ability to shift your thoughts and feelings upward on the scale and returning yourself to the middle of the river, instead of the jagged rocks on either side. It's a conscious choice to let go of the ego's demands to become a reactive negative field of energy, through negative thoughts, words, and actions. When you're on the rocks, it must become your immediate wake-up call to return to the middle of the river and its beautiful flow as quickly as possible.

Always remember, you never produce anything truthful, lasting, or worthwhile from this place. Unconditional Love does not live here. Your true self is a piece of this Unconditional Love and your best life possible comes from living in, and as, this energy. From here, you can't get it wrong.

So today, if you find yourself on the rocky shore instead of the flow, remember who you really are. Rise above petty arguments; apologize if you are out of sorts. Never try to defend a bad attitude. Own up to it and you'll find others coming to your aid, instead of resenting you for being less than your best self.

Shifting yourself up the ladder is the practice. It does take time, depending on how off-course you've let yourself get. But remember, the light is always there to bring you back home. Seek it, know it, and live in it today. One successful day will lead to another and another. Before you know it, you're in the flow as your normal, natural state of being. Stay on the path and watch your life become bigger and better than you ever imagined.

CTA: Remember that you are a piece of the divine. You are meant to be in the flow. You feel it when you are not. Let this be your guide to get back where you belong. All you'll ever need is found here!

Have a great day!

FEBRUARY 7

The Magic of Exercise

I see so many of my friends on Facebook already enjoying the magic of this spiritual practice. Yes, we do it for the health and well-being of the body, but it also feeds our soul and frees our mind.

The mind-body connection has been known and touted for centuries. All the great spiritual masters knew the power of exercising our human vehicles. We must all add this miracle of life energy to our daily lives.

So many of us have given up on daily exercise because it either does not fit into our busy lives or we have become stuck in the habit of complacency.

I think when you change your perspective to the truth—that we are meant to have physical exertion in each day as a crucial part of the overall well-being and success in our lives—you will begin anew and take up exercise as part of your life's path.

The benefits of exercise are immeasurable and its effects flow heavily into every area of our lives. We feel better, we look younger, and we open up new channels of our life force. Ones you may never have felt or known. Your mind becomes clearer, your decisions more sound. Your smile becomes more pronounced in each day because you have found a new wellspring of growth, determination and perseverance. Your moods are steady and keep you in a higher vibe. This vibe brings you more life, more health and more opportunities to give of yourself and to yourself. All of this from one simple decision.

If it has been a *while* since you've been off the couch and started a new regimen, now is the time. It's *always* about starting. One determined choice per day.

We all crawl before we walk, so no guilt, shame or self-judgment should be part of the new routine. Quitting is no longer an option, because *you* have decided to add this holy elixir to your journey. I promise that if you stay determined and fixed on daily success, your life will change and your experience will lead you to bigger and better things, people and places.

Now, the following is not a shameless plug for our 30-minute total body workout known as Focusmaster Fitness, located at 828 Hoosick St., in Troy, NY, the best kickboxing style workout on the planet, LOL, but being part of the fitness industry has taught me one very important truth about all of us, *we need it*! It is the battery charge for all we are and all we do. Our individual temples that house our true selves must be well maintained in order to know a balanced energy and a balanced life. It's essential.

There are so many areas of fitness to choose from. Walking, running, yoga, spinning, group fitness, personal training, rollerblading, swimming, hiking, and on and on. The fitness world is your oyster. Start with whatever appeals to you, but take it slow and build as you go. Exercise is just like any other life choice, one step at a time, one day at a time, and consistent right choice making.

The connections you will make and the new energy you will come to know are so worth the daily effort that you will never look back. Heath is our wealth. Without it, you will never realize your true, unlimited potential.

So today, go for it! Just start. If it's been a while, or even your first journey into the world of health and well-being, begin with a simple walk around the block. Your body will resist this new change and your old mindset will protest for a while, but in no time, a new you will break through. A higher minded you. A powerful you. A you that you may have never been introduced to. The *real* you.

CTA: You can do it. It's just a choice. I believe in you, now it's your turn! Go get it!

Have a great day!

FEBRUARY 8

Taking Risks

This will mean different things to different people. Taking risks is what personal growth is all about! We've done it all our lives, from the time we risked walking over crawling, learning to swim, starting school and so on. This is a practice we should never stop. Never.

I'm not talking about dangerous, stupid risks. However, they are the spice of life for many as well. I'm talking about getting out of your comfort zone on a regular basis and stretching to the next level of your life experience. There's so much to stretch for, yet we decide to play it safe most of the time. Playing it safe is the path to mediocrity and a lower life experience.

Taking a risk for some might mean getting back into the work force or taking a new chance at love. Taking risks are nothing more than saying *yes* to life! When you make the decision to risk being yourself and using the talents God has given you, you will be surprised at how well things turn out. You are always given help along the way when you move in passion and confidence. And for those of you that claim you have no confidence, this practice of taking risks will build those muscles each time we do it.

Fear, and its illusion of being you, will become a thing of the past when you start to see a stream of personal success stories. You need to start with the mantra of "*I got this.*" I've written about this phrase before and by all means, adopt it in every area of your life. This phrase turns on a switch of success in your brain and your body. You will proceed through this risk of yours with a suit of positive armor surrounding you. Taking risks is just overcoming the small you in exchange for a larger you. It is such a rewarding practice and the key is to start small and build. It's the very same way all people of greatness have done it.

Believing in yourself is the key to taking risks and that part of you is what grows when you take risks. Getting out of your box is the practice of actual Living. We are growth-seeking beings by our very nature. We are intended to grow and it is our responsibility to weed our garden of fear and replace it with seeds of confidence and truth. We have all we need within us to do just that.

So today, make that phone call, go see that person, make peace with your old fearful self, and move forward with a decision you've been putting off. This is the sign you've been waiting for. Take that risk. If it doesn't work out, you will have built the muscles to do it again. Never give up, never give in.

CTA: Go get that life you've always wanted but were afraid to move on. You can do it. Begin today with one small risk. It will be a powerful day for you my friends

Have a great day!

FEBRUARY 9

Taking Action

The big Kahuna of all success in this physical world of ours is *action*! No matter how great an idea you have, it will stay in the fantasy world of your mind until you decide to take action. Consistent action.

Successes in anything, including the daily obstacles we face, demand this force. Action is just intention in motion. When we live our lives intentionally, using the magic of inspired action, we will know success on an ever-increasing level. This means giving yourself a bit more time to let your spirit weigh in on the situation (no matter what it is) and then jump into motion and kick its butt!

Whether it's your dream you're working on, a new job, a new relationship, a financial difficulty, or improving your business or your life, inspired action is the rocket ship to success. The secret is to *just start* from where you are, with what you have and move! You do not have to see the whole staircase to take your first step. Just begin.

I have found that just taking the first step is like starting the engine. It will then lead to the next, and the next, until we find ourselves in the flow. When we see progress, we will want to keep going and the path will become clear for you.

Improving any area of your life begins with right-minded choice followed by the actions that it will inspire. Don't ever be afraid to make a mistake or get sidetracked by momentary failure. That momentary failure is there just to steer you to another choice.

Thomas Edison tried 90,000 different ways to invent the light bulb and said those were not failures, just 90,000 ways *not* to do it. That kind of determined thought is why you may even be reading this entry, illuminated by his inspired creation.

So, no matter what you intend your life to look like, think about it from your higher place first, let your imagination run wild with ideas and then implement them with this type of action.

If your problem, your goal, or your dream is big enough, you must move on it and move on it now! One step will lead to a thousand and you'll find that each time you succeed based on *your* action; you will have prepared yourself for bigger and better things. You will have taught yourself that you can handle anything that comes your way with grace, inspired thought, and creative, positive action.

Positive thought is never enough; we need to put it in motion. Gather like-minded troops to help you if you need it, but don't wait for it! Move forward in any small way. It will prove to be a victorious path and an enlightening journey for you. You are an amazing being with incredible power!

CTA: Unleash that power today and every day of your life and choose to only live in its light and you will be sure to bask in the glory that has always been *you.*

Have a great day!

FEBRUARY 10

Becoming Aware

Self-awareness is the key to mastering your mind and yourself. Our mind loves to create scenarios about everything, positive and negative, without any regard (most times) to actual facts. It is therefore our responsibility to be a constant gardener of our mind and thoughts. What we many times make up in our thoughts comes out in our words and actions. This creates our lives. Weed that garden every day and only let out the good stuff.

Self-awareness is the path to transforming an average life into a life filled with true happiness, joy, and victory. When we decide to embark on a new way of life because our current way leaves us anxious, depressed, or full of self-sabotaging behavior, we must always start with self-awareness. We must be brave enough to study our self-talk, the way we speak about others, and our pattern of behavior. This can be difficult at first because we have to admit to ourselves that we have been on the wrong path for a long time, sometimes, most of our lives. Do not let this stop you! Let the uncomfortable feeling propel you instead of shrink you back to your comfortable stagnant self. It is on the other side of discomfort that we find lasting, positive change. Remember that in every area of life, short term discomfort leads to long term gain. If you are at a loss as how to start, you need to become a seeker of the positive information that will transform the way you speak to and about yourself first, and then how you see the world outside yourself. Loving yourself does not come easy for a lot of us, based on past experiences and conditioning. You must be willing to let go of old ideas and beliefs in exchange for the real truth of who you are and what your true purpose on this planet is. Remember that if you consistently fill your mind with right thought, it won't be long until you find yourself living and feeling so much better.

CTA: Today is the day to start your new life. Life does not have to just happen to you and it's not random! Create your life like a master painter. Paint some beautiful strokes today in mind and deed.

Have a great day!

FEBRUARY 11

Personal Power

The very first book that I read from cover to cover was not in school. At 23 years old, I was the classic underachiever just out for a good time, lots of laughs, and debauchery (some of this is still very true). But, like most, I always seemed to have the desire for more. I was in the mall waiting for my buddy, who shall remain nameless, while he was finishing up his purchase of pinstriped, pleated jeans at the world famous Chess King. I went into the bookstore nearby and noticed a book with the very title I am writing about today; *Personal Power* by Tony Robbins, the world famous life coach. I read the back cover and was immediately interested in the whole premise. I was amazed to see myself at the checkout counter purchasing an actual book that I wanted to read. To this day, the words in this book carry me forward because of the truth they revealed. What is personal power and how do we get it? The book said that we already had this personal power and that in approaching life from a higher, more positive perspective and actions, we are able to succeed in every area of our lives. I thought of it as potential magic when I read the cover and it turns out that's exactly what the results of using this approach feel like. It's certainly a power we need to develop and nurture, but it's a power that is our natural state of being. It's the power of our spirit; the invisible part of us that animates our outer shell. And when we learn what the basics of our power are, they seem very familiar to us. In short, it's learning to live every area of your life from the inside out instead of the opposite, which is what we are all taught as truth. The truth is that we are all unlimited and have no bounds except those that we impose upon ourselves. It's learning to surpass the liar in our head and go forward with courage and the conviction of our true limitless abilities. When you begin to practice living by your true nature (from the inside out), it will be more like discarding all the unnecessary baggage that you have been carrying around since childhood. It's like taking off a backpack filled with weights. You see, in order to live a powerful life, it's the energies of this power that we must exhibit outwardly every day; the energies of love, kindness, generosity, humor, collaboration, and most importantly forgiveness.

You'll use the other power energies such as perseverance, determination, and faith to get to your goals and dreams, but they will all be fueled from this inner place of truth rather than the outer lower energies of "I can't," "I'm not good enough," "I'm not pretty enough," victim, victim, victim. These energies have never produced a bit of true power or greatness.

CTA: Today, live from the inside out. Practice being who you really are... an unlimited spirit of power. You can truly accomplish anything from this place and it will be a beacon for others to follow. Spread the wealth.

Have a great day!

FEBRUARY 12

Personal Development

What is so important about personal development that's different from professional development? If we do not constantly hone our person, we will walk through our entire lives with an old bag of tools; typically just the ones that were left to us by our parents or friends. Most often, this bag of tools is very incomplete and they never work for every job we will encounter in our journey and, in most cases, so incomplete that we screw up our jobs in a daily basis, leaving behind rickety relationships, bad feelings, and mediocre experiences. Even when we become so-called "experts" in our professional lives, we are missing the all-important tools of the inside that affect all we do, including our profession. You can be the best doctor on the planet with the skills taught to you in school, but if your bedside manner stinks and you exhibit no empathy or compassion from your inner toolbox, you are not the best healer that you could be.

This is true no matter what we do in life. Your foundation is built on sand and can give way at any time. Most people find themselves at a loss when something goes wrong and they never look at themselves as part of the issue. The world of personal development offers a variety of authors and personalities that, I assure you, you will connect with. You will learn everything you need to know about how to live a life of true power. We absolutely need to be teaching these principles in our schools so that our kids are truly prepared for what life throws at them. As it stands now, it is sorely lacking.

The good news is that all we need to do for ourselves these days is to go on our smart phones and simply download an audiobook or one in written form. Start with one! One can change the entire course of your life. Much like a new exercise program, it's all about the decision to start. For me, audiobook was the way, perfect time to learn; while you drive. Let your car be your temple of learning. We do not need to make this complicated. A small shift makes a huge difference. Remember that you are the only tool you have that can create a great life. One you will look back upon when you're old and say...

I did my best and I left a legacy of love and truth for myself and those around me.

CTA: Today, take that courageous step forward and buy your first personal development book. Anything from Wayne Dyer or Eckhart Tolle is a great place to start. All personal development books share the same truth, just in different, easy to understand ways. It will be the best investment in yourself and your life that you can ever make. Go get it!

Have a great day!

FEBRUARY 13

More on Personal Growth

Personal Growth is the purpose of life and when we live from that truth then we start to seek a different path and live from the space of the heart rather than the dictates of the ego (better known as our lower self or the lower energies of competition, envy, jealousy, hatred, and lack). The starting point to moving in the upward direction is when we realize that our inner world creates our outer life. There are many paths to this upward direction but it's all about the information we ingest each day and how we process it. Garbage in, garbage out is what most people live. We need to start feeding ourselves wisdom instead of the daily dose of ego related information that is so prevalent in our world. It's all out there for the seeker who really wants to live to their true potential rather than spend this precious lifetime in mediocrity and inner emptiness. Get started by constantly feeding yourself great inner information a bit every day. The internet offers an awesome selection of personal growth books and audiobooks from the great light bearers of our time like Wayne Dyer, Eckhart Tolle, and Deepak Chopra. Empty your cup of what you have been fed as truth your whole life and fill it back up with the stuff that great lives are made of. Be extraordinary and live life to the fullest using the best tools in the box. At the end of your life you will have left a legacy of love, kindness, generosity, and truth.

Life's constant changes can be a real challenge for all of us, but when we realize that all there is in this physical world of ours is change, then we can begin to flow with the changes rather than resist them. Resisting change only causes more suffering and anxiety within us and can get us into a position of where we get stuck, not knowing how to move forward, when we cannot go back. Changes in life are really blessings in disguise, but we will never receive the blessings if we do not move forward. This happens in a big way when we lose someone we love or you find your chosen profession changes or is lost, or especially in a broken relationship. Our only way to stay unstuck is to realize that there is a diamond to be found in the seeming bag of negativity you have been handed. It's there... It's always there. You need to move forward at all costs and lean on those around you who love you. They will be your stepping stone through the tough part, and with faith and courage you will find the diamond. This diamond is personal growth and it's there to show you that change is good if we keep our eyes peeled for its personal meaning for us. It is true that time heals wounds but it's the love from those that are put in our lives for these times of change that shows us we are never alone and forward is the only way.

CTA: If you have the opportunity to be that bridge for someone in your life that's going through a difficult change, jump on it. It's there for you too. Spread the wealth always!

Have a great day!

FEBRUARY 14

In Power or Out of Power

This is crucial for you to know. When you are able to recognize your own state of mind and energy, you have just grabbed the power switch, maybe for the first time.

We are given free will as humans. Free will to believe or not believe free will to choose, free will to live our lives how we like. How we do it best, is by breaking it down, one day at a time, intentionally choosing how we will approach the day, instead of giving up our power by unconscious default. Unconscious default will always include your ego, or false self. This is the side of you that betrays and sabotages you. You think it's the real you but it is not. You inherited this conditioned you by the outer world and its many perspectives. *You*, my friends, have the ability to shift your entire life to a much higher perspective and this one will be the solid foundation for a whole new and better life.

Choosing to create your days individually, on purpose, with a positive, self-assured outlook, is turning on your power switch. Any thought in the opposite direction, slows you down, stagnates you and brings your dreams to a halt.

Here are some examples of power thoughts that you need to install immediately into your mind's computer and consistently have them on the screen of your day:

1) I can and I will.

2) Obstacles are just opportunities to get to the next page. I can overcome any obstacle.

3) I believe in my abilities and I have been prepared for everything in front of me. I will proceed with faith that the right road ahead will be shown to me and everything I need will be there at precisely the right moment.

4) My tribe is strong and if I help them to grow, achieve, and live happily, this is what I can expect from them. My tribe is ready and we are bonded by a higher purpose. I am strong. We are strong.

5) My intention to give love in all its forms and symbols will be my calling card. Doors will open automatically with this life-giving key. My path is steady and sure. I am helped every step of the way.

6) There is no failure, only growth when I decide to move forward in faith, divine determination, and harmony with those around me. I am in my true power. All prosperity and true success lives within me. I am what I am seeking. My true power is always on.

CTA: Choose to be *in* your power and keep shifting back into it if your ego mind lures you away.

Have a great day!

FEBRUARY 15

When Your Power is Off

Your faith and daily attitude are what turns your power on. When your power is off, we sound something like this:

1) This day is going to suck.

2) No way can we do that.

3) I don't have what it takes.

4) I'm not like you.

5) That's not realistic.

6) I'm so overwhelmed.

7) I can't.

8) I'm not good enough.

9) I'll never get that.

10) It's them, not me.

11) I'm not loveable.

12) I'm too good for them.

13) I hate those people.

14) They don't like me.

These are only a few of the lies we believe and take on every day. We become the lie and then go about spreading its energy. This energy does not build great things. It only builds mediocrity and low-energy life choices. You have the choice. You only have to make this choice, one day at a time.

We are not guaranteed tomorrow my friends. Doesn't it make sense to spend each day giving away your true self as your life's true purpose? Wouldn't you want to be remembered for charging the hill of life instead of running the other way? You are an amazing piece of all that is. You are not separate from this power. You only think you are. You can claim it anytime you want. You just have to stay awake to this truth. Hopefully these words help you to grab your power switch and never turn it off again.

CTA: Today, get in the power seat! Act only from the truth that you can accomplish anything! Charge the hill! Claim your inheritance and never look back. Seize this day! Then just do the same tomorrow. No need to see the whole staircase at once. One step will lead to the next. Before you know it, you're on top for good.

Have a great day!

FEBRUARY 16

The Power of Your Apology

When you finally recognize that we all share a dark side called our ego, you will see that just like ours, everyone else's gets out of control from time to time. We actually elevate others ego when our own is out front and expressing its energy.

Our job is to recognize when we are out of our true self, indulging in our darker energies. When we express these energies, we pluck the same string in others and an ugly drama is formed. If left unchecked, we usually add more and more dark energy, like anger, fear, hate, jealousy, right and wrong, and the cherry on the cake is usually a pile of good old-fashioned judgment.

This is *always* a recipe for disaster, at least short term. Harmony, love, cooperation, encouragement, and forgiveness are out the door in these times and bringing the drama to a close can be a real challenge.

The fastest way to any resolution in these situations is, of course, the Apology. An apology is simply recognition of the temporary insanity of our ego and its effects on ourselves and others. This ego of ours is nothing more than clouded perception or contrast of the truth. You are wearing a pair of foggy glasses that only let you see the negative.

When we speak and act from our view through these lenses, we say hurtful things, raise ugly perceptions of others and usually damage potentially wonderful relationships.

The ego will always tell you the same story... It's them, not me! They caused this! This is not my doing! While this may or may not be true, our overreaction and elevation to a ten on the ego scale *is* our responsibility.

In these times of self-reflection, we must first get back to our center, calm the heck down and seek out our spirit side for the highest answer and resolution. This is also known as the High Road.

The apology is right up there with forgiveness when it comes to a spiritual solution. It frees both parties of a drama in literally seconds! The ego will want this squabble to last for days...sometimes a lifetime!

Never, never, never let things go down this path with friends, family, coworkers, or even strangers. You give away your power of light to the darkness when you choose a grudge, further expansion of the drama or cutting people out of your life because of what could have been easily resolved with a simple, heart-felt apology. You may not be wrong about the core issue, but you are wrong for using your ego (false self) to try and solve the issue. This is what you are apologizing for.

When we do this, an amazing thing happens. The other party, in most cases, will instantly lower their sword as well and a solution based in truth will emerge. The dark energy is cleared and a higher place is reached. You will be respected for your higher choice and will be looked upon as a wise, mature member of your friends, family, and coworkers. Blessed are the peacemakers so the saying goes.

Always be quick to apologize when the temporary insanity of your ego kicks in. This energy we all possess has no place in our lives, other than as a signpost to get back on the high road. Use your ego as a GPS that leads you straight back to your best self.

CTA: If you've used this ugly side of you recently to win an argument, negatively compete, back bite or spread a dark perception of another, *apologize*! Free yourself from this energy. Take off the foggy glasses and see the truth: that we are all struggling with the same stuff, just in varying degrees.

If you are on the receiving end of an apology, be quick to forgive, for this power is one in the same. It releases you from a low place and you can fly again. Move forward today as a champion and do the right thing! Apologize and Forgive.

Have a great day!

FEBRUARY 17

The Power of Surrender

This is a great practice that leads you right into the flow of grace and goodness. Surrender in this context does not mean giving up, lying down or stagnation in any way. It simply means to let go of trying to control everything in your life, in exchange for trusting spirit to guide your path.

This can be difficult at first. Many times we are brought to a place where we realize that it's time to give up the struggle and pain for the gift of letting go; allowing things to be as they are, without judgment.

The phrase, "so be it" is a great one to get you to this place. The very next thought you must align yourself with is, "I will trust instead of doubt, I will surrender to my higher will and have faith that I will be brought through this, with great success and a better way forward." Then breathe deeply and exhale out the worry you've been holding.

You see, when all your human logic and limited understanding puts you into an emotional corner that you feel you're never going to get out of, this practice of surrendering your troubles to your higher source will reveal to you the unconditional love and support you cannot see with your eyes, but feel in your heart. Trusting this power will not only bring you through your trial, but it will bring you treasures you did not expect. These treasures will include new understandings, hidden meanings, higher purpose, the ability to see things from a higher perspective, real trust in the flow of life, and a guided path.

These are but a few examples of the blessings to come for you when you decide to trust and allow everything to move forward without your usual controlling nature and emotional roller coaster. It's like jumping off the ride for a while to let nature take its course.

CTA: Practice jumping off the ego train as quickly as you begin to feel its negative energy. Don't allow the scenario to build. That's the easiest time to jump.

Have a great day!

FEBRUARY 18

The Power of Prosperous Thinking

Our every thought carries with it a vibration of energy. We feel these vibrations and we describe them as moods or mind states, but they are so much more powerful than we have been told. It is our very thoughts that create and shape our life experience.

Our physical reality always begins with our thoughts and what we choose to believe about those thoughts. Examining the beliefs we've held onto for our entire lives will give you valuable insight to what you have attracted into your life and how you can change what you dislike into what you really want.

Let's take the energy of lack. Lack is the voice that tells us we are "less than" in some way. Whether it's good looks, money, self-esteem, personality, talent, or whatever your ego voice tells you you're missing. This is known as a lack mentality. Sure, we've all felt these energies and have known this voice, but it lies to you. These are all lies you have chosen to believe about yourself. The longer you hang onto these "stories of lack," the longer you will continue to vibrate that energy. This energy keeps you stuck in the very thing you complain about. It's that old worn out record that even you don't really want to spin anymore, much less others wanting to hear you spin it. It's your usual script.

The opposite energy to lack is the energy of prosperity. Prosperity always begins and ends with a grateful mind that is led by a grateful heart. When we choose to shift from our old story of woe and defeat into the truth that you are blessed in so many ways, your life will begin to shift as well. Your dominant energy field will have shifted into a higher realm. With it, prosperity in all its forms and symbols will enter your life.

CTA: Prosperity is a state of mind that becomes its own energy field. Counting the blessings you have in your life must become a constant practice in order to shine light over the dark thoughts of lack and bring a renewed positive vibration to your personal field of energy. This is the ladder out of lack. Start climbing and never stop.

Have a great day!

FEBRUARY 19

Chase the Passion: The money will follow

Rule number one on your journey to more prosperous destinations is all about *your* passion.

Most people are just chasing the money, but money easily comes and goes with this method, jumping from job to job just for a few bucks more. While this is perfectly "normal" in today's society, it is not "natural." You are meant for more.

Discovering your passion, whatever it is, is extremely important for an abundant life experience. Do you have one? Are you aware of your God given talents? Where and what are you naturally drawn to? What do you do that helps or prospers those around you? What do you really love to do? These are important questions to ask yourself. Finding the answer must include a good feeling when you say it. Feeling good when you do something unique to you is the biggest clue.

It could be anything! Nothing is out of bounds, even if it seems impossible for you at this stage, don't ignore it! It's possible. Anything is possible. You yourself are a miracle. You are a piece of the miraculous that created you and all you see around you. You have this very power to create a dream life that includes doing what you love for a living, and doing it very well.

The thing about the energy of passion is that it brings to bear all your creative juices! It focuses your higher power and attention on giving something that is genuinely from you; your gift to humanity. It's part of why you are here.

From passion, obstacles are so much easier to overcome. Challenges are viewed as steps to the next level of success and goals are the juice that gets you going each and every day.

Passion, therefore, is the natural way of prosperous growth. Give your very best away as your gift, whatever form that takes. It could be writing, art, music, crafting, inventing, building, selling what you love, service, sports, and the list goes on infinitum.

CTA: If it makes you feel good, do more of it! Learn more about it and how others have turned this into their own profitable art form. Model their path if they are successful, but do it your own, unique way. This is the way you will run right into your calling.

Have a great day!

FEBRUARY 20

The Limited World of Lack

How many times do you complain about money? How many times to you speak of your lack and limitations? How often are you acting like the world is against you in some way? How jealous and envious are your thoughts, words, and expressions? And how often do you place more of your attention on who's above you, rather than how good you have it compared to many others?

These are the questions that will root out your current beliefs. Only then, when you shine the light of truth on the dark thoughts of lack, will you finally expose the lies you've been telling yourself. These lies only to keep you stuck in that very poor, low energy vibe. Lack is limited thinking, when the truth is, *you are unlimited*!

You, and only you, have the power to rise. It's the intentional, daily practice of the opposite train of thought, words, and actions that will break you free from this horrible, lying mind state.

The path of change begins every morning upon awakening. You must begin, carry yourself through the day, and end your days with gratitude. Being truly grateful for what you already have in your life. Giving thanks to those in your life who love you and whom you love. Giving thanks for your health, happiness, and even new prosperity not yet seen. These are the acts of a grateful mind and heart. Give thanks for your bright future, for it is sure to arrive in this faith filled mind state. Give thanks for blessings yet to come, because they are always coming. Give thanks as if what you want is already here. Acting in this faithful way will bring to you all you desire. A new attitude of gratitude is your path to a truly prosperous life.

CTA: Begin the inner shift away from your old lack-filled thoughts, speech, and actions. Begin to only speak prosperity to yourself and anyone you meet. Always remember that you attract who you are. Are you prosperous? The answer, my friends, is absolute. You are of the highest order. Start being it.

Have a great day!

FEBRUARY 21

The Power of Writing Your Intentions

The power we have as humans to direct our own path and realize our goals and dreams is the very stuff that makes our temporary journey so worthwhile and fulfilling. This all starts by you being intentional about it.

Although the gift of hindsight tells me I was always intended to be right where I am in my journey, my intentional journey only really began in 2006 when I made the life-changing choice to write down what I wanted the rest of my life to look like.

At the time, my partners Jimmy, Gene, and I were going full steam, trying to build our business through the blood, sweat, and tears of perseverance, determination, and striving. It was a crucial part of all of our journeys, but then, we as a group took a turn. A great turn. The turn of higher knowledge and understanding.

I now know that it was more of a shift in our conscious understanding of how the flow of life really works to our advantage when we work with it and direct our own thoughts, intentions, and energies in the correct way.

Part of this shift requires you to write down a list of your biggest life desires, or intentions. I've decided to share my list from 2006. I imagine they would be very similar to many of your own desires, so feel free to use this as a model when you write your own down.

It went like this:

1) I intend to expand and grow continually, internally and externally, by uncovering my true, unlimited self and living from this higher energy.

2) I intend to create new and exciting relationships wherever I go. These will be quality relationships based on truth. These relationships will help me to expand and others to expand. I will prosper others and it is sure to return to me.

3) I intend to live life to the fullest and give my best self in all my experiences.

4) I intend to increase the flow of wealth and prosperity into my life and the lives of those around me.

5) I intend to spread peace, love, joy, happiness, laughter, prosperity, praise, gratitude, and generosity as my personal energy.

6) I intend to spread wisdom and truth to help others realize their own true power.

So, there you have it. Six intentions that culminate as your personal mission. Once you write them down, put this list where you will see it every day. Live by it. Speak from it, give from it, every day. Your life course will have been charted and you are on your way to your best life possible.

So, eight years after writing these six simple but powerful life intentions, I can gratefully report that this practice has given us an amazing life. We are living our dreams come true every day and we are aware and truly grateful for all of it. Even the stuff that came in an ugly wrapper.

CTA: Today, chart your own course. It is inside of your DNA. Bring it forth, write it down, and just follow your own path.

Have a great day!

FEBRUARY 22

The Power of Your Smile

This one amazing power that we all possess is the door opener of true greatness.

Our smile literally has power. A lot of power. When our smile comes from a place of love, friendship, excitement, beauty, and confidence in ourselves, we have the power to heal ourselves and others.

When you walk into a room full of people with a smile on your face, what are you saying? You're saying, I'm happy to be here with all of you, open to all of you, and I'm already communicating my intention of good will. The response to your silent communication will be instant and most often will result in the disarming of any ego or gatekeeper being present in others. This is crucial in any and all interactions in our day if we want to live a great life for ourselves and give our best self away in the process.

Our smile has the power to open doors, move up the ladder in our jobs, attract all goodness from others, create meaningful relationships, let others know our feelings for them in an instant, attract a mate, create laughter, and so much more. Our smile even releases endorphins in our body to elevate our mood naturally. Think we're meant to smile a lot? The evidence says overwhelmingly yes!

Coming into any situation with your smile can change the energy and the mood of others automatically. This is part of spreading your wealth. A smile is a tool of giving and receiving. Every great person in history that has operated their lives from the heart will tell you that the one personal tool that has brought the most happiness and success to them is their smile. In my personal life and business life, it is my favorite tool.

CTA: Today, turn that frown upside down and give the world your very best from the second they see you. You will find you elevate your own energy, state of mind, and even your health! Plus you'll elevate others to the same. We are here on earth to prosper each other and what we give out will always come back to us tenfold. Smiling is the fastest and easiest God-given way to create a beautiful day and an amazing life.

Have a great day!

FEBRUARY 23

The Power of the Spoken Word

We are all very powerful creators. Nothing creates our lives more than the power of our spoken word. This power can, in seconds, destroy someone's day or even someone's life.

When we realize that most of us give no attention to the thought that precedes our spoken word, then we can begin to understand how we can either tear down or build up our lives and the lives of those around us. We must all become the masters of our minds and thought life. If we give up our true, heart-centered voice for the voice of our ego, then we have no command of our ship and we will end up always heading toward or crashing on the rocks. We all need to become the watcher and witness to our thoughts, which become our words.

If we practice the art of being mindful first and give some space between thought and our spoken word, we become the master creator and will be conscious in all our choices. This allows us to act from our best place, where all success lies.

We need to know the voice of our ego and our spirit. This is crucial to living a great life. We all know these voices and usually the ego likes to be our spokesperson. The ego is in charge of all your lower, non-creative, judgmental, fearful, victim minded energies. It's the voice of arrogance, martyrdom, defeatism, revenge, hatred, lack and separateness of spirit. This voice creates nothing good. Nothing. It does create drama, divorce, alienation and unhealthy competition. It creates envy and self-loathing. It destroys lives.

When we decide to start choosing our thoughts and become self-aware, we have decided to be the captain of our ship. This one decision will transform your life forever. Just go in this direction. Don't question it. Your ego is very convincing that the energies it spews will get you what you want, but that's the lie.

So today, practice the art of being mindful. Mindful of when the ego is present and wants to speak. Hold that thought and be sure to hold that tongue. Listen instead for a deeper voice. It's there.

CTA: Just give yourself and your mind some space and the right choice will emerge. Live today from the good place and sweep the egos demand to speak out of the way.

Have a great day!

FEBRUARY 24

The Power of Acceptance

This one power can free you from all suffering. It's also the hardest one to practice for most of us.

Acceptance is an energy of love, therefore it is of the highest energy there is. Once you begin uncovering this power you already own, you will have shifted your entire life into high gear. You will be in the flow of all goodness. It's living life to the fullest and being free. Free from worry and fear. Free from drama and negativity. Free to express who you really are, and free inside yourself, a.k.a. inner peace.

There are two forms of acceptance you need to work on. The more you strip away judgment from your life and replace it with loving acceptance, the more inner peace, confidence, and power you will know. Your life will change right before your eyes.

Ok, so here are the two we are all challenged with to some degree. We have the power to be both, and that's the gold. It is who you really are. Practicing both as one of your life's intentions will release a power in you that gives and creates all the good stuff.

1) Acceptance of yourself. From this day forward, accept yourself completely! Supposed flaws and all! You are a sacred piece of the energy of God. You insult your true self by not trusting it. Love yourself and let go of the self-judgment, self-sabotage, and self-criticisms. They are lies of the ego. No more! You suck the life energy out of yourself when you do this. You are trusting the thoughts of your false self instead of your true self. You betray yourself anytime you believe these lies. You are beautiful and incredible, get with it! Be your own best friend from here forward. You are lower than no one and higher than no one. Always give yourself love. You're the best of the best. Literally.

2) Acceptance of others. Accepting people as fellow souls, all here on their own divine mission, that we know nothing about, will help to shift your mindset to the higher realm. Everyone needs to be loved. It's the life energy of love that sustains our very existence.

The feeling of being accepted brings freedom to both parties. True communication from the heart is found here. Judgment only brings suffering. Acceptance gives life. Do your very best every day to accept others the way they are. If they are in your life, they are both your teacher and your student. Accepting them will be your key to the meaning and purpose of their presence in your life.

Judging others says more about you than them.

CTA: Today, choose love as your calling card. Be a great ambassador of kind acceptance. It's a much more fulfilling life experience and surely you will get to know some truly amazing people that you may have previously judged out of your life. Judgment is a plague. Drop it like it's hot.

Have a great day!

FEBRUARY 25

Acceptance of What Is

This is the big mama for most of us, but it brings divine freedom like no other choice you can make. Decide from this day forward to trust and accept the circumstances and experiences that come into your life, without judgment. If it shows up in your life, it is there for your higher good. Some of these experiences will show up in an ugly wrapper. Accept those too. Some of your life's experiences will offer no apparent lesson or even make sense to you. Trust that there is a reason and lean not on your own understanding in these times. You may not know while you are still here, but the answer will come. Trust it and accept what comes.

Always move forward, *always*! Your soul is here to grow. Some of our darkest moments yield the most beautiful gardens. Live as much as you can each and every day in the present moment. Live in the now. It is where all your power of choice is found and your power to create. Choosing in each moment to create positive, loving interactions and energy will always attract the good life to you. You choose to stay in the flow when you accept what is. You don't have to always be happy about it, but remember it is there *for* you. You'll be grateful for it later. Why not do your best to give thanks in advance for your new growth. It's coming. It's always coming. Your job is to cooperate and become more guided by this benevolent source. The more you choose to accept, the freer you will be and the more conscious and awake you will become. It's the gold we are all seeking. You are the miner. Chip away the ego and its demands to judge everything and everyone. Free your mind and shine your light.

CTA: Today, print this one out if you can and put it where you can read it from time to time. Practicing this particular entry will free you. Never give up. Never. You are too important to all of us.

Have a great day!

FEBRUARY 26

Brighter Glasses

The ego only wants us to see the darkness in ourselves and in others. That is why it is our duty and purpose to seek the light and be the light for ourselves and others. You cannot bring someone out of darkness if we choose to live there ourselves. Spread some light and everyone benefits.

True prosperity and wealth come from a natural place within us all and when we choose to give this away freely in our daily lives, it only grows and expands. Never bury your talents and dreams. Always give what you want and need for yourself.

What you focus on and put your mental and/or physical energy toward always grows. Make sure you spend each and every day focused on the positive and moving forward with good thoughts, deeds, and actions. Everything else takes care of itself and you're rewarded with great relationships and an extraordinary life. Works every time.

CTA: Put on your brighter glasses and see the light.

Have a great day!

FEBRUARY 27

The Victim Mentality

The opposite of a winning mentality is the victim mentality. This is usually a learned way of living that comes from childhood surrounding or spending time with complaining, negative minded people. What the victim is looking for is love or constant reinforcement from outside themselves. This of course is the worst trap a person could find themselves in because once they realize that those around them can no longer support the behavior, they know no other way but to ramp up the drama in order to get the attention they desire. It's a vicious negative cycle that sucks the life from the victim and those around them like an energy vampire. Remember that life is like a mirror and it gives back the reflection you are presenting. You can only break the victim mentality by loving yourself first and the giving it away freely in the form of positive speech and actions. It will change you from a vampire to a person that everyone wants to be around.

CTA: Practice not complaining about anything for a day and see the things that you would have said and done and you will be aware if you are Dracula to others or a magnet for the good stuff of life.

Have a great day!

FEBRUARY 28

Putting Off Your Success

Procrastination is the biggest dream killer there is. We all do it and we've all felt its wrath. It's not very difficult to overcome once you realize that a small change in course can change your entire life. Once you hear that familiar voice saying, "Ahh I'll do that later or tomorrow," you're on your way to another missed opportunity to succeed. You see, huge success is nothing more than small successes consistently accomplished. When we practice small successes in our daily lives they always add up to creating a dream come true. The trick is to stay the course and celebrate and notice each small success as you go. Remember, the time will pass anyway and it's what we do with this gift of time that matters. Acknowledging our small successes will be your fuel to continue and it obliterates the mentality that crushes dreams and leads to nowhere but a mediocre life. You can either create a road filled with potholes or a smooth stretch of highway by the small decisions you make to take action. Baby steps eventually create milestones and in the end... a life well lived.

CTA: Notice your self-talk and what it's telling you. If it's procrastination, pull a George Costanza and "Do the opposite!" Action plus passion equals success! Get out of your comfort zone every day and push the envelope of what your mind tells you is possible. No dream is too big for the person of action.

Have a great day!

FEBRUARY 29

Fear is Just a Feeling

Fear is the Mac Daddy of all emotions that keep us from moving forward in all areas of our lives. Especially fear of the unknown. Most people will trade an amazing life experience for stagnation and mediocrity, solely based on the totally false notion of things being worse if they try something new. The best acronym I have ever heard for fear is "false evidence appearing real." This is true when we do not question the scary scenarios we create in our heads as to what "might" happen, instead of believing in ourselves and our true unlimited nature and ability to succeed. We are meant to succeed! I'm not talking about the natural type of fear that keeps us from burning our hand on stove or doing something potentially life threatening. I'm talking about that inner liar that tells us we don't have what it takes. That's the lie. The way out of the trap of fear is to consistently challenge this liar in our heads and go forward with faith and confidence. Remember, if you are brought to it, God will see you through it. But we have to do it for ourselves in order to deny the liar and realize the truth.

CTA: You are not a victim but a victor. Fear is an illusion that stifles our life force and kills our dream for a bigger and better life. So today, push yourself to do or say the things you need to in order to get to the next exciting level of your life. Deny the lie! You are amazing. Live from that truth and you can do anything!

Have a great day!

MARCH 1

Assuming

We all know the treacherous waters of assumption and how most often our minds betray us when in the midst of it. Remember, when we assume something, we are in the theatre of our minds, creating a scenario that we judge as fact, before we have the facts.

We all do this on a daily basis and most often we get our tails in a sling and regret the story we told ourselves and others. These are stories where our ego is happy to fill in all the dirty blanks about someone or some upcoming experience. Assuming, more often than not, creates the havoc and drama that we say we are so desperate to rid ourselves of.

As mentioned so many times before, it always comes back to us and taking responsibility for our end of the bargain. Our thoughts, if left unchecked and unquestioned, will become the words we speak and the subsequent actions we take. Why is it that so many of us always assume the worst when the best is just another assumption. Many will say that always assuming the best about someone or a situation, is just folly or looking through rose colored glasses. So many have built their lives around the practice of looking at their lives and the world through glasses covered in mud.

We do have a choice in the matter and manner we assume things. How many times in your life have you assumed something about someone that you are completely convinced it's fact, only to learn how wrong you were. Hopefully in these cases, you did not let your assumption be known to others, broadened through gossip about the assumption and then have an innocent person nailed to the cross. I've done it many times. Many times. We need to learn this lesson once and for all in order to live a life of happiness and harmony.

When we choose to indulge in gossip, judgment and negative assumption, we are hanging out in the hell of lower energy, attracting to us all that goes along with it. Which I assure you, is never what you really want. You say you want a drama-free life? You want to live a happy, fulfilled life and leave a legacy of love and kindness? Then you must learn to guard your thoughts, question everyday if they are 100% true. If they are not, do not speak on them, act on them or dwell on them as truth. In most cases assuming only leads to strife. It is how wars are started in our lives and our world.

CTA: Today, practice the art of no judgment, no gossip, and no assumptions. See how well you do. It may be a wake-up call for some who often say "it's them, not me." Change your thoughts and you will change your life. Drama is always the result of assumption. Drop it like a hot coal from your hand every time you are tempted to assume the worst and you will begin to live life as it was intended. You'll be rewarded with great relationships, great opportunities, and an awesome life. And that, my friends is the truth.

Have a great day!

MARCH 2

Our Triggers

We all have negative triggers that, when pulled, force us to go into a certain defensive or offensive mode. These triggers come from the ego's desire to be right or protect a certain mental position. Usually these triggers go back to our childhood when we were taught the way by well-meaning parents or the perceptions the outer world has shoved into our belief system. You would know these triggers by the way you feel when someone says something counter to your beliefs or way of thinking.

For most, being right is more important that having a great relationship with those who don't share in our beliefs. Wars and drama are all started this way. Triggers are like guitar strings and when someone else plucks their negative note; your same string is plucked, causing you to go into either a silent Cold War with this person or an outright battle.

I can bet with relative assurance that you have a few wars raging in your head about someone you work with, live with or even love. This is our ego at work, judging, convicting, and condemning others in silence or gossip. This is a massive trap for those trying to live a great and fulfilling life.

We need to recognize our own ego first and know its voice before we can set its demands aside and let in the truth. This is accomplished by giving yourself a lot of space between when your trigger is pulled and your usual reaction to it.

Be the witness behind your reactions instead of becoming your reaction. I guarantee you'll see some very ugly thoughts and desires for revenge, jealousy, envy or even hatred. These thoughts and reactions suck up our time, good energy and even our lives if we let them. Remember the goal: loving life and spreading your light. These two gifts to yourself and others are overshadowed each day by our triggers. Having an emotional roller coaster life is the norm on planet earth and our ego is usually the guy at the controls of this roller coaster.

Practicing the art of dismantling our old triggers is actually the art of rising above. Rising above the sour note when it's plucked, will give you the power to eventually cut these strings from your guitar all together. What this will do for your life is amazing and it's what all great masters and spiritual leaders call freedom. This freedom from the ego and it's low energy promises will give you the power to do anything and accomplish anything you desire. It's the stripping away of old habits, triggers, and energy. You'll attract new friends, relationships and opportunities that are truly worth having.

So today, when your negative strings are plucked by yourself and your negative thoughts, or from one of those negative guitar players in your life, be silent and witness what your ego would have said or done. Start trying to let go of your need to respond or even create negative scenarios outwardly or in your mind. Letting negativity pass through you instead of sucking you in is the goal. You will get better as you practice being a bending reed instead of a negativity sponge. Know that you are affecting your own higher energy by lowering it to your battle stations. Keep YOUR day up by letting the crows fly below you.

CTA: Like anything else worth having, stripping away your old perceptions, habits, and lower energies takes time, patience, and forgiveness for yourself and others. Non-judgment is your path to this freedom. Make this day great on purpose! What do you want it to look like? Go get it. Spread the good stuff today and you will sleep well tonight.

Have a great day!

MARCH 3

Being Offended

I think we all know that our society today has become one of a victim mentality. Everyone is offended about something. Being easily offended is an off-shoot of a victim mentality. When we choose to be offended, our ego is in control. The ego demands we take offense, suck it in, hold on to it, and then either retaliate with overreaction or more commonly, hold it until we can find the first ear in our path that will listen and also overreact to the story of being offended and then the drama has begun. Chances are you'll want to keep the story going for a while and spread it around a bit more.

All this time you spent wrapped up in this negative vortex, churning your stomach and causing you to react to everything that day through this negative lens. This one offense has created an ugly day for you. Because *you* chose to be offended.

When you finally decide to live your life from your true power, you will never have the need to be offended. You see, when you're offended, you've given all your power over to an opinion or action of someone else! What they think is none of your concern or business.

Hear me now...don't ever give your power over to anyone! You are beneath no one and you are above no one. Live in this truth; you are what you believe yourself to be and will live your life from that perspective. You are magnificent! Your life must come from and be lived from that perspective. From here, you can do anything. Bowing to the opinions of others and then believing them and taking them in as your belief about yourself is actually choosing a lower energy life. You are so much bigger and better than that! The *real* you is never offended because it is a self-assured, confident, harmonious being. All the other is the work of your ego. Live in the higher energies, my friends. It's the only way to fly and it's where we are all meant to be. So today, notice the demands of your ego to be offended or to control others. Deny this voice and instead, *choose* to laugh, love and have fun. We literally have no time for the other.

CTA: Next time you feel offended, become very present and watch your mind for the normal reaction to bubble up. Notice what the real issue is. Could it be that your ego is telling you that you are somehow below or above this person? The truth is that another's opinions only have power over you if you give it away to them. Becoming someone who is grounded and self-assured in their true nature recognizes that so many are still asleep in this lower mindset. If you rise out, you'll be able to show others the way. Rise today. Become the witness to your mindset and make the necessary adjustments.

Have a great day!

MARCH 4

Loss of a Loved One

This is undoubtedly the hardest of life's experiences for all of us. Whether it's a parent, a friend or especially a child. I write this entry today in honor of my good friend Jimmy Westhead and his wonderful family. Jim just lost his daughter to complications of diabetes and it was unexpected, which certainly makes it even harder for the family. My heart, my prayers, and my love go out to the Westhead family during this time. May you all extend the same to them, as they are truly like a second family to me.

When we lose someone close to us, it is important that we grieve, mourn, and let the emotions out. This is our natural way of healing. During this time we must all gather around the family who has experienced the loss.

When my partner Jim Pettit lost his brother, he had to deliver this horrible news to his mom. It was one of the most difficult moments of his life. His mom was of course devastated and could not bring herself to even attend his wake. This was how hard it was to accept his passing. Jim told his mom one of the most profound statements that I will share with you and I hope when the time is right, Jim Westhead will hear these words and take them to heart.

Jim Pettit said to his mom, "Mom, we are going there today to celebrate your son's life. While we will be in the midst of mourning Joe, our attention and focus will be on celebrating this awesome son, brother, and friend. And when you go there today Mom, everyone who comes to this celebration of Joe's life will be there in the spirit of love, only Love. These people will come and hug you and each of these hugs will take away a bit of your pain and suffering. This is why we must go, Mom. Joe is now free and he is with Dad. He is now at peace and no doubt wants you to be as much at peace as you can be with this knowledge that he is ok. He does not want you to cry for long and suffer for long, for he is at peace in a place of sheer beauty and unconditional Love. He is surrounded now by loved ones and he has a new job of watching over you and continuing to love you from a place that is not so far away as we think. He will always be with you and you *will* be together again. Be certain of this fact."

His Mom was in fact, surrounded by this healing love from everyone and it did help her to move forward. A little bit of her pain was taken away by each of the loving hugs she received that day.

Jim just lost his mom, dad, and brother all within a few years' period. My buddy knows about loss and my own life has changed through his experience.

After the loss of Jim's dad, I learned so much and felt that loss so deeply myself, that it prompted me to call my dad and tell him that from this day forward we must end each phone call or visit with an "I Love You." For some reason, to that point we didn't say it. We just let each other assume it. Not good enough. Not good enough at all. To this day and beyond its a regular expression of love we share. Thank you Jim Pettit.

Each of Jim's losses opened his heart wider and wider, as did all those around him. And I am so grateful for this experience.

So, to my dear friend Jim Westhead, your family and all those reading this entry today; please know that the Love we share is the truest part of us. In times of loss we must cling to our families, friends, and our faith. Faith in knowing that our loved ones are free and at peace in an awesome place that we know as our true home. We will all go home when our work here is done. We must celebrate the lives of our loved ones, while they are here and when they are called to go home. Jim, your daughter is still very much with you. She lives is your heart forever and now she watches over all of you. God bless you my friend. God bless all of you.

CTA: Never let others wonder if you love them. Today is the day to tell them. It will change your relationship and raise it to a new level. That's what love does in all areas of your life. Give it freely.

Have a great day!

MARCH 5

Jealousy

This one energy ruins more relationships than any other.

The voice of jealousy tells you that you are not enough. It says others are more than you in some way and you must be insecure about others for some reason, whether it's beauty, money, popularity, etc.

Insecurity in yourself is a lie about yourself that you keep telling yourself. This keeps jealousy firmly in place. Usually for a lifetime.

As with all of the lower energies within us, we must be steadfast in breaking our agreement with this lie, so we may become self-assured and confident in our own skin at all times. No need for jealousy.

A jealous mind will always create another show in its life that will produce more reasons to be jealous. It's a vicious cycle unless you intentionally decide to grow past this self-sabotaging behavior.

The jealous mind will also lead you right into other victim minded behaviors like controlling others. Trying to be sure your spouse or significant other doesn't find another more attractive. The fact is that this whole field of negative energy and behavior of trying to jealously control others is the very energy that makes them want to leave you. Controlling behavior is the number one enemy to great relationships. Jealousy is in the same energy basket.

I saw a saying the other day that read, "maybe it's not so much about becoming something new, as much as it is about stripping away what is not needed." This is the key to living your life to the fullest, at the highest energy on the scale. We *must* strip away these old, self-defeating habits and low energies. It's like cutting off sand bags in order to lift your hot-air balloon.

If you are brave enough to look inside yourself on a daily basis and see where you have been spinning old, worn out songs of woe and drama, you will be on your way to positive change. Many people say they want to change, but it's the journey inward that creates what you're looking for.

Sweeping out the basement of our past and stripping away the shitty energy of our egos is the daily chore. This chore pays huge dividends, my friends!

CTA: Today, take a peek in the basement of your mind and begin the spring cleaning. A cluttered mind delivers a chaotic life. Let go of all that stuff that never serves you.

Have a great day!

MARCH 6

Doubt

Doubt is the opposite of Faith. Usually we use this mental position on ourselves and it kills all our aspirations dead in their tracks. We need to move beyond this low level thinking in order to realize our true potential.

Doubt is usually based on our past inabilities to create the lofty dreams we see for ourselves and as we know, the past is gone! We should never use our past selves to create our present and our future.

When we doubt, we've decided to be less. Less than what we came here for. Less than we are meant to be and less than what God intended for us. When we doubt our abilities to do better and be more we are doubting our true power. At this moment, we have shut off the faucet of higher energy.

Our higher energies of creativity, perseverance, determination, overcoming obstacles, and victorious new levels of life are shut down like a garage door when we choose to doubt ourselves. This is true also when we doubt those around us.

When we decide instead to have faith in the fact that we all possess seeds of greatness, and that faith itself is the miracle grow for these seeds, we will begin to unfold and grow as was always intended. We need to push beyond the weakness of doubt into the light of victory and success in all areas of our lives. This happens one brave step at a time.

These brave steps are just you, punching fear right in the mug and taking back your power. This power is granted to all of us. We just need to walk on a little water every day and see that we can indeed move up the steps to a bigger, better life.

The next time self-doubt surfaces in any situation, decide in that moment to take action anyway! Move past the old decision to play it safe or small. Go the extra mile in spite of fear and doubt and you will see that doubt is just a smokescreen designed by your ego, designed to keep you trapped in old, past beliefs. Move upward and onward, my friends. Kick the butt of doubt in all areas of your life!

CTA: Today, be brave! Push past your doubt in some area and feel your spirit soar. Then just keep doing that.

Have a great day!

MARCH 7

Staying Ahead of Disappointment

This practice is a great one that I was inspired to write about by my beautiful sister Beth, who has truly transformed. I am very proud of you, Sis. You give your all in everything you do.

Disappointment comes when our outcome is not what we expected. Everyone knows this energy. It sucks the life and enthusiasm right out of you and brings you to the basement of your emotional house.

We must change our viewpoint when it comes to receiving news or having outcomes of any kind that are less or different that we had been attached to in our minds. Notice the word "attachment" in that sentence, because that is always the precursor to disappointment. We become attached to a movie in our minds. This movie has all the details included. T's crossed and I's dotted. And if things do not go according to the script you've developed, the movie quickly turns into an epic drama instead of a love story.

Staying ahead of disappointment means that you must stay detached from a particular outcome. That does not mean you give up the goal. It simply means that you stay open to having the very best outcome that is for your highest good and let God help you with the final outcome. This is also the path for anything good.

Say for example you're looking for a new home and you found what you thought was your dream home. Right price, great location, and many of the qualities you've had written into your movie script. Eureka! You've found it! It's perfect and you're charging forward in anticipation, enthusiasm, and excitement. Bags are packed and then... Another offer was accepted. You swirl out of control and head to the basement of your emotions. How long you stay there is the lesson and your spiritual practice.

My mantra that I've adopted when disappointment comes, is this; "Ok, it is what it is. I trust you have something even better for me. I will move forward in faith and gratitude for an even bigger outcome. That is surely for my highest and best good."

This, my friends, is how you stay ahead of disappointment. It's faith; faith that you are not moving forward alone. Your job is to trust that when you stay in your power and choose to stay faithful in the Universe and its higher choices for you, that you have nothing to worry about and nothing to fear, and most of all nothing has been lost.

Stay in the vibration of gratitude and positive expectation or at least shift back to it as soon as you can from your usual reactive state when the energy of disappointment arises. Stay powerful. Use the mantra and move forward in the spirit of the winner you are.

Anyone you have ever read about, who knew true greatness has used this same formula for his or her success. It's familiar to us in the phrase, "pick yourself up, dust yourself off and start all over again." I would change the last part because it's not really starting all over again, because you have certainly learned things along the way that were meant to continue shaping the best outcome for you. It's always up to you and your relationship with the flow. It's not always on your time frame either. Be ok with that. Continue to hold true to your vision and stay faithful to the truth that you are guided by the highest energy there is. You do not work alone. When teamed up with your higher self, you will always get what you need and so much more.

CTA: Today, if disappointment enters the room, shift into high gear as soon as possible. It may take a bit of time because of your old script, but choose to rise above it and stay in faith. Faith that you are part of the energy of all creation. When you remember to remember, you'll be back on the road to success.

Have a great day!

MARCH 8

The Punitive Mindset

This one can be tough for all of us, but letting go of this mindset will not only free your mind, but it will open your heart to the true power of understanding, higher knowledge, mercy, and forgiveness.

The punitive mindset comes from our inner judge. This judge loves to hang em high as the first order of business. This judge does not need much, if any evidence to convict and cast a guilty sentence. Many times this punisher convicts us and gives us a life sentence of guilt and shame. And we let it. Other times, it goes through the day with us, doing drive-by verdicts of guilt and convictions to everyone in our path. Family, friends, and total strangers. All guilty of some crime in our minds. You know this judge. We all do. We call him the dishonorable Judge Ego. This judge has only one verdict for you and everyone else. Guilty! What a horror show.

Being punitive, or the act of punishing is always the realm of lower thought. What causes the violations is also the same energy as the judge of it. And so it continues. Negativity draws upon itself, from the acts it demands of us. Once we judge, we will be judged. It's a vicious cycle that has gone on since the dawn of man. Once we decide as a people to go beyond the ego, we will know earthly peace. And I believe this is happening as we speak. Despite the chaos in the world, well maybe even because of the chaos in the world, we are finally waking up to the truth of what the ego had been doing to us, and as us.

The macro of this plane we live in is merely a reflection of the micro, which is each one of us, as individual parts of the whole. When we as individuals become self-aware and understand that our small contribution to the energy of this planet absolutely matters, we will know our true purpose. Our purpose is to wake up. Letting go of judgment is a huge step on this path to personal and global freedom. It always begins with us.

Listening to the demands that our ego makes within us and being aware that this voice only destroys life, will be your wake up call. This voice keeps you judged and convicted by constantly hammering you with your own past convictions and tells you that you must continue to feel guilty, sad, shamed, angry, vengeful, and defeated. It's *all* a lie! And it's a life killer.

Yes, we are dual natured beings while we are here. Our job is to recognize that our true selves are the unconditional love part. When we leave this ship we call our bodies, we leave behind the ego nature. The ego nature was part of our survival instincts, within us for that purpose, but it got wayyyy out of control and became a thought and then a belief that this was, in fact, us. It is not us, my friends, and we must learn to leave it behind like a polyester leisure suit from the seventies. Don't be caught dead or, especially, alive in it! See the ego as contrast to the true path forward.

Being punitive is but one of the lies the ego instructs us to become. Being aware of its nature is the first step to taming it, lessening its effects and ultimately letting it go. Doing so is the key to living an amazing, love-centered life while we are here.

It's not about becoming something more than what you currently are. It's about chipping off the unnecessary parts that are not Love. The real you is revealed, not created. You've always been there. Shedding the ego is of the highest spiritual practice. Love in all areas of your life is the quickest path to this shedding. Making the choice in every moment to choose love, understanding, truth, and forgiveness is the underpinning of that love.

CTA: Today, make the choice to shed some light on the antics of your ego. Watch the activity of your inner judge. Call it out when it lies about you or others. Know that there's always another voice to choose. It's called truth.

Have a great day!

MARCH 9

The Power of the Silent Blessing

For the next two weeks, I want you to do yourself and the rest of humanity a huge favor. At every opportunity, when you're in a line at the store or the mall, watch what your mind wants to say about those around you. I assure you it's either got you deep in an internal story and you're paying no attention, or you're judging others around you. Not necessarily in a negative way, maybe just assessing and making assumptions.

Listen to how your mind makes up a little story about others. It puts them either below or above you. You're perhaps saying, "will you hurry the hell up?" Or many thoughts in between.

So instead of letting your mind go where it wants according to its usual pattern, I want you to give each and every person you put your attention on a silent blessing. It would sound something like this, "I bless your journey with light and love." Simple.

Now, there could be an irate customer behaving horribly or loudly, and I still want you to do it. Why? Because that's what they need. And that's what you want to keep entering your own experience. Your prayers are thoughts in the right direction. When you pray for anyone, you're also praying for yourself because we are truly all one. Different choices and paths for sure, and some extremely different, but what we all want, whether we know it or not, is light.

Your silent blessings change the very physiology of your being. You rise in these sacred moments. Your soul is driving the car. This only brings beauty to your life. After the two weeks of practice, you'll never go back. You will have tapped into your true self a bit more. Stay on this path and be grateful you are able to find it every day. It will lead you to an amazing life.

CTA: Today, give what you want to see show up in your own life. Thoughts are energy. They have greater power than you've been told or chosen to believe. Just give your best. Your best is always love.

Have a great day!

MARCH 10

Complaining: The art of attracting the negative

We all know how to complain and some have unwittingly chosen this as a life path.

Complaining is voicing anger, frustration, and negative energy outward, because we feel something in our past, present, or future is not as we would like, or is causing us to suffer in some way.

Here's the truth, you get what you think, speak, and act on. If you're a habitual complainer, you can expect to keep getting more of what you're complaining about. You're attracting it to yourself, whether you believe it or not.

The issue is that you've built a groove in your brain that automatically spits out complaints and complaining energy, which is negative.

Sometimes we feel that only by complaining, do we get what we want. Here's more truth; when you get what you want by complaining, it will be a short-lived victory. In the long run, no one wants to be subjected to a constant complainer, except for *other* constant complainers. And we all know what these groups look like and feel like; a horror show. If you find yourself turning people off or you're not attracting the good stuff into your life, you must look at your thoughts, outward conversations, and actions. It's always about your perspective and the lens you view life through.

The good news is that complaining is just an old dug-in habit. The experts will tell you that you can change a habit in six weeks if you're willful and diligent. This habit of complaining is so worth that effort. You will feel better, you'll attract new people and opportunities into your life, and you will see for the first time, how life was meant to be. This one decision, to starve your complaining habit, will be life-changing.

CTA: Today, start attracting the good stuff into your life. Anytime you are tempted to complain, give yourself some space and ask yourself what good this complaint will bring to you. You'll find that it's always love and loving energy that bring you life and all the good stuff. The more of this you give, the less you'll have to complain about. This I guarantee. Practice, practice, practice. It's the only journey that's worth it.

Have a great day!

MARCH 11

Starving Your Ego

We all have what is called the ego, or false self, while we are here on earth. Personally, I believe it's here to give us contrast, so we are able to grow our light, by knowing the darkness. We all know this low, dark energy and voice of the ego, it's the one that causes all the trouble for you.

This is the voice that tells you you're not good enough, others are better or worse than you. It's the one that judges everyone else, but also judges you. Its incessant demands upon you to be easily offended or upset by the words or actions of another are the common chant by this life saboteur.

This voice tells you to watch out for this one or that one, because of something negative you've been told, and now, you just take it in as 100% fact and act and speak accordingly.

This voice loves to spread bad news and gossip and loves to be the mayor of martyr town. You also know this voice as your friendly neighborhood complainer and storyteller of woe.

This is the voice of the liar. It is not to be trusted and it must be starved out of your life if you are to ever know true peace of mind, daily happiness, harmony with all, and loving, supportive relationships in all areas of your life.

Your job is to begin being an astute observer of this voice and how different it sounds from your true voice of the spirit within. The spirit is more subtle and is easily heard when we get to know the difference. Quiet time is essential for you to begin to identify the opposite tones and vibrations of the true and false selves.

Once you begin the noble practice of starving the ego of its power over your life, your radiant light will begin to assist you in the process of clearing out old lies, fears, and judgments you've been telling yourself for way too long. You'll begin to see others as fellow souls, instead of outsiders who deserve to be judged for their different journeys.

The practice of starving your ego happens one awakened choice at a time. Becoming the witness of your ego instead of becoming your ego will be your path to its starvation.

Shedding the unnecessary dictates of this low energy voice will bring you the inner and outer freedom that all the ancient spiritual texts speak about. It's all about being awake and aware and then becoming a conscious choice-maker. This will lead you to the life of your dreams. Unloading all the garbage always streamlines your life.

CTA: Today, begin or continue to cultivate your silent witness. Watch your ego as it begins to create a maddening scenario in your head about someone or something. Does it want to judge you? Or perhaps lash out at someone for some assumed offense? Be vigilant, give space for the other voice of truth to be heard and then move forward in a consciously chosen, positive direction. When you begin to see the new results in your life, you'll never look back. Out with the old, in with the real YOU.

Have a great day!

MARCH 12

The Blame Game

Probably the most popular game on the planet and the one that cuts the deepest; destroying relationships instead of nurturing them.

We all know the face of blame. It seeks its victim first and asks questions later, or not at all. Blame is seen every day and many times it's we who are pointing that finger.

Most have been conditioned to use blame as the first line of thinking. Instead of first trying to find a solution or quick resolution to an issue or problem, we find ourselves in the role of hunter, looking for our prey. Solving the issue is secondary or not even the main focus. A guilty verdict needs to be assigned and the guillotine must fall first, in order to have satisfaction.

Who did this?! Where's so and so?! I'm pissed and somebody's going to pay! Sound like somebody you know? Well, we've all been in this position. Sometimes it's to cover our own tails because we don't want to take responsibility for our part in something, or we have a domineering role that we play, and the ego is at the helm.

Anytime the blame game is played, things usually get really ugly. Blame teams are formed and mob mentality ensues. We see this on both a small scale in our own homes and we see it on a global scale everyday on the news. The news is in the very business of blame. All of which keeps the ego in power and the wheels of negativity spinning. We can and must do better.

Always remember that to cast stones of blame, we must always look in the mirror first, to see when and where we may have done similar offenses. I assure you, you have. When we see something positive or negative in another, we are noticing something we too possess or have possessed.

The way out of living a life with a very pointy finger is to recognize that when *we* do something wrong and we feel the wrath of blame coming at us, what we really want is forgiveness and understanding. Not condemnation.

We are *all* mistake-makers here on earth and we all need to feel the blessing of forgiveness when wrongs are committed. Always ask yourself what you would want and how you would want it said to you. Blame usually has an ugly tone with nasty body language to go along as a side dish. It never feels good. Only to your ego.

The art of putting yourself in another's position before the ego demands the finger be pointed and blame be assigned, is your best way forward. Most often the things we find blame for, we are guilty of ourselves and we refuse to look at it. Just because you have overcome and learned your lesson from a past, similar mistake, does not give you the high ground in which to cast blame. In fact, your job is to recognize the similarity and offer some kindness instead. Even if the offense means a parting of ways, you can still be kind.

CTA: Today, catch yourself before that finger of yours comes out of its holster and harken back to when you may have done something similar. Choose to respond with your higher self, rather than with your lower ego nature. I promise you that the results will be totally different and love will have never left the room if you choose the high road.

Have a great day!

MARCH 13

Our Distressing Disguises

Mother Teresa was once asked what she saw as she walked the streets of Calcutta, where poverty and suffering is an everyday reality. The earthly saint answered, "I see Jesus in his many distressing disguises."

What she meant by this is that she was able to see beyond the human disguise and clearly recognize a fellow soul; a connected soul. Despite the outer shell that would frighten, sadden or be judged by most, she saw past this and went into her true sight of unconditional love.

This true sight of hers understood immediately, accepted immediately and entered their world on their terms. Her gift was always the same, Love and Light. She gave her gift without any expectations or reservations. She was fearless because she knew who she really was and wanted others to know their true selves.

Mother Teresa led an amazing life and she healed many during her journey just by her mere presence. We too have this power. This was her life's message. This is the message we must pay attention to over all others. The more we as individual souls spread this energy, the higher we will all climb and be healed from the horrors and distressing disguises we all see every day. Many times we are in this disguise.

We need not sit back and wait for the next Mother Teresa to take the helm and do the work so many of us admire. We must do the same each day in our own personal worlds. We all possess the gifts she gave away so freely and without reservation. We have all been given many talents and gifts to share, but the one that offers you and others the most healing and life-giving energy is unconditional love. Love without expectation or judgment. This is the fountain of life we all must consistently give and receive in order to live a meaningful, purposeful life.

So today, if you should come across anyone in a distressing disguise, instead of judgment, offer the good stuff. See this worn-out shell as merely a suit of rusty armor that has done its best to protect a damaged soul. Do your best to offer a step up in their day. Your own soul will be opened up and will let you know exactly what to do or say. Trust it. Look into the eyes of a distressed soul and you too will feel something you've known yourself. Then ask yourself what I would need in this situation. The answer will be forthcoming and your action will be a gift from the divine source within you. You'll ask for nothing in return, but you will be given the gift of an expanding self. That, my friends, is the gold you seek.

CTA: Today, notice how your ego wants to judge another as less or more than you in some way, based solely on their outer appearance. This is a powerful step forward in your rise. Once you've become the witness to your ego, it opens the door to higher choices and a more beautiful path.

Have a great day!

MARCH 14

Life After Divorce

So many of us have lived through the experience of divorce. My parents were divorced when I was twelve. Personally, with the gift of hindsight, it was a blessing. Not because my parents were always fighting or did not care for each other. In fact, they remain friends to this day. I feel blessed because it caused me to play a new role in my family, one that I believe led to growth I would have not otherwise known. I am grateful for this gift that most might consider a tragedy. This gift taught me many things about relationships and the importance of truth, nurturing, trust, letting go of the little things and so much more.

I remember well the day my sisters and I were told of the impending break up. It was hard to hear, but in our hearts we knew it was right. I remember not needing to judge the situation as horrible, but instead my role was to comfort my mom and accept what was. It was weird, but I knew instinctively my part. This was 1978, so divorce was really just becoming more prevalent in society, on TV and in the lives of my friends.

Today I am aware of many friends who have gone through a divorce or are currently in the middle of the process. For you, I say don't worry so much. It's going to be ok. You will be ok and your kids will be ok. Your job is to create a new positive reality for everyone involved. This will start with a new vision for this new chapter for your life.

If you have children and you want the best for them, it's all about assuring them that they are loved, protected and that will never change. That is what they really want and need to hear. You'll need to have a positive vision to share with them when you make the decision to tell them. If you do not have a positive vision to share with them, they may create a very scary one on their own. This is a very important part of the process.

Let them in on the plan forward. The less you leave to their negative imaginings, the better. Give them the truth wrapped in positive loving kindness. There is no need to bring out the dirty laundry. This talk is all about the continuation of love and security in their lives. That's the real goal. It made all the difference for me.

Now, for you personally, once you've attained a loving understanding within your family, you need a new vision for your life. What will that look like? This also must begin with positive focus and a vision for your new chapter.

In order to create a new life that brings bigger and better results, you need to take a good hard look within. Be honest with yourself about the things you did right in your past and where you seem to always fall short. Look at where you may have been controlling or controlled. Be honest about your choices during the last relationship and what you would change about yourself to bring about better relationships in your new chapter. It's all about being a truthful witness to your normal patterns and where they bring trouble to you. If you do not grow past these old worn out patterns, they will simply recreate the same havoc in your new chapter. You cannot go forward expecting better results with the same you that helped to create the past ones. This is your time.

If it is at all possible to remain friends and let go of the past when children are part of the picture, it will do wonders for the path forward. Speak in kindness not hatred, for you are helping to shape your children's perceptions of healthy relationships and emotional choices. Love and kindness instead of transferring pain, vindictiveness, and bad examples. Always remember that your life and the way you live it is your example. Never be afraid to seek the help of professional healers during this time. They will help you through it and keep your perspective in the higher realms. This life is ALL about relationships. This seeming ugly wrapper has gold in it for you and everyone involved. Do your best to be a great ambassador into the new chapter. The right words will come to you as you trust in the process.

CTA: So today, for my friends who may be facing this page turning event, take heart. No blame, no shame and no judgment. It is what it is, and what you do from here is everything. Choose to rise above the pettiness of the past and forge a new positive reality for yourself and your loved ones. It's all about growth. Choose to do just that and you will have chosen to live at a higher level. Your gifts from here will come back to grace your own path. Hope this helps.

Have a great day!

MARCH 15

The Hole In Your Heart

I am compelled to write a bit more on the loss of a loved one after a message sent to me yesterday from a friend.

Many will extol the waste of time that is called Facebook, but for me, it seems to be a pretty positive place where feelings, love, support, and raw emotions are shared. I see more truth here than we will ever see or read in the mainstream news.

Recently, I have seen and sent messages of hope, love, and healing to those of you struggling with the loss of a loved one. This is never an easy time and a broken heart is part of the process, I'm afraid.

There is however the truth of a broken heart that must be known and held onto in these times. A broken heart is truly a vehicle of higher blessings. It certainly will not feel like that in the beginning, but rest assured, the blessings will come and the road ahead will become easier. Hold to this, for it is truth.

We will all experience this blessing, first felt as great pain. Our heart is not just an organ that pumps blood through our system; it is a sacred vessel that holds our deepest pain and our greatest joys. It sings to us and it gives lessons that we need in order to fulfill our personal dharma, or mission while we are here.

The gold you will gain from your heart being cracked open, will show itself in due time. Never rush the process. It is here for you, all of it. That may not sound comforting in the early stages of this difficult life change, but perhaps knowing the truth, that your loved ones are now in a new position of helping you to heal, from our true home, where they now reside.

They want you to live! They want you to move forward and they know that you love them dearly and miss them. Always remember that your separation is only temporary and you will be reunited when your mission here is complete.

CTA: Today, begin a new relationship style with your loved ones who have gone home. Yes, it will be different. Speak to them often and instead of using your physical ears to attempt to hear an answer, you must feel what they would have said. The more you move in this feeling direction, the more you will know that they are with you all the time. What feels weird at first will become your new way of spiritual communication. Your connection is the same, Love.

Have a great day!

MARCH 16

Healing After Loss of a Loved One

Divine healing is a cooperative endeavor and you, my friends, have a crucial role to play. Your job is to shift from the mindset of loss to the heart centered place of gratitude. Holding the memory of your loved one in a very special place of being grateful for the time you had with this blessing in your life.

It doesn't matter how short or long this blessing lasted, it is more about how your soul has benefited from your sacred union. A grateful heart is the path to easing your pain. This is the very peace your loved one wants you to know. It is a gift that you will have for all eternity. Never doubt that.

Your loved one shines their light through you now. Let it be a glorious light, a beneficial light and a grateful light; one that you will be able to share with others who have or will know this same human experience. That is part of your new purpose.

As your heart begins to heal, you will have new powers you did not previously know. You will have a broader view of life and your divine mission to serve. All of this is a gift to you that came in a seemingly ugly wrapper. Many of our higher gifts come to us in this manner.

The sooner you are able to feel gratitude for what you still have in your heart as the beautiful memories of your loved one, the sooner you will be able to help others through their painful trials.

Being a channel of understanding and love for others is the gift you are being given. The more you use this new gift, the more meaning you will be giving to the life of your loved one. Theirs is the love you are spreading. It is part of you.

While the tears and sadness may be with you for a bit, please hold to your faith and trust that your life is meant to go on and go upward from this transition and that you *never* really lose your loved ones. They are happy and at peace and their message to you is that their supreme desire is for you to know the same peace and happiness. They are whispering for you to live and live big while you are here. They want you to remember their best selves and carry that forward as part of your new mission as a more loving, compassionate person, toward yourself and others.

So today, take heart in knowing that love never dies. In fact, it is the only true force that is eternal. Never stay in pain for pain sake. Never get too comfortable in the pain, but let it take its course because it is a totally natural part of the process. Pain, however, is not what you want their memory to be about. It is not what they want their memory to be about.

Life is about living and you know very well that your loved one, who is now home, wants you to rise from this, give thanks for the growth in your spirit and give this new gift of a deeper understanding to others. Let that be your way through. Giving is always the way through. It is the true healer. Find a consistent way to give love and your heart will be healed.

CTA: Let their light shine in you today. Go out and show your loved one that you will not stay down, but for them you will continue to rise and move forward in the energy of your true nature. They will thank you for it. God Bless.

Have a great day!

MARCH 17

The Thief In Us

There is a thief in all of us. This thief robs you and others each and every day, and gets away with it. *You* let the thief get away with it.

This thief steals the following from you, but only if you let the thief: your joy, your self-confidence, your self-esteem, your gratitude, your true vision, and understanding. This thief is also a liar. The thief whispers lies to you so often, you've decided to believe the lies. This is how the thief easily robs you without challenge.

You've decided to believe the thief when you're told that you're too fat, or too old, or too skinny. You've decided to believe you are unlovable and will never find someone to love or that will love you. You've decided to feel fear and worry as your constant companion. These are just attributes of the thief; just a little daily side dish from the inner liar. We all know it well. We can decide again. You own the power to do so.

How our thief steals from others is just a reflection of how we allow the thief to steal from us. We decide to believe the thief and steal others' joy when we speak and act from the perspective of this robber. We put others down, treat them as less than us is some way, try to control or manipulate others. We judge freely and gossip behind the backs of others. When we do this and decide to become the thief, we rob our own soul. We rob the souls of others. And we decide to do this every day. This is how the ego remains in control of our lives. We must rise from this old paradigm to a vastly better way; the way of the heart.

Your heart is the center of truth. When you are living from it, you know it. It feels good. The opposite is true when we let the thief lie to us about ourselves and others. We totally change our energy and pinch ourselves off from spirit. In other words, we feel lousy. Our insides churn with anger, fear, envy or hatred. We cast guilt and shame upon our own selves and live our lives in darkness, much of which we create ourselves. If you are reading this page and it resonates with you, your time to change is now. Today is the day.

Our power to rise is always in the present moment. Choosing new thoughts and actions. Choosing to love yourself and give love as your new calling card. Letting go of the past and trusting in your higher power to help you create a powerful new future. Becoming a person of gratitude and giving thanks many times throughout your day, instead of complaining. Giving your new best in all you say and do. This is your path away from the thief.

CTA: It is *your* daily choice to live from your higher self or to have another day robbing yourself and your happiness, and subsequently robbing from others. *Give!* Give the energy of love to yourself and others as your new life choice. It only leads to an amazing ride and meaning in all areas of your life. Why on earth would we choose anything else? You own the key! Use it!

Have a great day!

MARCH 18

Ten Phrases That Keep You In a Low Vibration:
Discard them from your life

1) I'm always broke.

2) Just my luck.

3) Why me?

4) It's them, it's not me.

5) I can't do it.

6) No one likes me.

7) I'm offended.

8) Must be nice.

9) It's too much work.

10) I'll never get it.

The higher vibration that brings you everything you'll ever need is above these thoughts, words, and subsequent low actions. You must leave this place for higher ground. You must be brave enough to leave this comfortable, self-defeating mindset. It brings you nothing you want but everything that goes along with this energy. Chaos, illness, old before your time, little or no support system, and no apparent way out. You'll never see a way out in this mindset. You must rise.

CTA: Today, seek and ye shall find. Download or pick up a book on self-improvement strategies, there's so much available to you. Love is always the answer and it has an opposite phrase for each of these former choices. It's called the truth of who you really are and were meant to be. It's different than you think. Learn and grow.

Have a great day!

MARCH 19

The Art of Loving Yourself

We are all here on a collective journey as well as a very unique and individual one. We are here to uncover our true nature and also recognize it in others. Comparing yourself to others and their journey is a game of your ego.

Too many times, we want to affix a marker on where we think we are in our lives, compared to others. When we indulge in this negative game, we either find negative judgment of ourselves, which leads to self-esteem issues, or we make ourselves more than others and thus, perceive these fellow souls as less than us. This shuts off the connection to our own true self and the potential for having a beautiful relationship with those we judge as less than. There is no more than or less than where we really call home.

When we go about finding our self-worth by comparing ourselves, our station in life, our beauty, our prosperity, our talents, or any other facet of our lives to that of another, we only rob ourselves and others of the truth.

In order to live your life in victory and your true power, you must cease this destructive practice and replace it with love.

Love yourself enough to be your own best friend. If you are dissatisfied in any area of your life, you simply must begin to intentionally improve in those areas. No amount of comparing or complaining will get you there.

Once you recognize where you want to be, the only power that will get you there and keep you there is love. Love includes many facets. Knowing we possess the power that creates worlds, what does that leave out? You are of this power called Love. Love brought you into this world, love sustains you, and love creates all goodness and meaning in your life. Love is determined because it knows how to succeed. Love perseveres because it is eternal. Love takes risks because it is an endless stream and it knows the quickest path to your deepest desires. Wishing you were anything else than who you are, pinches off your flow. Being that you are now your own best friend, stop sabotaging yourself.

Loving yourself must be first and foremost in your life. Why? Because the act of loving yourself brings you into alignment with the energy of the loving force that created you. The more you deny this by self-hatred or loathing of any kind, the more you separate yourself, or pinch yourself off from your true power.

Once you completely accept yourself (supposed flaws and all), offer compassion to yourself instead of listening to your inner critic, and begin to let love rule your being, you will never hang your head low again. You are a piece of the highest! We all are. Treating ourselves and others by this perspective will change your life forever. Uncovering and unleashing your true power and potential will bring you to a place where the only person you compare yourself to, is the you of yesterday. Leaving the lies you've believed yourself to be is done one day at a time.

Comparing your higher perspective to what you used to believe, instead of someone else's personal world, or view of you, will be your ticket to growth and a life well lived. We curse ourselves when we either believe in our own negative perceptions of ourselves, or worse yet, take on the negative perspective of us that someone else has given you. Lies are lies. Break the curse.

Our false self feeds us a daily diet of lies and negative energy, *but only if we let it*. Choosing to shift into a higher gear from the minute we wake up will be the choice of true living. Believing, knowing, living and spreading this truth raises you and it raises the world. We must all wake up to who we really are. Choosing to believe you are more or less than anyone else is just wasted life energy in the wrong direction. You always have the choice.

CTA: Unless you love even the parts you wish to change, they will not change. It is through self-love that we heal. So today, shine some love on those areas of yourself that you continue to judge and curse. They are a guide for you as well. Be grateful for their lessons and then let that story go for good. Spend that same time you would have spent cursing, into the joy of positive creating.

Have a great day!

MARCH 20

Jumping to Conclusions

This one human trait causes so many problems, it should be renamed, "foot-in-mouth disease."

We are all guilty of this practice. We have a smidgen of supposed facts and we create an entire scenario in our heads that we decide to believe as total, 100% truth. We then grab our judge's robe and gavel and commence with the trial, guilty verdict already decided. Sound like you?

So what do we do so we keep ourselves out of this trap of the ego? We give space and time to the issue. Space in our minds to ask if what our self-created scenario is in fact 100% true, or if some parts are facts and others are assumptions of our ego's desire to punish and be right instead of kind and understanding.

Time is also needed to sift through what is truth and what is your, or others perceptions of supposed truth. These can be treacherous waters. We've all sailed them at one time or another. Some sail these waters every day.

When we jump to conclusions, we are usually just reacting to whatever our first thoughts are. Usually we get so tangled up in this first thought, that we just let the verdict out of our mouths quicker than our higher self can stop us. This is how wars are created in your mind and outwardly in your life. It's also why we become disconnected from each other and from spirit.

When we are in a great mindset, we tend to automatically give space and understanding to issues that arrive, without becoming the reaction your ego demands. We speak with kindness, forgiveness, and from a place of connectedness. When we become the reaction of our lower nature, we blame, we curse and we lash out. When this happens, no one in the room is openhearted. We shut down; we close ourselves off and usually retreat into our own lower nature, where responses like revenge, vindictiveness and hatred live. This is never the place where true solutions are found. True solutions and growth come from the heart and the understanding that we all are mistake-makers. It's how we find our way.

When we choose to hold onto our own mistakes, we carry these burdens around with us like a constant negative companion, ready to whip us again and again for this same mistake every time we choose to relive it on our minds. Our attitude takes a sudden nosedive by constantly reliving old wounds. When we are judged by others, we also hang onto these perceptions as truth, and many times never let them go. We carry this backpack of mistakes like a heavy load of weights our entire lives; time to let go of the load.

CTA: Today, give space between your normal reaction to everyone and everything and your actions forward. Most often you need to stay quiet and wait for the truth to emerge. Patience goes a long way for this gift. Try it.

Have a great day!

MARCH 21

More on Assumption: Jumping to conclusions

Our higher selves would tell us to stop jumping to conclusions and keep our eyes and minds on the bigger picture. If you want to rise to your highest potential, you must give up assumption. You know it as jumping to conclusions. This is better known as the art of getting it wrong. You let your egoic mind spin a tale that you instantly accept as truth. Most often this is what causes drama to ensue. We cause our own drama when we jump to conclusions. The answer is to calm this negativity that you give voice to. You do this by giving some time between your ego's usual reactionary judgment and what you let out of your mouth. This time is of great value to you. The truth most often emerges quickly when we choose not to react and instead give space. Trust this process and give it a try. The more you practice this peaceful art, the more you'll come to realize how false your old way was. You'll be choosing light energy over dark. You'll know this as "feeling good."

After giving the needed space, you may reach the same conclusion as to the one you would have jumped to, but it's the way you approach the solution that is most important for your soul growth and the growth of another. Loving yourself and others as connected souls will steer you to the right approach. Treating others as separate or less than because of their mistakes, is a response from your false self. It usually does more damage than good.

If we are already in a whirlwind of stress from another, totally separate issue and a new issue arises, we will most likely begin grouping them together like targets in a shooting gallery. We begin shooting negative conclusions and punishing language in all directions and in every encounter. Hunker down in these situations; because the mess has hit the fan!

Only through your consistent practice of higher sight and big picture thinking will you be in the proper head to make better choices in how you approach situations and life in general. We all have days where our heads are in the basement. Learning to center yourself in these times will prove to be your higher path forward. Learning to compartmentalize our issues will help prevent us from shooting up the whole place at once.

CTA: Today, take off your conclusion-jumping shoes. Stay grounded in loving energy. If a storm comes your way, give some needed space before you respond. Being a reactive person instead of a mindful person only breeds animosity and low-energy relationships. You are not these reactions, my friends. They have been conditioned choices and habits that you can peel away like a banana skin to reveal the sweet fruit within. It's there. It's always been there.

Have a great day!

MARCH 22

What's the Real Issue?

How many times in your life have you had an argument, misperception or ego interaction, and then turned around and used that energy as your calling card for the entire day? We all have, and more often than not, we leave behind a trail of defeat, hurt feelings, and old, resurfacing wounds. How we choose to repair the damage we do is all about loving awareness.

Are you aware of the carnage your ego leaves behind? Are you aware that you even have a choice as to your approach? Are you aware that the very same results you seek can be better found through consideration rather than contempt? Uplift rather than punish? Recognition of our connectedness rather than seeing others as separate and deserving of your scorn?

One side is true and the other is false. One approach comes from being connected to your higher self and others, while the other is the flamethrower of your ego. Are you aware of which choice you make most often?

So often we carry ugly luggage with us from one place to another and happily unpack it in the lives of others. Instead of being aware of our own low energy mindset, we use it to plow over others as a way to vent or release the negative energy. Soon, WE feel better, but have left carnage in our path to getting there.

We must become better stewards of our own energy and subsequent behaviors. It matters more than you know. Your ego is very convincing. Never forget that. It will always tell you that your words and actions are justified. And when they come back to bite you, your ego will immediately move to defend your approach, instead of apologizing for being less than your best. That's how you know what energy you are in and emitting. One heals while the other hurts your relationships.

Defending the perceptions of your ego will only serve to widen and expand the negativity. While a simple apology releases it from both you and those you've hurt. Never be afraid to apologize, even if the message was right, the approach is what you are regretful for. The ability to apologize is a true strength of your spirit, not a weakness. Only your ego finds weakness in apologizing.

Keeping yourself free and nurturing the real gold that is your relationships is done through the power of forgiveness and apology. It *always* works when given by both parties. It keeps love in the room and brings the great, creative energy back to peak levels.

CTA: Today, if you are caught in the storm of your ego, dig down and find out what the real issue is. Do your best not to use these same glasses to view and spew the lower energy of one issue into your entire day. If you need to apologize, *do it*! If you need to let go and forgive another's dark moment, *do it*! Remember, we only hurt when we shut off the love to ourselves and others. Free yourself and others today with your highest self.

Have a great day!

MARCH 23

Overreaction: The learned behavior

Many of us were raised in a household where overreaction was just a "normal" part of life. We've seen our mom or dad go to ten at the drop of a hat. This was a learned behavior and energy they unwittingly soaked up from their parents. Lifelong habits of behavior are created this way. Unless we have the courage and insight to recognize these detrimental energies, we are destined to relive them again and again. It is time to break this habit.

Overreaction is simply fear-based energy. It's either telling you that you have no control over a situation in the present or future, or an old trigger of negative response has resurfaced in a new situation. We as evolutionary beings, have the power to change course at any time. It all starts through self-awareness and the burning desire to rise from old, worn out habits and behaviors.

I think we all recognize which parent has instilled certain automatic behaviors in us. It is in this recognition that the entry point to meaningful life change can begin. It's all about picking up a new brush to paint the rest of your life with.

Practicing inner peace is an every moment decision. Peace demands that you trust in your higher power. It says you must abandon the doubt and replace it with faith; faith in yourself and your God-given abilities to overcome anything. You are no different than anyone else who has made this decision. We all possess this power. It's in the very practice of what we want to see in our lives, that brings more of it. As you well know, the opposite choice works just as well. You've become an expert in drama and overreaction, haven't you?

The next time your overreaction trigger is pulled, decide to simply say no to it. You not only have the right to say no to overreaction, but a duty to your higher self. Your higher self always says "don't worry, I've got this." Your higher self says, no problem, together *we* can handle this. It constantly whispers, "stay with me, I'll guide you through these dense woods." It's in your inner communion with the power of love that unlocks the inner peace we all seek.

We all know that person who responds to the same frightening issue with grace, calm confidence, and the attitude of "it will all work out." They, my friends, are no different than you. They have just made a higher choice. This choice is *always* available to you as well.

Fake it 'til you make it. This is how you begin to fill in the old groove of fear, panic and the feeling of being out of power. Only by practicing calm, will you know calm. Only through calm, will you see the fastest and best way forward. Only through peace will your light begin to shine brightly in all you say and do. And only through faith will you be able to give your problems over to your higher source, the *one* that you are a beautiful, amazing piece of. Overreaction is just the energy created by our inner liar. Deciding to give calm a try, instead of immediate overreaction, will begin this trusting relationship.

Your lower nature loves to feed you the imaginary horror stories you create in the theatre of your mind. It's time to give over the reins to your soul; your true self. Give your horror-show director the boot! He's caused enough trouble for you. Hire your new director, the one who creates a beautiful new story of courage, confidence, victory, and lasting happiness.

Every time you choose this director in each day, in each interaction and in your every thought, the screaming, chaotic, ego-minded reactionary you used to describe as yourself, will begin to fade and fall away to reveal the real director that has always been on the set.

CTA: Today, when the old director wants to grab the bullhorn, give space to your situation. Breathe it away for a few minutes and make a higher choice. You will make a much clearer decision and be shown the path to the proper solution. You won't be going around the block in order to get right next door.

Have a great day!

MARCH 24

Our Earthly Regrets

How many feuds, silent cold wars, torn relationships, or present day shoot-outs do you have in your temporary visit to the school we call earth?

If you're like most, you have a few. How many do you regret and wish you could change? How dug in and attached are you to the reasons behind the ugliness? In most cases, these reasons will not be good enough when you face each other on the other side, or our true home.

What we fight over in this material world is usually just that, something material. We fight over "things." Sound familiar? Always remember that these "things," while they may represent something important in your mind, they are never as important as what is eternal. They are temporary. They are objects. Your attachment to them and the importance you give them must never be higher than your close relationships.

Is that object or subject more important than the love you once felt for the other you're now detached from? Will that object or subject come to your aid in a stormy crisis of life? Will it wrap it's arms around you in your time of loss or suffering? You know the answer.

My friends, at the end of your life, you'll never be able to cling to the treasured things or old grudges you held. They will all be lifted from you and your temporary ride. So what will be left? The real you. The eternal loving energy who could not care less about that thing. The one who wishes they knew that it's the loving relationships in your earthly journey that were the real treasure, the real issue, and the real lesson.

Letting go of prideful issues, feuds of ego-centric reasoning, and our physical attachments to things over loving relationships is the path of no regrets.

Most likely it's just the story you are now attached to. Let it go! Rise above this pettiness and release the horrible negative baggage you're carrying. You've never gone too far for you to accept responsibility for your share of the drama that haunts your soul and the others in the feud. These battles of the ego just cause harm and cast another shadow over your true light. The more shadow you release, the more light you become. It's your choice. Why hold into these burning hot coals when you have the power to simply let them go. It's only your ego that demands you hold onto this pain and mental suffering.

Living your life from the end means to see things from a higher perspective of what's truly important. Love is important. Forgiveness is important. Becoming detached from things is important. Giving is important, gratitude for all you are and all those you have in your life is important. That "thing" or low-energy reason for your separation from a loved one is *not* important. Don't wait until the end before you realize it; especially when none of us knows when that end is. The time is now.

CTA: Today, call that person; write a letter if you have trouble with confrontation. Get rid of this ugly shadow you're holding on to. What good is it bringing to your life? Is it better than love?

Have a great day!

MARCH 25

Drama: The unnecessary choice

If you want to live the very best life for yourself and those around you, it's all about releasing old, negative energies and conditioned habits that create the drama in your life.

Change is constant on planet earth. That's all there is here. We are part of this ever-flowing current called the human experience. In order to fully live in this amazing flow, you have to move with it. Accept what is in every moment and choose to ride the wave. Fighting the current or sitting on the shore, is where we suffer and cause others to suffer.

When we hit the rocks or have decided not to trust the flow and paddle against it, we are stuck emotionally. Tangled up in some drama, temporary loss, fear of loss, defeat, anger, jealousy, rage or one of the many misperceptions our negative story creator has just written for us in our mind. We can also choose freedom.

When any of these storms of life arise, you must become *very* mindful; *very* present. Become the witness to the turmoil going on in your mind, without taking on the energy of it as you. Just watch it for a few moments, so you recognize what energy is at the wheel. We have a choice in every moment to *not* become the reaction. Always remind yourself that *not everything needs to be dramatic.* In fact, spiritual masters will tell you, nothing need be dramatic, just loved. It takes practice, but this practice is what brings you the good life.

We can look at things from a much higher perspective. We don't have to become our old reactions to daily turbulence, or what you consider to be turbulence. You can shift.

Every time you choose to be dramatic, guess what you can expect to be created right before your eyes? Most often in seconds. You've chosen the roller coaster again.

Your tone, your words, and your momentary lack of trust in your true self are the issue.

What could be handled in a calm, confident, loving, solution-oriented way has been turned into a full-blown soap opera because *you* chose that old, habitual, lower energy as your path. You'll say you didn't, but you at least took the bait from someone else's drama, or assumed a guilty sentence for someone and won't rest until their conviction is handed down. We also do this to ourselves. The time to awaken has arrived.

CTA: Become the witness to your dramatic self. Are you at a ten on the agitated energy scale? Where would you rate your energy, from "calm and content" being a one or "agitated, aggressive and over-reactive" being a ten? Your true path will lead you to one. Keep going there.

Have a great day!

MARCH 26

Listening to Love

The perceptions you think and then outwardly offer in any situation will dictate its energetic course almost immediately, taking you down a pleasant road or a turbulent trail.

The tone and words you use will be like a conductor in an orchestra. If you choose a loving course to solve life's issues, you will have chosen the fastest way to solving them and learning from their guidance. Understanding, empathy, and compassion are the higher perspectives that lead to lasting solutions over temporary fixes..

Your ego will always argue against this course, calling it weak or ineffective. Pay attention to this voice. It's the one that betrays you. Always ask yourself what would work best on you. Is it judgment from another that will change your mind? Or would *you* rather be understood, given mercy or empathy? Would *you* rather be motivated? or told that you are less than in some way? Giving what you would want is giving the truth.

If you choose personal judgments, negative assumptions, and punitive energy as part of your spoken word and usual course of action, you've decided that love has no place here. You have decided that your ego is best to serve this situation and you can't possibly fathom how your light could solve the very same issue.

Assumption, judgment, and some kind of condemnation or competitive tone are what create the drama and negative vortex around you. Dramatic energy and your reactionary, self-created scenarios bring you the drama that you claim to hate. What *you* give is what you get.

You may not even be aware of your own energetic state, tone, or habitual pattern. This state is your spiritual responsibility, to yourself, your health, happiness, and well-being.

You are also responsible for what energy you give away. You're either prospering or you're polluting. If you go through life never truly knowing yourself, you'll get stuck in these dramas all the time. You've been unwittingly choosing them. You think they are somehow necessary. They are mostly conditioned habits. Spiritual growth comes from simply deciding to choose higher paths for the same issue. Shining your light where you once chose dark energy to solve your supposed problems. What your ego thinks is a "problem" is really an opportunity to higher and better ways forward. You'll either learn that the hard way, when the drama has died down and you look through all the wreckage, or you can always take the shortcut your spirit is offering.

CTA: Let your heart lead the way today. Practice makes beauty.

Have a great day!

MARCH 27

Living Life Too Seriously

We all understand being serious. We all know that there's even different levels of this particular energy when we, ourselves have become it. At mild levels, we use serious as a focusing tool. We say, "all right, let's get this done." We stay pretty even with our overall, good feeling energy, but we briefly use serious as a kind of snapping us into the moment. It can be a great tool for that.

If we decide to stay in serious during our tasks or thinking, however, serious tends to attract some other, similar energy friends to the party. You see, serious is a constricting energy, based in fear. Thus, the longer we hang with serious, the more of its energy builds, and we begin to attract thoughts and emotions that support it.

We know this to be true when you're rolling along feeling good and an uncomfortable issue arises. Your conditioned mind will throw off its usual, reactionary juices, filling your body with anxiety or the energy of panic. You then snap diligently into *serious*! If you are not mindful and present to your own energy in these moments, you will always *become* the reaction in human form and flailing actions. You know this person. It's you, right? Me too. It's what we've all learned to become in these times. We have a higher choice, however.

You see, serious energy like this can be very needed and helpful in life-threatening situations, but it usually causes more problems than it solves. Why, you ask? Because constricting energy of any kind limits you to your human self. It pinches off your connection to all knowing. Higher knowledge, wisdom and of course, love. These are really what you want in all life situations, especially the life-threatening ones; calm, confident knowing, instead of unsure, unsteady reactions.

So what you really need is expansive energies. Serious is one that, if held onto as your vehicle forward, just slows you down like a set of new brakes. It's friction against your spiritual wheels.

Let's continue this one tomorrow.

CTA: Go with the flow. Today, choose to be in a state of love and calm.

Have a great day!

MARCH 28

Too Serious *continued*

So what do you do instead? You say, I need to be serious in order to do my job! I need to be taken seriously and seen as a serious person or I won't be respected! My friends, it's always your freed energy that attracts what you need for your day, who you really want in your life, and your life goals.

It's expanding energies that carry you to your dreams in the fastest, most beautiful ways. Using lower energies for your daily ride give you lower results. Plus, we all know how feeling too serious repels, rather than attracts. All you attract when you're indulging in your lower, more serious energies is fear from yourself mirrored back to you as fear from others, resentment because there's little or no love in the room and not much forward motion because there's no true collaborative harmony. The energy isn't good. Get it?

If you're feeling too serious for too long, you must make an intentional shift. It doesn't have to come all at once! It should be stepped up. Take a breath, give thanks for recognizing where you are energetically and decide in that moment to rise! You need to realize you are walking in mud when you're too serious. The waters cannot flow freely when you are deciding to be the hard rocks instead of the flowing water itself. You must begin to command your energy if you want to command your life.

One of the great truths of life is that we are beings of energy. Quantum physics agrees with this truth. Going inside and becoming aware of which energies within you create which results is the path to spiritual and physical freedom, my friends. Learning how to steer your personal field of energy is the gold you seek. Inner peace will be your constant vibe when you finally grab the wheel. Sound better? Thought so.

We spend way too much of our precious life energy in these constricted states. They are nothing more than your old, conditioned, learned, mental habits. They are meant to be shed by you when you realize you no longer need to move in a slower vehicle. Low = Slow.

So today, try a new vehicle forward. Yes, others will respond to your seriousness. They will feel fear. They will respond with fear. They will work or be around you in fear. Or they will respond internally to you with resentful, hurt energy because they feel no connection to you. No love or reason to love. None of us feel good when we are in this vortex of energy. No collaboration, just separation. No creativity or at best, constricted creativity. The only part of you that gets fed by this energy is your ego. It gets to feel superior to others here. It gets to dominate and conquer at the expense of your spirit and your connection to others; never a good foundation to build anything upon. It's sand at best.

CTA: Today, loosen the grip of serious. The fastest vehicle you can ever be in is gratitude. Love is inherent in gratitude. Gratitude keeps the brakes off. Gratitude says, "I get it!" It doesn't have to be this serious thing. I can choose to stay in the vibrational harmony with my higher self, the one that is eternal and realizes that it's all just temporary. That it's love and giving love that frees us, keeps us free, and tells us the truth in every moment. This energy is the creative one. This energy builds greatness all around you and, especially, within you. This is the realm and workshop of everything you really want life to be like for you. So, if you're going to be too serious about something or someone today, be serious about loving yourself too much to stay serious, and give love to others, so they don't have to be too serious either.

Have a great day!

MARCH 29

The Assumptive Mind

In everyday life we must make many logical assumptions in order to move into the unknown of the day. In our relationships however, assumption has no place. Not if you want to live in the higher realms of love and peace as your life's expression.

All of our assumptions are unique to each of us, based on our past experiences for the most part. Past successes and past consequences, both negative and positive.

Most often we believe only to expect more of the same. Sure, we do our best to climb out of habits that have brought negative circumstances and outcomes into our lives, but we unknowingly leave out the most important ingredient, changing our thoughts and core beliefs to the ones that serve us, rather than sink us.

We each have gotten to be experts in our old habits, thoughts, and beliefs. They have become comfortable to us. We were never told to question the beliefs or perceptions that were handed to us. We just became them. The problem with this is that you're using someone else's map for *your* life. Time for a peek under your hood.

How many times during your day do you assume the worst will happen? How many times in your day do you assume the truth of a situation only based on the spoken word or perception of another? How many times in your day do you assume someone doesn't like you, or is upset with you, and it's a misperception? One you later regret. How often do you think of the future as a scary place because your normal life pattern assumes fearful outcomes or failure? How often do you spread your negative assumptions to those around you, creating dramas and low energy? Are you even aware you do this with your negative assumptions and negative future forecasting? If this sounds like you, you're in the majority. Time to help yourself and those around you.

CTA: Today, hang up your negative meteorologist hat in exchange for great energy and harmony with all you meet.

Have a great day!

MARCH 30

More on The Assumptive Mind

The choice of higher living is non-assumption. This is akin to non-judgment. You need to awaken to the fact that you are a creating machine; creating your life in every moment. There is not a moment, except during sleep, that you are not creating your personal reality and life experience, so realize that the way you think is always the precursor to the assumptions you make. Most of them lies and fabricated mental meanderings. a.k.a., your imagination.

If you were raised in a very judgmental home with lots of drama, you will tend to think and assume in those terms. You see, you must begin to become the witness to the thought and belief pattern that you've assumed to be true. Do they still serve you or are you living a less than desired life? You are the machine that creates your new path forward. You've just been creating in the wrong direction. Not your fault necessarily, but it is your responsibility. You are the gatekeeper of your own potential. You are also the key.

Changing how you think about things takes time, but that's all you have. Make the most of it in your favor my friends. Get to really know yourself, how you think, how you normally perceive and give, and how your assumptive mind is actually betraying you and causing lots of problems in your life.

Beginning to shift yourself into a more positive mindset will demand that you stop assuming. Never create a story around something until it creates itself in real time. Stay in the present moment and be aware of who's steering the ship that is you. In other words, you're most likely assuming you have things right 100 % of the time. That's your ego. It's the judge. It judges you and everyone else. Plus, the ego's favorite game is assumption. The ego will help you create wild scenarios! So vivid that you explode with anger, rage, jealousy, envy, revenge, sadness, depression and all the other hell holes of ego-centric thought. You are always serving one side of yourself predominately. Make sure to honor your light. Your light will have an entirely different solution forward than your ego. One may offer partial success with some emotional carnage, while the other brings forth the beauty of compassion and truthful understanding. One offers the ego satisfaction of being right, while the other choice, benefits both parties through loving kindness.

Let's continue this one tomorrow.

CTA: Let go of all assumptive thoughts. Be in the moment. By doing so, new patterns will form, bringing you greater peace.

Have a great day!

MARCH 31

Assumption *continued*

You also have the power to at least assume the best. Give others the benefit of the doubt; especially when you only have one small piece of the story. Offer non-assumption with an eye on finding the truth with an open mind and kind energy. If you go in like a battle hardened detective with the energy of already assuming some kind of guilt without proof, you always run the risk of damaging relationships. How many times has this been you? Me too; many times.

Being a well-balanced person demands a balanced, open approach to daily life. So often our assumptive mind is changed by the mood we're in. This makes you vulnerable to the ego's imagined version of what is. This is because you are unaware of how much your mood is playing a role in your decision-making and your ability to respond intentionally instead of with the overreaction of your lousy feeling self.

Did you ever realize that you've hurt someone's feelings by your assumptive mind and its negative force field, only to regret ever having that false scenario in your head as absolute truth?

This is a huge way we, as humans scar ourselves and those around us. We must be aware when we get caught up in assumption. Assumption happens so quickly and is so convincing that we choose to become the outward reaction of it in a split second. You have just lost the witness and become the thought. Get it?

You never have to become what you think, just because you think it. Awareness, patience, and giving others the grace of non-judgment is therefore the path past assumption. Remember, these are all the beautiful energies that you would want coming your way if there was an issue with you right? Give what you like to see in your own life. Life's a mirror, remember?

CTA: Today, begin the journey into your own life pattern. Is it mostly about judgment, reaction, assumption, retaliation or martyrdom? Or is it about non-assumption, non-judgment, and giving your light instead? You can always choose to be either in every moment. One heals you and others, while the other steals your joy and happiness and robs the spirit of others.

Always look at what you're doing and how you're doing it. What you say and how you're saying it. How much assumption is involved? You can always get the truth by being guided by its very energy, the energy of love. Chances are, if you're using your ego as the means, you are assuming much of what is true, instead of just asking for it nicely. Peace, my friends.

Have a great day!

APRIL 1

A Crooked Path to Success

Ask any entrepreneur how they finally reached their goals and you'll find a common thread: a crooked path.

What do I mean?

When we admire someone for the success they've achieved, we tend to think of it as a linear path; steps in a straight line until their goal was attained. Similar to running a race, jumping over each hurdle while the tape at the end is in sight. This is more the exception than the rule. You've not been witness to their daily struggle and crooked path. You've only known where they began and how they are now in the catbird seat. The stuff in between was the real gold. This is what they would tell you.

Reaching any goal in life, especially the goal of bringing something totally new and unique to the world, will be a crooked path of uncharted territory. Unique hurdles for a new outcome. Each one, honing new skills you did not know before. Each closed door meant to lead you to a better one to go through. Sometimes having to break them down instead of easily turning the knob.

The crooked path can seem like a pinball machine, knocking you around, when in fact, the pins are just rounding out your sharp edges for a smoother road ahead. Letting you know that you are a trailblazer, not a casual hiker following a trail blazed by another.

The myth of a straight, smooth road to success is why most people give up on their dreams. They view it as too hard, or not worth it. "There must be an easier way to make a living" is where most people will stop and choose the safe road. Safe is fine for some, but it usually does not lead to greatness or new gifts *you* are meant to bring forth from within.

The rocks on either side of the supposed straight path will be the ones you learn your greatest lessons from and the ones that uncover your gifts. Never shy away from challenges. Yes, they will feel uncomfortable. Sometimes bringing you to the edge of a very scary cliff, but if you are faithful, awake, and doing your best to trust, you will recognize this cliff as an illusion to get you to turn back instead of plow forth. There's always a gift for you within each challenge. Always remember that you are much stronger and inherently wiser than you give yourself credit for. You are part of the creator of all miracles and you must believe yourself capable of the same power. Because you are.

Let's continue this one tomorrow.

CTA: Today, embrace the roadblocks to your goals and dreams. Know that they are just opportunities for you to gain more knowledge.

Have a great day!

APRIL 2

A Crooked Path to Success *continued*

In my own case, I travel in a group of crooked-path adventurers; each of us offering a unique perspective on the rocks and the best way to read their message. If you are blessed to have an adventurous traveling partner or team, you are indeed well equipped. If you are traveling alone on your personal quest of greater destinations, you will need others to get there. This is where you begin to build your network of fellow climbers. This is done through having a passionate dream that you are well able to articulate from a solid plan and big vision. Everyone likes helping a big vision come to pass. You must share it every time you need to enlist a talent you may not possess yourself. This is how we connect and are meant to harmonize with our fellow brothers and sisters in this earthly game of growth.

You, my friend, must be willing to fail on a daily basis without the self-defeating judge as your traveling companion and voice that you've let guide you in the past. That judge will kill your dream as fast as a wink of your eye. That voice must be the one you hear as contrast, not the one you give your power over to.

Set your sights on a worthy goal. A goal that benefits all of mankind and not one that is just meant to line your own pockets. Your goal must be a gift to others, filled with your love and passion in order to succeed long term. When you choose this path, you will have engaged the power to literally move mountains, even though at times, it will seem like you can't lift a pebble. Stay the course! Trust. Give your best, no matter what the evidence in your immediate view is saying. In every worthy endeavor, you will make loads of mistakes. You will encounter loads of twists and turns. It's how all good things come to us. Rarely is it a straight road. In order to truly know the light of success in any area of your life, you must know its opposite and overcome it. You don't have to live your life "as if."

CTA: Today, jump out on your own crooked trail. Listen to and learn from the rocks you hit. They are as much, or more responsible for your dogged determination and subsequent successes. Celebrate all successes, big and small. It is always a clear recognition of what the darkness shows us that leads us back to the light of all success. Use love as your constant GPS on this road. Love for yourself when you feel like listening to the judge, and love the challenges that are there *for* your rise to the top. Give thanks for all of it. It's all part of the delicious, divine journey into who you are meant to become. Go get it. You can do it. Never give up and never give in. You are incredible.

Have a great day!

APRIL 3

The Power of Perseverance

Perseverance is the juice that keeps you going when there is no evidence yet of what most people would consider success. In any worthy endeavor there will be great challenges, highs, lows, and everything in between. The only way we will ever get to our goals is with the power of perseverance. The more we push past seeming obstacles, lulls, slow times, finances, etc., the more we strengthen our power of perseverance. It's just like building new muscles. Small successes, done consistently will become big success over time. The trick is to always do what you can, from where you are, with what you have, and in the slow times relax in knowing your dream is growing through your constant positive gardening and stewardship. If your vision and goal are big enough to you and worthy of the effort, you will persevere. In times of pressure, remember the vision. Stay the course, stay focused only on succeeding, and you will. If you feel a big challenge at hand, you need to make it much smaller in your mind and speech first and then move right into inspired action that will blow you past it. The more you persevere, the easier it will become to see challenges for what they really are: opportunities. You need to consistently beat back the illusion of obstacles. Big vision, great goals, and purpose will always win the day when you decide to keep going despite any evidence that may seem contrary to your dream. Kick the butt of challenges every day. After all, true greatness has always been the prize of perseverance. "I can and I will" must become the mantra of the seeker of success and a higher level of living. Go get it today. You can and will succeed. Have a great day!

CTA: Practice perseverance in your challenging moments. Move through gracefully instead of pushing.

Have a great day!

APRIL 4

Be the Silent Witness

You are not your mind. You are not your thoughts. You, the real you, are the silent witness behind both. "What the heck does that mean?"

When I first heard these words from author Eckhart Tolle, I asked that very question! But it soon became the most powerful wisdom of my life.

We are the ghost in the machine, the witness who needs to grab the wheel of our thought life and steer that sucker like Mario Andretti! You, my friends, are that driver.

Mindfulness, self-awareness, the watcher of our thoughts, these are many names for the same powerful practice of not only watching the pattern of our own thinking, but shifting ourselves into the driver's seat. We *must* do this or we will stay in the passenger seat, or worse yet, the back seat, with our lower, ego self at the wheel.

When we go through life in this lower, unconscious state, we don't realize that WE have this incredible power within us, dying to get out and steer your vehicle to an exciting new place called *living*! I assure you, it's so much different than what we have been taught.

The practice of becoming the silent witness is an ongoing, lifelong practice that is known as awakening; awakening from the sleep of ego-centric living. Arguing, fighting, competing, taking sides, holding grudges, martyrdom, victim minded, unhealthy, negative energy living is at the wheel when you are asleep in your ego.

Learning to watch how your low energy thoughts have affected you and your life in the past will become totally apparent to you when you learn to witness your mind and how you have unwittingly geared it your whole life.

When you begin to awaken from this nightmare style of thought and living, you will probably feel bad for past deeds, actions, and thoughts. Do not get stuck in that stuff. That's also the ego trying to make you feel shame and guilt for these things.

Forgive yourself first and foremost. Apologize to those you have wronged and get on with your new life!

Dropping the baggage of the past is only one of the massive benefits to becoming the silent witness of your thoughts. Reshaping your life from a new perspective of finally freeing yourself from low-level living to a whole new you is what you get from assuming total responsibility for your life. Finally driving your vehicle instead of just going along for a mediocre ride. Have a great day!

CTA: Today begins your new practice of witnessing your pattern of thoughts. Am I a complainer? Let's see. Am I a controller? Let's see. Am I more interested in winning or being right, instead of kind? Let's see. You get the picture. Change happens in every moment and it all depends on you.

Have a great day!

APRIL 5

Acceptance of What Is

When we finally realize that the purpose of our physical life here on earth is spiritual growth, we will begin to see our daily interactions as either a learning or a teaching experience. We are brought to what we need to know or where we need to grow.

Experiences that we judge as positive or negative are two sides of the same coin. In other words, they are both there for our benefit. Acceptance of what is, is the first step toward reaping the rewards of the lesson or message from this physical experience. And there's always a message.

The art of acceptance is one of the greatest tools of personal growth that we have, yet it is one of the most difficult to master. Acceptance is usually a process for all of us, especially when we lose a loved one, lose a job or go through a break-up. In these cases, our personal process kicks in. Everyone's personal process will be different, but we can learn to process these realities from a much higher perspective.

You see, our perspective and what part of ourselves we draw this from, will make all the difference in the world, when it comes to accepting what is. If we are prone to the lower energies of our ego, we will have a much longer, more dramatic, and drawn out process in getting past a seeming negative situation. We will cause ourselves to suffer way too long. Sometimes we train ourselves so well to suffer that it becomes our go-to emotion. You see this in people who are unable to accept even a little discomfort if things do not go as planned or as they thought they should.

The ability to not only handle what is, but to master what is, emotionally, is the realm of our higher self. In times of loss, we choose faith instead of falling. We choose forgiveness instead of revenge and we choose to rise above the small voice of defeat with the voice of truth.

Losing a loved one is the highest of all challenges. The process of moving forward will take time, and it should. Proper grieving and mourning is actually an enrichment of our souls. You may never be quite the same, but the truth is that we never truly lose anyone. It is just a temporary separation. Your process in times like this must eventually shift from mourning to gratitude. Gratitude for your time together and all the wonderful moments you had. This act honors the beauty instead of focuses in the loss. This experience allows you to be a rock for someone else in your life who will need your loving perspective. This is part of the purpose. To give.

Loss of a loved one is at the top of the list for accepting what is. Everything below that should be much easier to handle. Just the menial things we get so upset about on a daily basis, is just the habit of non-acceptance. This is what causes us all the needless suffering, anger, disappointment, and low-energy experiences. The ability to accept what is and then immediately shift our focus from problem to solution is the art we must master.

You are not necessarily agreeing to the situation, you are accepting that it has come to you and that instead of your normal reactionary response, you choose to use your higher power to solve, move past, ignore or forgive the situation. When you decide to stop overreacting to the smallest of slights, attitudes, disappointing news or any other challenges, you have chosen the best and the fastest path forward. Staying in your true power requires this self-mastery.

CTA: Today, practice the art of acceptance. Instead of your usual ego-bound reactions, choose to instead stay in your happy place, realizing that change is the constant here on earth and it is in our response to it that we either grow our power, or we have decided to relinquish it to someone else or a temporary situation. You always own the power, my friends. Get to know it and you'll know a great life.

Have a great day!

APRIL 6

I'll Figure It Out

A powerful statement from a powerful person. Is this a statement you regularly use in your life? If you do and you've been successful at doing just that, you are a solution-oriented thinker and self-starter. Good for you.

No matter what it is in life; a new project, goal, dream, or challenge, these four words will become your intention and your consistent guide to success.

Trusting yourself is a higher energy of your spirit. Self-doubt is its low energy opposite and the realm of your ego. If you are used to doubting yourself and always looking to others to solve your issues, you need to shift.

Trusting yourself to find solutions to issues, taking inspired action to solve them, and then moving forward will be your path to change and the upward climb. And boy is it satisfying!

Being your own best friend demands that you learn to make your own decisions and trust in them. Making mistakes along the way is how we all learn. There is no greatness in anyone who has not made mistakes. Mistakes are our guideposts to the truth in anything. Our job is to quickly learn the lesson, adjust our sails, and keep going. Each time you do this, you become stronger, wiser, and more confident. These are the jewels of trusting ourselves.

Thomas Edison said his journey to create the light bulb was blessed with 90,000 ways "not to invent the light bulb." He never gave up and his mindset was always about the title of this entry, "I'll figure it out." It's like giving a command to the universe that you absolutely will succeed in whatever the goal is. The Universe (or God) will then conspire with you to assist in the solution. In other words, God helps those who help themselves.

Believing in yourself is just a way of acknowledging that you are of the highest order and the highest order can create anything. You are this power, so why would you not exclaim it in your self-talk and outer speech. Once again, the truth shall set you free. Have a great day!

CTA: Today, decide to be the powerful person you were meant to be. Own the life you were meant to have and know the power that is really you. Move forward and make some great decisions today. Trusting yourself is step one.

Have a great day!

APRIL 7

Your Unique Gift

You have a unique gift that no one else on this planet has. No one! Your job is to discover it, improve it, and give it to the world as your gift. Is it your personality, your craft, your voice, your empathy, or your unique understanding of something? It is there my friends, and whenever you use it, magic happens. Being present and witnessing yourself and your thoughts is how to find your purpose.

I read an inspirational post this morning that said, "hell is when you cross over to the other side and meet the person you were supposed to become and didn't." In other words, you only regret the things you did not do that you knew you should have done. Believing in yourself, trusting that you are not alone in this journey, and moving forth in faith is the way all great people have figured it out. You are one of those great people. Inside you, there is no greater. Trust that and you will live an amazing, adventurous life. Have a great day!

CTA: Today, whatever comes your way, say yes. Say yes to the fact that you can figure it all out. Use others in your sphere if you need higher advice, but you be the driver! Start your day with determined faith and you will end your day in satisfaction.

Have a great day!

APRIL 8

Learning to Receive

Receiving is the art of allowing goodness into your life. You would think that would be the norm, but so many struggle with this.

When we begin to look at ourselves as an energetic being having a human experience, we will begin to understand how we work and how life works. Energy needs to flow freely in order to have the highest potential. We as beings of this omnipresent energy need it to flow freely through us and as us.

We all tend to have erratic energy because we do not understand how to balance it ourselves. We know that when we feel good, the energy is tipped to the positive flow and everything feels great. Conversely, when we pinch off the positive flow by choosing our darker, lower energy of the ego, the mess hits the fan, right? This is the knowledge that can save your life.

The art of receiving is simply being grateful for all that enters your life. If it seems negative, the flow helps you transmute the experience into an opportunity to learn and grow. This is how we become open to whatever comes our way without fear or anxiety. Always remember, if it comes to you, it's always intended as a gift to you. May not seem it at the time, but it is a gift for your soul; the eternal you. The human side of us sees good and bad. The flow of Universal Spirit sees it as growth for you. If you learn to allow it to be, understanding that there is indeed a diamond somewhere within, you will have chosen the higher path to understanding the true meaning of the lesson and intentionally trusting the flow to bring you to a better place from it.

Look back on your life and remember how many times the so-called "bad" thing that happened led you to a higher understanding, a better path forward, or a new and better relationship.

When you become aware of how the flow of energy works and its purpose to raise you up because it wants the very best for you, and from you, then you will begin to take the steps to cooperate with the flow and become aligned with the energy of it. Yes, that is also called being positive. Positive energy is just another name for Love.

Learning to receive Love is very difficult for some. They have a voice inside them that tells them they are not worthy, or have done such horrible things that they shut off the love to themselves. This is a life killing choice. The thing about God, Jesus, Universal Flow or whatever you may call this benevolent energy, is that it is truly Unconditional in its love for you. It knows you better that you know yourself. You simply got stuck in your ego and fell asleep to the truth of who you really are. You are part of the flow. When you leave this earth plane, you will return to it. This flow knows only forgiveness and every other subset of love. It does not condemn you; it forgives, nurtures and shapes you. Your job is to just let it in.

Letting in the flow means forgiving yourself for past mistakes. Sin is just an old religious term for mistake. We all make them, but not all of us accept forgiveness from ourselves and our inner judge. Get past this horrible lie and all of the lies of the ego. Move upward and onward to a new you! It does not matter who you are or what you've done! You can always choose to jump into the flow, which is the path to all you need and desire. Have a great day!

CTA: Today, your job is to let in the love. Whenever it comes your way in the form of compliments, praise, hugs, laughter, fun or peace, let it in. Feel the flow. Then give it back in the same forms to others. When this is your choice, giving and receiving the very best, you're flowing, my friends. You'll never go back.

Have a great day!

APRIL 9

Commit

In order to have the best life possible, and I mean the best in all areas of your life, you must develop your commitment muscles.

Fully committing to something means that you have your heart in it. It means that you consistently give your full attention and great energy to whatever you love and value. This always begins with your relationship with yourself.

Making a commitment to personal growth and steadfast practice will be the catalyst to having it all.

Having it all includes the following; great relationships, marriage, partnerships, friends, family, peace of mind, calm confidence, creative outlets and expression, health and well-being, prosperity, and financial freedom as well as a continued flow of giving and love in all of it.

Committing to excellence is what we are talking about. When you decide to be excellent in all your words, actions, and deeds, this becomes the dominant energy you emit. The more you commit, the better you emit. From this place things become easier, *much* easier, because you are creating life in all you say and do. All good things will return to you multiplied when you commit.

If you are a steady stream of positive energy by your constant awareness and choice, a steady stream of positive will be your life experience. Challenges will still arise, but you will be able to easily know the way forward and through. The result of your commitment and faith will always guide and protect you. Always.

CTA: Today, dare to commit. Say yes to learning and growth. Say yes to a great life, generously created by you.

Have a great day!

APRIL 10

Being the Change

You've all heard the saying, be the change you want to see in your life, but what does that mean?

Being the change means first, knowing what you want. Is it peace? Become more peaceful. Taking time to "be" instead of "do" is the beginning of this one. Quiet contemplation of the energy of peace and meditation to calm your inner self on a regular basis will create a peaceful inner space that you will come to know. It will become an integral part of you and your new improved energy. Others will feel peaceful in your presence and you will have become the change.

Is it happiness? Happiness is the mind-state of someone who is content. Happy with their career choice, their home life, and good friends. This has everything to do with your relationships and what you give to them. In this change, you must be your own best friend first. Loving every part of you. Even the so-called flaws. Constant gardening of your inner life will blossom outward into all your relationships. This is all based on giving your best. Both to yourself and everyone you come in contact with. Even the challenging ones. You change inside and everything on the outside changes too.

Do you want wealth? Again, it's an inside job. Always giving and being in giving energy will bring back to you what you give. Wealth is more than just money, but giving money is part of it. Be generous always; with your time, your attention, your money, and your talents. The wealth you seek comes from you and the inner treasures you were blessed with. All your treasures are meant to be given as gifts for the enrichment of the whole. This includes you.

Any change you seek will have initial hurdles, as you stretch some new muscles. Just like starting at the gym for the first time, there will be some pain, stiffness, and sore muscles from your efforts. Don't ever give up, the change will come according to your perseverance and will. The good stuff you seek is natural. It's all about discarding what we may call "normal" behaviors and energy, but it's what is "natural" that works every time. In other words, your higher energies.

Always remember that any positive change in your life will come as a result of your inner improvement and development. No change on the inside, no change on the outside. It's always up to you. Change your thoughts and actions and your life changes.

CTA: Today, begin to become the change you wish to see in your life. If you need to have a few Ground Zero conversations to set new boundaries for your change, do it. Empowerment, new confidence, and a new direction will be the result. Then, the sky is the limit. Let me rephrase that; there are *no* limits.

Have a great day!

APRIL 11

My Daughter the Young Sage

Wisdom is something that is usually gained by a lifetime of experiences, both good and those perceived as bad. We are enriched with an inner knowing of what is truly important and what is the folly of the ego.

Sometimes, however, a very special person is born who seems to possess an old soul. One who has been around this block a few times and gets it naturally. In our lives, we have been blessed with such a wise old soul that popped her head out of my wife's womb (she's going to kill me for saying it this way) nineteen years ago today. Kate had been teaching us lessons for many years about how a great life should be lived and the important things we need to keep as our life's compass.

Kate, you are a remarkable human being with a heart as big as the Universe itself and a soul that is meant to show others the way. Your amazing sense of humor and open, kind nature is the stuff that endears and attracts the right kind of people into your world. We are so proud and honored that God chose us to be your parents.

So my entry today is about wisdom. It can be learned or it can be a gift that must be nurtured right from the hips of your mama! LOL. Have a great day! Love you Kathryn Grace Keary!

CTA: Celebrate those wise souls who grace your life today. Let them know how much you appreciate them.

Have a great day!

APRIL 12

The Art of Non-Reaction

We all know very well how to "become" the reaction to outside forces or the negative scenarios we create in our own minds.

When we have allowed our ego to take the stage, we will always bring to life just what this negative voice tells us to do. When we become this reaction, it means that we are consumed in an instant with a burst of energy that needs to get out. In this case, I am talking about negative energy.

Whether it's fear, jealousy, hatred, drama, revenge, anger, the need to dominate over another or the need to always be right, the ego always demands action; usually in the form of overreaction. When we get caught up in this space, the mess hits the fan and everyone involved needs a raincoat, because it's going to get ugly!

The practice of non-reaction will seem to you at first like just ignoring issues. However, the wise person understands its power. The spirit, or your higher self, offers calm in the midst of any storm. It "responds" instead of reacts. This means that you allow the negative scenario to be seen for what it truly is, the ego at work. When we are aware of this, we call out the lie while it's still in our head, debunk it as just another deception of the negative mind and rise above it to a higher place and path forward.

CTA: Today, whether you decide to confront an issue or not, based on this new information, your outer speech and actions must now be calm, insightful and coming from a place of truth and understanding. From here, love is in the room instead of the other voice.

Have a great day!

APRIL 13

More on Non-Reaction

When we see our world from a higher perspective, the everyday dramas that used to consume our attention, reactions and lives, will fade and your old desire to jump in this negative pool will fade with it. This all happens one non-reaction at a time. Before you know it, you will find yourself in the flow of the good stuff.

One of the best mantras you can consistently use in this practice is, "I don't go there anymore." The quicker you remember these words, the better your chances for non-reaction. It is always a choice my friends. You either have a bad habit of giving voice and action to your ego's demands, or you choose to rise above the lies and stay in calm confidence.

Calm confidence is always the alternative. From here, the heart has its say in the matter. Whether it's a totally made-up scenario in your head, or the desire to lash out, the heart will be your guide to shine its light on the lie and guide you to creative, constructive solutions instead of reactive ones. We all know how the reactive ones turn out.

CTA: Today, make the higher choice of non-reaction when the ego starts its whispering. Be the silent witness behind your thoughts. Notice what your reactive mind would have said and done first. Analyze your thoughts and see how most of them are assumptions, half-truths, negative judgments and outright lies. Choose not to defend and hold onto poisonous thoughts. This poison of the ego always wants a victim, whether it's others or it's you. Never give into the liar and never become its reactive puppet. You are in control. Just takes practice like everything else in life. Become the master of your mind before it masters you.

Have a great day!

APRIL 14

Breaking From the Pack

When you finally decide to take charge of your life and rise above what most call "normal" living, you will be breaking from the pack.

We have all been conditioned by whatever our surroundings have been to this point of our lives. We've inherited a lot of our everyday mindset from these surroundings and many times the information, knowledge and wisdom that come from these places are less than adequate and most often very lacking.

A huge part of having and knowing a great life comes from having a solid foundation to build upon. This foundation must be grounded in truth in order to have anything real, worthwhile, and lasting.

The truth is that when you choose a path of being self-made, you will have chosen the upward path to your divine self and inheritance.

Surrounding yourself with these types of people and higher information, will fertilize your own efforts and help you grow at a much-accelerated rate. It's like adding miracle grow to your life.

If you find yourself wanting more love, prosperity, quality friendships, and higher spheres of influence, then you must "become" these energies. This always begins with a deeper personal understanding of them. It's like anything else we want to be or do in life; we train ourselves.

The beginning of any path upward starts with new concepts. Always remember that you can never grow new types of flowers in your garden by using the same old seeds. You must learn in order to grow and become. Seeking this knowledge and continually ingesting high-energy concepts will bring it all into view.

CTA: Seek a new book on self-improvement or spiritual awakening. Good stuff will always bear beautiful fruit in and outside yourself.

Have a great day!

APRIL 15

The Power of a Great Role Model

Do you have any positive role models in your life right now? Are they sharing with you a better way forward than you have known thus far? Are you reading any books on self-improvement or in the area of your dreams? What is it that you want? Do you know anyone who already lives it? All of the above are entry points into higher knowledge and wisdom for you. Your job is to begin turning over stones and soaking in new and better information.

All that I write about each day, I learned first by reading and listening to the wisdom of higher knowledge. It certainly is not the stuff they taught in school. What you will gain from surrounding yourself with—and learning from—higher-minded people, is a new awareness. First, you will become aware that you don't know everything you need to, and second you will learn that it will be some hard work to change some of your old thoughts, beliefs, and patterns. This is the challenge you must accept and keep accepting in order to rise above mediocre living and less than desirable results.

Be brave enough to look at your life from above and see who your friends have been, their outlook on life. Do they even think about it? Talk about it? Do they want more for themselves or are they complacent in living a below average or average life experience. Are they quality companions or do *you* need a change?

This is where you decide whether you hold the reigns to your life or if you're giving them up to someone else's powerless view of life, including how *they* think you should live. Time to decide.

Learning to be temporarily uncomfortable in order to get what you want in life is where the gold lies. Most people will do anything to avoid this short-term pain, so they stagnate and stay where they think they'll be more comfortable. The problem with this is that you'll *never* get what you want in this place. This is the mediocre mindset and the path to inner death and despair.

We are meant to grow. We are here to grow. If you are not growing, you are dying. We see so many in society who have given up on growing. You can see it in their eyes and you can feel it in their low energy. This is not life as it was intended. Breaking our agreement with this old worn out path is what you must do. Leaving surroundings or people who want you to stagnate with them is the choice of a powerful person who knows what they want and are willing to make whatever sacrifice it takes to get there. Seeking higher knowledge and your own inner treasure is the way forward. If these words resonate with you, it's your time to change.

CTA: Break an old agreement today. Perhaps that person you've been misjudging for some shallow reason. Say, "no more!" I'll at least wish them light and love instead of silent barbs. Stay free.

Have a great day!

APRIL 16

Take This Positive Action Today

Today, go online or visit the bookstore. Go to the self-help or spiritual section and read up on what the authors and their books are about. If the subject resonates with you, pick it up and digest the wisdom fully. Re-read the parts you don't understand until you get it. Stay on this path and surround yourself with truly positive people. Soon you will find yourself on a new road; one that will lead you to your best self and true living. You can do it.

CTA: Just start.

Have a great day!

CTA: Understand that if you have the confidence to face your fears, you will be given the tools necessary to achieve your goals. Believe it!

Have a great day!

APRIL 20

Self-Reliance *continued*

Taking up self-reliance as a life path is truly rewarding and you begin to spread it to others just by living it. Self-reliant people are compassionate and caring, because they know what it is like to struggle and fight against what is. They will be the first to help push you through the lies your ego uses to keep you stuck. Self-reliant people want others to rise with them because they love surrounding themselves with quality people. Self-reliant people never think of themselves as victims. They know that discomfort comes wrapped around an inner diamond, just for them.

My friends, don't wait until there are storms in your life to get to know your true unbounded self. Once you realize that your true self is fearless, eternal, and unlimited, you will want to dive right into your power, take the reins of your own life and move forward, undaunted by the smokescreens of your ego.

Always remember that it is in your small victories that you can and must become aware. Celebrate every time you overcome a seeming obstacle, fearful thought or a once limiting belief. These small victories will lead to bigger ones and soon you'll be in the flow. Your new thought and action pattern will become one of a champion; a very self-reliant champion! One that sees temporary challenges as huge opportunities to learn and grow. Then, you must pay it forward. That's part of it.

CTA: Today, have a more self-reliant day. Any of those things you used to not handle well yourself, handle them. In fact, kick their butt and celebrate. You are an amazing, powerful spirit in human clothing. Start acting as such. You'll be amazed at what you can do.

Have a great day!

APRIL 21

Your Unguided Intentions

Whether you realize it or not, the circumstances, outcomes, and amount of life energy that flows through your life are all coming from your intentions. Most people here on earth are living their lives by their unguided intentions or unconscious choices, better known as the ego.

What this means is that they are on autopilot and not deliberately guiding their thoughts and intentions. If this is you, and you want to take control of your destiny, you must begin to live on purpose and with intention; *conscious* choice-making in every moment.

This means that you sit down and write out what you want the rest of your life to look like. This is always the first step toward any success.

Most of us speak about and think about the things and circumstances we *don't* want. You see and hear these kinds of conversations every day. Living in fear and having fearful thoughts as a constant companion. Your mind, if left unguided, will whisper tales of failure, scary scenarios and judgment of yourself and others. Also sound like you?

Here's the cure my friends; from here forward, chart your course. It begins with your thoughts. Think and act only on your desired life. Once you've written the story of how you want the rest of your life to look like, that and that alone is your *new script*. Burn the old one symbolically in your mind and then declare your new intentions.

Unless you take the time to write down your intentions, you'll be flying blind and your ego will remain as a menacing co-pilot in your journey. Acting and speaking only on the principles of your higher self will ensure a steady path in the right direction.

Let's continue this one tomorrow.

CTA: Disengage your autopilot. Be present. Take time to think about your goals. Commit them to paper. Then, live each day with the intention of reaching those goals.

Have a great day!

APRIL 22

Your Unguided Intentions *continued*

Love, prosperity, generosity, stories of your victories and blessings, laughter, joy, and many acts of faith, easy forgiveness and quick apologies, uplifting others and random acts of kindness. These are the gifts you give to yourself and others on a consistent, intentional basis.

Once you get into the flow of your intentional life, you will begin to feel much more alive. Your overall energy will have shifted to a higher realm, where all possibility lives.

Intentional positive living is not just a happier mindset, but it literally brings to you a life of beauty and wondrous synchronicity.

You will have new relationships with more loving energies surrounding you. You will see cooperation at every turn and you will see your dreams come to pass. All of this from one decision to live your life intentionally in this direction.

CTA: Today, take an hour out of your day or evening and devote it to writing your map.

What do you want?

Whatever you write, make sure it is vivid and clear. Make sure you see it every day and make sure you give thanks as if all of it is already part of your life. Then give the energy of each intention away every day in your positive speech and actions. Your life will change right before your eyes and in ways you've never imagined. This is the gift of life. You are in command and you are assisted by the truth all along the way. On this path, you can't get it wrong.

Have a great day!

APRIL 23

Believe In Yourself

Taking the reins of your own destiny will require that you believe in your God given gifts to overcome obstacles all along the way. But how do you do this when you have that inner voice telling you to constantly play it safe and small? Baby steps.

When any seeming challenge comes your way, recognize it as an opportunity to stretch rather than constrict into your normal box. That box is a trap that you keep yourself in. The voice that keeps you there promises safety, but what it *really* is, is the illusion of fear. You overcome this voice one baby step at a time. Doing the opposite of your normal, fearful self. You jump instead of hide.

One small step in the direction of your dream life will soon prove to be larger and larger steps, until your belief in your abilities grows to higher and higher levels.

Always remember this one very important truth about life; "God is *for* you!" This means you have the greatest of all power within you, and the only thing stopping you from living an amazing, huge life of wonder is you.

If you decide to rise, you will be helped every step of the way. God helps those who help themselves. Why would you go through life playing it small, when you inherently have all you need to rise? Fear is the opposite of truth. It's a lie. You'll see this when you take the brave steps to grow.

Let's continue this one tomorrow.

CTA: You must take the initial step on your journey if you want assistance from a greater power. Move!

Have a great day!

APRIL 24

Believe in Yourself *continued*

Yes, you may stumble along the way, but that's normal when you choose to run instead of crawl. Getting back up each and every time and getting back in the ring will prove to be the key to your new, exciting life.

Obstacles are just a test of your will to grow. Blow them right out of your way my friends. They are there for you on purpose. The so-called easy road is the mediocre road. Nothing great ever happened on that road. You deserve the best, because you are part of the highest. Treat yourself as such. Love yourself enough. Be grateful for this gift.

Celebrating the small victories along the way will be like getting a new colored belt in karate. You've earned it and now you choose to continue to go for the next color. You're expanding! With every new belt, you've learned new moves, new skills, and new ways to kick fear out of your way. You are now on the path to your highest potential and life experience. This all begins with the choice to believe in yourself, your *higher* self.

There is no growth in your comfort zone. You can always be content wherever you are. In fact, being content with who you are and what you have is a blessing. It offers the gold of inner peace. The goal is to always be content and grateful for where you are, but still keep the inner flame of intentional growth burning.

CTA: Stretching and growing is part of your divine purpose. Giving it all you have is your part of the bargain. Never let yourself down. Believe in yourself and your ability to co-create your life with your higher power. Start creating something new today.

Have a great day!

APRIL 25

Charting a New Course

Charting a new life course is always done one step at a time. New territory will always feel uncomfortable to you. Never let that deter you! Do one thing you feel is out of your normal comfort zone today, feel your normal, fearful self say, "you don't have to do this, why risk it? Stay in your little box and be safe!" And then... Take the action anyway! You will feel the flame of your true power burn away the voice of fear, and then, you have entered the realm of your spirit. Your higher, wiser, unlimited self.

Dare to believe in yourself! Take that chance! If it doesn't work out, try another route, turn over another stone! Never stop growing!

Never give your life over to the fearful voice of your ego that tells you things like, you'll never do it! You'll never get that job! You're not smart enough! You're not good looking or young enough!

These are all lies of your lower nature. Choose to rise above the inner liar and take the spirit up in its daily offer to live life the way it was meant to be lived. *You are the power*! Believe it! Get to know it by using it! Make that call, go see that person, put a smile on your face, and take charge!

One baby step at a time will lead to a whole new life! It is yours for the taking. Make sure you stay grateful for all you have now and the rest will fall into place as you choose to keep moving forward.

CTA: Never give up and never give in. You'll see! Life is meant to be awesome! You must simply do your part. Be bold! Jump into the flow today!

Have a great day!

APRIL 26

Rising On Purpose

Deciding to move into a new, more positive direction in your life always begins with changing your thoughts and how you process them.

If you were to rate yourself on a scale of one to ten on how well you do every day in the art of positive thoughts, positive inner dialogue, and subsequent positive speech and actions, what number would you give yourself? Then ask someone you're close to, to offer their number for you. See how close they are. Not from a judgmental point of view, just for the purpose of introspection and self-awareness. Getting to know your regular energy pattern. Does it lean more positive or negative?

Just thinking about *how* you think is the beginning of becoming self-aware. Until you do this, you will never know your own energy and what you are giving the world as your calling card. Most people are certainly a mix of both, but only one reveals your true self. The one that attracts all goodness and fulfills your life's goals and dreams. This pattern of yours means much more than you think.

Always remember that you receive what you give. Life is like a mirror. How you see and treat yourself is a huge factor in what you are giving off as your vibe. Loving yourself is of the very highest priorities. Being self-assured, knowing the truth that you are a piece of the eternal gives you every reason to stand tall and take your honored place in the blessing of human life. When you choose otherwise, you are just betraying yourself. Sabotaging yourself. When you know better, you must rise to better. The gift of freedom is the reward.

CTA: Look in the mirror and express your love for all of you. Unless you give love (light) to every part of you, the darkness hangs on. Shine for yourself and for the rest of us.

Have a great day!

APRIL 27

Working on Your Thoughts

For those of you who find yourself naturally attracted to seeking a higher, better, and more meaningful life experience, the only way is to intentionally and consistently work on your thought life.

Your negative attitudes, judgments, speech, and acts only smother the light that is the real you. The persistent daily practice of letting go of your old negative judgments, inner dialogue, and outer speech and actions will be your path to higher places. It's always an inside job. And only you can clear out the garbage.

You will be challenged along your new path to change old beliefs that no longer, or may never have served you. You are charting a new course, maybe even with new people. New beliefs, especially in yourself, will be part of the practice.

You must be willing to shed the past and get uncomfortable for a time. You're using some old muscles you've forgotten about. How long it takes to shift your sails is however long it takes. Truthfully, it's more about the great unfolding that happens to you on this road. That's the real prize. The real you, being revealed to you, in only a way that you will know and understand. Others will notice your growth, but it is you who will truly feel and know it. Then you get hungry for more. It's called becoming enlightened; "To add light to your life." You'll feel old layers of the unnecessary, false self falling away.

CTA: Be brave enough to look inside and shine the light on where you must grow. Let go of the dictates of your ego today. Be kindness in a physical disguise.

Have a great day!

APRIL 28

More On the Art of Giving

The greatest reward you will ever feel in life is when you give from your heart. There are many ways to give in life, but the most meaningful moments in all our lives, is when we give without the expectation of any form of return. That, my friends, is the golden ticket; giving simply for the sake of giving.

There is no other action you can take in human life that will ever enrich your soul, and your life, as much as heartfelt giving.

Giving your focused, caring attention to another is one of these gifts. Listening to another with a completely open heart and mind. Attention without judgment of any kind, with the sole purpose to understand another completely. And then respond with any kind of loving assistance you can offer. You have a very unique way of helping people. Always remember that. Never shy away from this gift. You have a very important role to play. These giving and receiving moments are what make your life so meaningful. Why on earth would you not want to consciously bring this practice into your daily life? Giving your very best, also gives to you.

From the consistent act of giving, you will begin to attract new friends, business relationships, in fact, better relationships in all areas of your life. Then, this will open many new doors of opportunity for you. At this stage, you must carefully make conscious choices on what you want your life to be about and look like. Then just direct your one pointed attention in that direction and watch your world change. Everything you want in life always begins with giving.

Giving your time, your money, your heartfelt attention, heartfelt advice, hugs, gifts, thoughtfulness, kindness, and overall loving energy, will bring all you need and desire right to your door. Giving is the secret to a great life.

Taking, on the other hand, brings you the total opposite. One is the highest on the scale of positive living and the other is a magnet for a mediocre, drama filled existence. It's always just a choice.

CTA: Today, just give. Give the energy of love in every form, symbol, text, and spoken word. Let others feel how you feel toward them. Never assume others know you love them. Letting them know should be an everyday occurrence. Surrounding yourself and everyone else with the highest life energy in the Universe is your magic ticket to an amazing life. Punch that ticket every day and watch your life transform. Spread the wealth.

Have a great day!

APRIL 29

Raising Your Thermostat

Each of us has a very unique temperature on his or her personal thermostat. In other words, our personal energy field.

If you're like most, this temperature fluctuates quite a bit during your day, and subsequently, your life.

No matter what you do in your day, if you are constantly just reacting to the circumstances that come up, instead of consciously steering your thoughts and actions, your temperature will be like a roller coaster, up and down the thermostat.

Most of us unfortunately stay in and consistently return to a lower temperature. Let's say 50 degrees. Sometimes it's higher when good things come our way and then other times we're in the teens, due to negative dramas, low expectations, and low self-esteem. We all know the twenties. It's really cold there!

My friends, *you* have the power to consistently raise your temperature to new heights and a much warmer median temperature. All it takes is a decision. This decision must get more consistent, until it's your only decision.

Letting go of your old, negative beliefs, habits, and speech puts your hand firmly on your own thermostat for the first time in your life. YOU raise your own temperature! No one else can do it for you.

CTA: So today, notice your energetic temperature when you wake up. Set it intentionally higher if it's low. Give thanks for the great day you intend to create and ask the Spirit to guide your thoughts, words, and actions.

Have a great day!

APRIL 30

Your New Tools

There's an old Chinese proverb that reflects our need for continuous, lifelong growth. It goes, "House done, man die." This means that if we let ourselves stop growing we will slowly die inside. So the lesson is to never stop growing. In fact, we must seek it through all we do. If you're in a rut of stagnation, you must begin to use the ancient tools of wisdom to build a new house. A beautiful house that makes you and others feel totally at home. For this amazing new home, you will need the following tools. You must be steadfast in taking out the right tool when you need it, but always have these tools handy:

1) Self-Love. First order of business. You are a piece of the Universe itself. Treat yourself as such. You can't give away your best if you don't yet know it.

2) Gratitude. Be grateful for the gift you are. You are a miracle. Be grateful for everything in your life. Even your past, for it has brought you to this place of awakening. If you are reading this passage, you are being called to rise. Be grateful. It's how you will begin to see a new light. Then it will grow into becoming you; your real self. Be grateful. Every day. On purpose.

3) Give. Give only love, in all its forms and symbols. Kindness, generosity, forgiveness, prosperity, passion, creativity, collaboration, and charity. Give an open heart and the gift of your non-judgment to all. Be a healer instead of a harmer. Be the peace and love you want to see in your life. Give it all away freely. Your life and the lives of those around you will become truly amazing.

4) Stay Humble. Remember that all you become in your higher climb will be a gift from above and within. You are the divine channel. Starve your ego and let your light shine through. Having humility gives deference to God, your higher self. It says that you truly recognize where your talents, love, and goodness all come from.

CTA: Today, maybe for the first time, pick up some new tools. Try them out and use them throughout the day. Practice leads to meaning. Meaning leads to purpose, and purpose leads to a great and wonderful life.

Have a great day!

MAY 1

Taking the Drama Out of Your Problems

The so-called problems in your life always have two sides to look at. One side offers pain, suffering, and the dreaded Drama. The other side offers opportunity.

On earth we live in what's called "duality." Everything has a dual nature, including us. While we are here, we are dual natured, both positive and negative. The side of us we feed most often is the path we have chosen for ourselves. Unless you know this, you probably have just fallen prey to whatever conditioning and perceptions you have surrounded yourself with in your life up to this moment. You may not have even been aware of your negative approach to life.

This knowledge will be your new starting point. When we know better, we choose better and subsequently, live better. Feeding your spirit is feeding your true self/nature. Starving your ego, or false, negative self, will let in your light.

My friends, your problems are always opportunities in disguise. There is always the seed of growth in them. Watering them with your higher power is what propels you into wisdom and new understanding. This is the very purpose for your visit here. Learning and growing.

So often we get tangled up in the lower emotions that crop up when trouble arises. We have our usual, go-to reactions. Panic, despair, immobility, fear, anxiety, and depression. These are all on the Lazy Susan of negative choices. I'm sure no one ever told you growing up, that you have a choice as how you can respond to what life brings to your doorstep.

CTA: Today, begin to shift. Spending 10% of the time on the problem and 90% on the solution is where you find peace and right thought. From here, your solutions come naturally.

Have a great day!

MAY 2

A Practice In Non-Reaction

The next time a problem arises in your day, try the following:

1) Give it space in your mind and body. Do not "react." Instead witness what your normal response would have been. What path does your mind want you to take? What words does it want you to speak? What actions, if any, are on the table? This is how you learn what you've been taught and what you would have given out as your energetic response. Remember, you are either expanding the problem with your response or you are moving to a higher ground and solving the issue.

2) Immediately use power phrases in your mind as top priority. "I am prepared," "I am able to handle anything, including this." "I am not alone. My higher power is in the driver's seat." "If I am brought to it, I will be brought through it." These are examples of power phrases. Chances are, you've been using powerless phrases as your first response. Most of us do. No worries. Change has come.

3) Be the first one in the room to express faith; faith in optimistic thought, optimistic words, and forward motion to solve the issue. Only this way will you sow the seed of growth for yourself and those around you. You will have become the light. This is the power. The real you.

Always remember this one thing: prayer is also the words you speak during the day. You think it's only the words you pray in private, but there is no separation from what you pray in private and what you say to yourself, about others, and with others. Your actions are just prayers in motion. What you give out in everyday life is prayer. You are constantly asking for your future, in what you give in your thoughts, speech, and actions. This is why it is so crucial to be self-aware.

Stop focusing on the problems of your life and start focusing on building your life through positive, faith filled thoughts, actions, and speech. When these become your inner and outer prayers, your "problems" will turn into grateful opportunities. You are being blessed instead of cursed. You have the power switch. Remember to use it and constantly give thanks for it.

CTA: Today, turn the corner. Start with your thoughts. Drive some trust and faith into your problems, trust and faith that it will all work out. Only by acts of faith, will your energy begin to shift. Go after that problem and let it know who's boss! Blow it away with inspired action and see the clouds disappear. Taking action tells your problem that its days are numbered. Once you gain momentum in this direction, you have taken the reins of your life. Spirit will become your constant knight in shining armor. That spirit is you! You are the knight!

Have a great day!

MAY 3

Life's Delicious Menu

Life is very much like a restaurant menu. So many choices for each dining experience we have in our temporary physical journey.

We are humans with five human senses, but we are also spirit energy. Our spirit energy is what gives life and animation to our human framework. Our spirit is of such a higher energy, or frequency, that our spirit "feels" life, in lieu of touch, taste, smell, sight, and hearing. We can *feel* another's pain or joy. We can *feel* if something is right or wrong for us. And we *feel* when we have chosen to order from our ego side of life's menu, or what spirit would recommend as a much more succulent dish. Your intuitive self is part of your true power.

We innately know this to be true, but we've been conditioned for so long to live in our lower nature, consistently choosing the slop from Chef Ego. We are even told from the highest levels of our human society that spirituality is politically incorrect to express. Not only is this shameful, but it's lying to keep us asleep to our true nature and connectedness to each other. Time to awaken to the actual truth and your *own* power.

You are spirit on a brief visit to the human experience. When you leave this experience, you simply shed the meat suit and go home to your family and friends who've gone home before you. It's not the big deal we all make of it. You are so much more than you believe yourself to be. You are spiritual royalty, but you treat yourself like a pauper. You believe yourself to be lower than others, or higher than others, but those are the choices from the dark side of the menu.

What you choose to say and do while on your visit may be more important than you know. In other words, you'll wish you'd lived the human experience by the delicious side of the menu as your guide, instead of feeling separate, lost, hopeless, fearful, angry, and all the other low energy choices on the ego side of the menu.

Let's continue this one tomorrow.

CTA: Be true to yourself. Order from the finer side of the menu and let your intuition guide you in choosing those menu items that will bring you the most joy.

Have a great day!

MAY 4

Life's Delicious Menu *continued*

We always have the choice to live from the fine dine side of the menu instead. Always remember, that in every one of your thoughts, acts, and spoken words, either side of the menu could be served for the very same life issue. So why would you choose the gruel when you can choose one of the award winning chef specials? The price for these delicious specials? *Free!* This side of the menu is the *real you*. The other side of the menu costs you in more ways than you are aware. It costs you lost love, it costs you in lost friendships, lost opportunities and lost life energy in general.

Here's the menu you look at every day. I don't have room for all, but you'll get the picture:

Chef Ego Specials:

Hatred, fear, jealousy, anger, envy, competition, self-loathing, self-hatred, self-judgment, judgment of others, drama, separation, anxious thought, depression, low self-esteem, arrogance, the daily thought, "you're just human, then you cease to exist," or hoping instead of knowing.

Chef Truth Specials:

Love, gratitude, positive vision, kindness, forgiveness, apology, persistence, determination, no-limit living, risk taking, joy, laughter, collaboration, sharing, compassion, empathy, team mentality, fun, adventure, excitement, passion, celebrating others, understanding, truth, honesty, integrity, character, and knowing that you are an eternal being of light energy with a simple mission to just share and give *all* of this menu away free of charge. Every day.

CTA: Today, when you're in the restaurant of your mind, or if you go out to eat, decide to consume and serve up the truth *only*. Soon enough, the other side of the menu will simply be inedible to you.

Have a great day!

MAY 5

Learning to Love Yourself Completely

So many of us struggle with aspects of ourselves that we deny. We do our best to hide our darkness, but it always seems to have a say in our daily lives, creating negative scenarios and prognostications in our heads at the very minimum, or outward havoc around us at its worst.

When we finally have the courage to take the real journey, the one within, we will finally begin to shine the light of truth on what's really bothering us. What really causes all the strife, anxiety, fighting, hatred, punishing, thoughts of lack and loss, martyrdom, vengeful thoughts, envy, and all the other lies that manifest themselves into our physical journey? It's always an inside job.

Failing to look inside yourself, your thoughts, beliefs and old, conditioned habits, as part of your daily rise to a better life, is like deciding to take a trip to a beautiful new destination, using a map that only brings you around the block to right where you are.

Awakening to how you created you and your life results to this point, will prove to be the most valuable information you can ever know. Becoming a student of yourself. How you think, the things and the way you say things, and your approach to life and those around you. These are the subjects really worth knowing.

When you begin this, drawing back the curtain to your inner life, you'll definitely see some darkness. That's ok! In fact, it's only in the recognition of the darkness that we can begin to use its opposite energy instead. a.k.a., your light.

Every dark energy we own as humans has the possibility of the opposite choice inherently within it. It's when we begin to look at how these dark choices affect our relationships, dreams and lives that we want to make higher choices for the same life issues.

Let's continue this one tomorrow.

CTA: Do you know what's driving your thoughts and fears? Take time to really ponder this. Once those triggers are identified, you can start to do things to overcome them, leading you to a life full of love and kindness.

Have a great day!

MAY 6

Learning to Love Yourself Completely *continued*

We begin to see that it's really about us. What we view as right and wrong. How we feel about others is always a reflection of how we feel about ourselves. If we are able to love ourselves completely, supposed flaws and all, we will then begin to live a truly remarkable life of love. What you are is what you are able to give and project outward. Get it? If *you* don't give love to yourself as part of your daily path, how can you expect to give it away? Your cup needs to runneth over with love. How full is your cup?

I'm not talking about arrogant, self-centered, boastful self-love. That is not love. That is your ego telling you that you are somehow better than others. More lies of your lower nature.

I'm talking about recognizing that we are *all* part of the same source. We come from the same home, and are *all* equal in the eyes of our creator.

This is loving the truth of who you really are. You are a divine piece of the miraculous. Never, never treat yourself or others as less than that. Have a healthy love of yourself and this fact. From this understanding alone, you free your need for competition with others, being jealous of others, wishing you were someone else or thinking you are somehow less than others. You are not. You are you! Be the very best you! That's all that is expected and hoped for by your divine source. You are a gift to all of us. Be that. Give love your own unique way. It will always be enough.

CTA: Today, begin the inner journey of untying the old knots of lies you've held onto as truth. Begin taking stock in your higher self. Learn its soft, subtle voice. It's there under the lies. Learn to slow your mind down by being still for a while each day so you hear it. It's very real and it will guide you always in the right direction by your surrender to it and your discarding the reasons you once believed the lies. They are no longer valid. They are the old story. Stop telling any stories of doom and gloom. Focus instead on all the light in your life, especially the light within. Love yourself enough to abandon the liar forever. Love yourself, trust yourself and have faith in yourself. Your creator does. Why don't you give it a try? You deserve it. It is the real you.

Have a great day!

MAY 7

"Hey Buddy, How Was Your Trip?"

This is a true story. You'll know the characters very well. It's longer than my normal words, so hope you take the time to read it all and enjoy it.

Two spirits from Heaven decide to go on an amazing trip to the physical world called earth.

They are both totally jazzed about the trip. It's a trip to one of millions of possible places and dimensions a spirit can choose to go to advance its eternal self. Like a vacation club for souls.

This place called earth is amazing they thought! You get to have a solid feeling experience. How awesome! You get this cool suit to wear called a physical body. It breathes for us. It grows in size as we go along an incredible experience called human life. We get to travel with others here by sacred relationships with others and we get to spread light on a place where darkness still lives. We get to heal and help others grow as they help us to do the same.

Your suit can be made to look singularly unique according to how one decides to create oneself and how well you take care of the suit. It can be dressed up a million different ways.

This suit called a body is your vehicle and your creative physical machine! You get to use it in all you do and say. It is your communication tool between you, this living planet, and everyone in your path. It communicates your message from home, or it can douse your own light and the overall light of earth if you choose to instead, communicate the darkness of this physical place, known as the ego. Both are always present here. For now.

Let's continue this one tomorrow.

CTA: Allow yourself to communicate freely with yourself and others, without judging or the fear of judgment. Live in a positive light.

Have a great day!

MAY 8

"Hey Buddy, How Was Your Trip?" *continued*

Your communication tool will know which one you're messaging outward by the way it feels to you. "Feeling" is your power, your sixth sense. Use this as your real guide. Friends from home will guide you this way. Always pay attention to it and move forward from it, knowing it's all only a temporary trip. This knowing will empower you to be brave and take risks. It promises that no matter how well or poorly you do on your trip, you always come home. No worries.

Your sixth sense is there to remind you that you are unlimited and you can do amazing things and beautiful deeds for the spiritual raising of this place if you choose to.

Your only way to struggle and falter during your trip, is if you fall prey to believing that you are the dark energy. You take it on and express it as yourself. You'll always know where you stand in every moment by what the energy inside your suit feels like. One makes you and others feel low and ill, while the other keeps you happy, free, alive, awake, and giving your light power to yourself and others. The guide tells them to instead, use your dark feelings as an alarm to tell you you're off course in some way. Investigate this energy and see how you can use your light to bring truth back to yourself. The light always brings you forward. It blazes a fruitful trail for you. Follow it. Use it exclusively. Your light will never betray you. Darkness will *only* betray you.

Once you awaken to this truth, you'll be able to intentionally help yourself *and* all the others. Don't forget where you come from, my friends! "It's where all your power lies," he said. You have unlimited choices of your experience there! All of which you have total freedom to create! Your own way! How awesome! You get to even choose challenging life paths if you wish. These challenges grow your eternal self in very special ways. They are gifts for you really. They are there to remind you of your power. Not to defeat you. They expand you through experiencing certain valuable aspects you did not yet have. Give thanks for them by overcoming them and not getting stuck in them. Use gratitude as a shield against the lies. Gratitude says that you remember the promise from home and that all of us here support you, love you, and want you to simply give your light to a darkened dimension.

If you wish it, you can choose to experience more darkness, in order to truly appreciate your home. Sounds crazy, but true. You get to create a family if you wish. You get to party with all your friends that you'll think you're meeting for the very first time, but your true self will know them as your closest eternal friends.

You get to help this physical place become a spiritual playground with your own unique gifts from home. Raising it to a planet of light, where it will someday be known as Physical Heaven. You get to participate in this living transformation. You have chosen to participate.

Let's continue this one tomorrow.

CTA: Listen to your inner self. Let it guide you towards the positive. Be grateful for each challenge you face, knowing that every challenge you overcome shows how powerful you truly are.

Have a great day!

MAY 9

"Hey Buddy, How Was Your Trip?" *continued*

The two travelers are told that they will experience a divine amnesia when they are brought into the physical by fellow spirit they will know as their mom. They get to choose their parents and the type of experience they are born into. They know they can overcome anything with their eternal selves, as long as they remember or awaken to its power from home.

They are warned that they will have a mix of experiences thrown at them, many of them negative. If they are not aware, then they will be weighed down by becoming attached to the negative physical energies and the adding of others negative perceptions and energies to their earthly selves, like layers of heavy clothes in winter.

He said, "if you are not careful, you will forget who you really are and there's a possibility that the layers of your darker experiences will cover much of your light for the whole trip." Oh! and one more thing, says the guide, "you will have all the guidance and assistance you need from here! Anything and everything you need is always supplied to you when you ask and use your power of faith in your home and true source."

If you do not use your emotions as a guide back to your light self, you may begin to believe that the emotional darkness is really you! If this happens, you'll be decreasing your power immensely! You won't trust that you have any power at all and you may walk the entire journey in what is known on earth as defeat, anger, self-hatred, feeling separate from your brothers and sisters from home, and you may even do horrible things and no longer recognize your true self. You will know no real control over your experience.

"So beware, my friends," he said. "But remember, you will *always* have your light self, for you can *never* be truly disconnected from who you really are. You can only choose, sometimes unwittingly, to cover your light with the lies of darkness."

"My advice," he said, "is to always and only trust the light you feel within. It's always there to serve you and you to serve it. When you do this, and seek to do it every day of your journey, you will know greatness. You will be greatness! You will be shining your royal light in order to remind others of theirs. This you must do to your best ability. Helping others out of the falseness of their winter layers will be the best thing you can do while you enjoy your amazing physical journey. The more you shine your light, the more layers of your own heavy winter ensemble will be peeled off, easily and gently, instead of harshly and violently."

Let's continue this one tomorrow.

CTA: Every day you must practice being present with your thoughts. Be true to yourself. Brush off outside influences that try to dictate your actions.

Have a great day!

MAY 10

"Hey Buddy, How Was Your Trip?" *continued*

Both of the eager travelers understood their tour guide and promise to do their very best in shining their light and remembering their true power. They both look at each other and hug. They wish each other an amazing trip and say, "see ya soon buddy!"

You see, a trip to the physical seems longer than it really is. In Heaven-time it's about a minute or two.

They now fully understand that when they leave to go to the physical, that it's really like a dream and then you wake up back home, welcomed back by your closest fellow souls. Free of any residue of the negative, and with a complete understanding of the gold they gleaned from their trip, and a full review of all of it, in Heaven time, a few milliseconds. How cool!

Both travelers want very different experiences to add different aspects to their eternal selves, so they choose different parts of earth to come into physical form. Very different experiences indeed. Separate languages, different cultures, various perspectives on earthly truth. Even various perspectives on the eternal and what they think the eternal is! Wow! So many have forgotten! So many believe that this place is all there is! So many have forgotten who they really are and what miracles they are capable of bringing forth! Too many are still in the divine amnesia and forgot to wake up! They follow the voice of their lower earthly survival mechanisms, the ego. They believe they are the ego voice. Holy mackerel!

So they came forth. Courageous, knowing, trusting, and up for the ride! They know they have a mission. They are here. They are just like you.

Let's continue this one tomorrow.

CTA: Wake up the true you!

Have a great day!

MAY 11

"Hey Buddy, How Was Your Trip?" *continued*

My friends, we each have a mission here. It's the same, but carried out many different ways. Each in our own unique space suit. Each with our own gifts to give. We must all choose to wake up and use our power in order to heal this cool place.

Where you take your journey from this day forward can be a totally new and awakened direction. *you* are one of these travelers. We all are. It's all about remembering where we are from and the eternal power we possess. Giving your true self to this world will awaken your own power more and more. It will also lead to healing and awaking others. When we all remember who we are, this world will be a positive, physical vacationland for all of us. No more war between anyone, for we will have awoken. We are all one. We just got caught up in believing a lie we must collectively rise above.

Waking up is a beautiful process of deciding to simply be a giver of your light. Just that. Nothing need be added. Give it through what you love to do. Give it through your spoken words. Cast out your negative judgments of yourself and anyone else. Choose to see and be the light. Just give what you really are my friends.

CTA: Today, follow the recipe.

Have a great day!

MAY 12

Your Script

Every one of us lives our daily lives by a familiar script. We have our roles we play on the stage of earthly life and we play them like Oscar-winning performers. This sounds great, unless the part you play is written *for* you, instead of *from* you.

Most of your lines in the daily play are easily acted out by you because you say mostly the same ones. You jump dutifully into your role as mom or dad (probably using your mom and dad's lines LOL), you play the role of employee or boss. You play the role of friend, son, daughter, wife, or husband. You're very good at playing the gossiper or the fearful worrier. So many roles and so little thought to your same old script. Time for a rewrite in some of your roles.

We love to imitate the roles of other actors who handed us their script. They said, these lines will serve you! Adopt them as your own! And you did. Never really examining the plots or the next page in the play. Assuming that the lines of an actor you trust will also bring you the Oscar. Not always true. In fact, mostly never true. These are just old scripts. Some worthy of your acting chops, but mostly lines and roles given to you by others. You, my friend have your *own* unique role to play.

If we are ever to live a life of original lines and truthful roles, we must intentionally write our own script in each moment.

Rewriting the destructive lines of your old script into an entirely new role will take lots of practice before even *you* believe in your new character. It will take lots of self-study to see where your old character has betrayed you and your worldly pursuits.

You can write anything you want into your new script! And you can and must begin to delete old words, phrases, beliefs, and theatrical acts that once defined you. You've allowed a very dark writer (we all know too well) to write the lines for you. Probably for your whole life, until today!

Let's continue this one tomorrow.

CTA: Write your script! Play the role that was meant for you and no one else.

Have a great day!

MAY 13

Your Script *continued*

You must become the director, writer, producer, and actor in your own play and your own roles. When you decide to finally grab the pencil and begin the rewrite, you'll need to know some new concepts and guidelines for creating the new script. Here are a few to get your pencil moving:

1) Fear betrays and constricts your ability to write new lines. Feel the fear and move forward anyway. Positive action dissolves fear. Belief in yourself dissolves fear. Developing new faith in your higher power and using it as your vehicle forward changes everything. Use it exclusively. Write your lines with the pencil of love. Love for yourself and everyone else.

2) You are *unlimited*! If you can imagine the life of your dreams, you must write it down first! How else will you keep your eye on the prize if you don't have a clear picture of what it even looks like? Do this immediately. Today. Who are your friends? Who will you write out of your play? What new beliefs and lines will you write in for yourself? Who do you want to be? What does your new character look like? What new friendships do you want to create? How will you treat others and give to others in your new role? Are you including happiness, harmony, inner peace, and all the new lines it will take to pull off the new role? Make sure of it! Write it down and live from it. When the old actor tries to grab the stage, give him or her the hook. Keep using your new lines. Soon they become you and redefine you. You will have recreated *you*. The old director will fade away.

Let's continue this one tomorrow.

CTA: Imagine the life of your dreams and commit it to paper!

Have a great day!

MAY 14

Your Script *continued*

3) Use beauty and creativity as your constant ghostwriter. If you decide to embody these energies, you will see and feel them both in your every scene. Speak on them, deliver lines that include them and solve your problems with them. Beauty is an energy and a subset of love itself. You know it when you see it. You know it when you hear it, when you give it, and when you are receiving it. Mostly you know it when you *feel* it. Write beauty into all your roles. Creativity helps you to imagine these new lines. Trust it. You are the creator. Never believe you are not creative. You've created your whole life my friends. You've just been using two writers instead of the real *one*.

4) You must *always* have forgiveness and the power of apology written into your role. If you don't, you'll constantly have writers block. Forgiveness and apology keep your energy clear, so you can hear the true writer within. Forgive yourself constantly for your old shortcomings as you consistently shed them. A heartfelt apology, when needed, frees you from pain you cause others. When you finally realize you are responsible for your words, thoughts, and deeds, apologizing is the release valve that keeps the pressure of guilt and shame from building up and overshadowing the writer within. It's only your ego that needs to defend. Keep yourself free and flowing with the good stuff.

CTA: Today, sit down and look at your entire script to this point. Begin the rewrite in the areas of your life you want to improve. It's all about what you're giving, or not giving, in all these areas. If fear is immobilizing you in some way, take action in spite of the feeling. It's only a feeling that's stopping your feet from moving, your voice from being heard and your pencil from writing new possibilities for yourself. *Just a feeling*! If it's not going to kill you... *do it*! It's the only way to silence that liar we all have believed is us. Trust yourself my friend. Trust your higher self. Your eternal self. It will never betray you. It's a much different voice. It's waiting for *you* to use its power. That power is the real you.

Have a great day!

MAY 15

Unconditional Love

On a recent Mother's Day, I thought how appropriate the subject of Unconditional Love would be. After all, that's what a mother's love truly is. Love is our eternal energy. It is the highest energy on the scale and it is also our true home. When we leave this place and all of the many experiences of physical life, we will return to a realm of unconditional love.

Our moms have been our beacon for this energy since they unselfishly carried us and delivered us into this world. It is their unconditional love that nurtured us in the womb and guided us through life. It is from this deep wellspring that we learned what it feels like to be loved and to be able to carry it forward into all we are and all we do. No matter what we did in our lives, good and not so good, the unconditional love from our mom has always been and will always be a constant.

If your mom has passed, her love for you is still a constant and surrounds you still in all you do. Her love for you still guides and lights your path. Be certain of this fact. If your mom is still here with you, you need to let her know how important and loved she is. You need to be the torch-bearer everyday of this unconditional love that she has shown and taught you.

Unconditional love is at the center of your heart and should be opened each day and let loose as much as you can. Let this day be one of immense gratitude for your mom and what her heart has given you all your life. She imagined you even before you came forth and her love for you will never die.

Your job from here forward is to be the beacon of this energy for your children and all those you love. Show them the way as your mom did for you. After all, it's our true nature and the place we are all from. Shine your light today and spread the wealth of your love.

Thanks, Mom, for showing me the way. I love and cherish you.

God Bless all of you.

CTA: Let go of judgment today. Let people and things be as they are without you needing to jump in and fix everything your way. Let go and let God.

Have a great day!

MAY 16

Take the Wheel

We are all beings of energy. We all struggle with the low ones and we all know the higher ones. The key to life is simply use the lower ones to be your reminder back to the higher ones. This is called living intentionally. Not on autopilot like most people.

When we live on autopilot, we are living in a lie. This lie tells you that your outside circumstances must dictate how you feel on the inside. It also says you feel that life is random and you have no real control of your life's direction. It lies about you being limited in any way and makes you doubt your own abilities. It tells you that you're separate from everyone else and that you are simply what you see in the mirror.

Most people live their whole lives this way. From the outside in. This is a roller coaster life at best, guaranteed to include mediocre results. It's limited living that is much less than you are capable of, and less than you deserve. You are not meant to live this way any longer. It's an outdated paradigm. Time to rise up the ladder, my friends.

If you adopt a true set of core beliefs that serve you, and you simply begin to live your life from these, you will rise. Your overall vibe will rise.

You must become consistent in your energetic rise and never go back. This is how lives are transformed every day. This is how we all awaken and how we intentionally grow out of ego centered thinking and shrinking. No more need to indulge in negativity as a life path.

Think of your rise as busting out of a cocoon and learning how to use your new wings. That's exactly what it's like to leave your ego behind. You flourish. You grow. You become the real you. This higher version of you knows no limitations. Has no worry, guilt, shame or fear. You trust in your higher self because you now realize your connection to the true power of spirit. Anything is possible for this version of you.

CTA: Today, grab the wheel of your life. Turn off the autopilot and drive your day and your life with intention.

Have a great day!

MAY 17

Truthful Intentions

Below are a set of core beliefs that have helped me bust out and intentionally live life in the present and to the fullest. If I happen to veer off course from time to time, I simply center myself back in these knowings. They always work because they are universal truths. Here they are:

1) We are eternal beings on a temporary human journey. We *all* return home once our mission here is done. Our souls know this mission. We must uncover this mission by letting in more light and choosing to be a giver of it as our purpose. Give it through what you love to do. Your mission will be included in that. The more light you become, the clearer and smoother your journey will be.

2) Look at others as fellow souls, not separate humans. We are all here in the soup. Treat everyone the same. Give love instead of judgment in all your interactions. Accept people just as they are. If you can add light to their lives, do it. Every time. Give up negative judgment of yourself and others. Be done with it.

3) Give up assuming. Never assume you have the full picture. You don't. You can't possibly. Live in the present moment and let things unfold naturally. If you're giving your light, things will always turn out for your best and highest good. Be open to it all and give others the benefit of the doubt until you have all the facts. You'll always be glad you did and you'd want the same in return.

4) Give only what you want to see show up in your life. This leaves a lot out! Like anger, drama, hatred, revenge, judgment... You get the picture.

CTA: Today, open your new eyes and infuse your loving intentions in all you say and do. Watch as the world responds to you with the same. You are in your true power.

Have a great day!

MAY 18

Living in Power

If your life becomes about only giving the inward energies you want to feel yourself, you can't get it wrong. Give love, kindness, your time, your creativity, your smile, your laughter, your joy, and above all, give gratitude. Gratitude for it all. Even the ugly bumps along the way. They help you get to the next level. That usually doesn't become clear for a few miles past the bumps. Don't forget that.

The more your mind stays in a state of gratitude, the more light and love will show up in your life. In other words, more to be grateful for. Your life is a mirror of what you give as your expression. Only give your best. That's the practice! Not always easy, but worth it. The only way to fly.

So today, start establishing your own set of core beliefs. Let go of all the old ones that no longer, or may never have served you. If you have any beliefs that make you feel less than amazing, ditch them. Give them the boot and begin creating your new personal world. In no time, others will begin to see your progress and make comments. You'll begin to feel different and just plain better. You must *be* the change. You must learn to embody and express your best loving energies as your calling card. Start today and never look back.

CTA: Let go of all the small thinking your ego wants you to react to. Become the light.

Have a great day!

MAY 19

Feeling Good

Any time we are seeking something in our lives, what we are really after is a feeling.

Think about it, no matter what it is. A new car, new positive friends, a new intimate relationship, a new job, personal wellness and health, creating a new family, and on and on. We long for the feeling of what these will bring us. We long to feel good, as much as possible. Feeling good is just another way of saying "adding light to your life."

When we feel good, we are feeling our inner light. We get great news or have exciting plans and our energy shifts immediately. We all know this to be true. We also know the opposite.

We all have our struggles with our dual nature of light and dark. Most of the time we rattle around our day, up and down, down and up, depending on outer circumstances, issues, and personal interactions.

Up until this moment, I'll bet you haven't given any thought or time to intentionally improving your happiness quotient or ability to feel good more often. I'll bet no one ever told you that it's you that allows negative circumstances to knock you off your game. Your game simply must improve.

During your life to this moment, you've been taught how to react in everyday life situations. We all know people who dutifully snap into melodrama and overreaction as their normal triggered reaction. Maybe this is you? If so, you need to spend some time in the lab of your own conditioned habits. Who in your family has taught you how to react? Nervous mom or angry dad? Maybe a sibling or the people you hang out with? Maybe all of the above. Time to break the cycle and take a new direction.

CTA: Today, practice your calm, confident self, you know, the one who gives just the good stuff.

Have a great day!

MAY 20

The Courage of Looking Within

How would others describe you during a negative scenario? Calm and confident? Or perhaps elevated and fearful? Maybe you get overly serious and jerk the wheel? Are you a peacemaker and diplomat? Or are you known for adding fuel to any fire in sight? Are you considered to be more of a problem creator or solver? How would your daily attitude be described? Low, dreary, withdrawn, competitive, dramatic or narcissistic? Or more on the positive side? Intentionally giving your best energy in order to keep yourself feeling good and to raise everyone in your path? These are very important questions to ask yourself.

Feeling good demands that you let go of the low energy you've become comfortable in. Low energy is dark energy. Dark energy makes you tired, sick, and old before your time. You continue to stay in these energies because you keep choosing to give them as part of your life's expression. You're choosing to stay a judge of others and yourself. You're choosing to gossip and give assumptive negative perspectives away freely and without actual truth. You're choosing to use darkness as much or more than you give light.

Giving light is how you create more of it within you and to the world. The more you choose this as your path, the higher you will rise. It's that simple of a formula. Not always simple to do. But that's the practice and way to a beautiful life, well-lived and feeling good. How badly do you want it is the only question. You feel good when you give good. Your smile. Your laughter. Your empathy and support. Love is what you give. When your heart grows, you grow. Your life grows. Your wealth grows.

CTA: Today, begin to intentionally become a giver of light in all you do and all you say. Don't take my word for any of what I write. I want you to just try it on for size. See if it's true. Make a commitment to be your best and give your best for one month. If you get off track, read this again. You can do it. It will change your life!

Have a great day!

MAY 21

Believe It Before You See It

Any goal or dream you have in life must start with your fervent belief that it will come to pass and the only thing between you and it is time.

Belief is the key to manifesting any idea, thought, or dream into physical reality. Belief backed up by consistent action toward the end result, coupled with dogged determination and faith. But it all comes from your belief that it is indeed possible.

Anytime you take on any new challenge, you have to be in the driver seat. Confident, self-assured, and ready. I promise you that if you hold strong to your belief, stay true to your vision and know that what you desire is in alignment with your higher self, your dream will come.

You will be adjusting your sails along the way as you hit obstacles, challenges, and seeming roadblocks, but these you will discover to be lessons on how better to sculpt the all-important details of your dream.

When you use the power of your higher self and your goal is congruent with these energies, you will find that the right people and things you need to propel you forward will show up right on time. No need to worry about the next 200 feet, as the way forward will be made clear to you.

Should you try to pull anything underhanded, unfair, and selfish, without consideration for others or any other low energy path your dream will meet sure defeat and death.

The best way to realize any dream is not to go into it directly seeking the money. Prosperity comes easily when you choose to act, deal, and live with sound character and integrity. These are the higher energies of living and expansion. Belief in these and action from this higher place, is what produces worthy dreams.

Dream big, my friends. Always seek higher knowledge and move forward with great character and personality. Your dreams will end up chasing you once you are in this flow.

CTA: Today, if you've had a goal or dream and it's become stagnant, lost or given up on, revive it or design a new one. Begin with your unwavering belief on your ability to accomplish anything and then move forward from a new, higher place. The place you were born to know.

Have a great day!

MAY 22

Trust

Trust is the safety net for all of us. If you have relationships you can truly trust in your life, you are wealthy. If you are a trustworthy partner, parent, child or friend yourself, you are the treasure of many. When you have trust in the unseen, you are indeed blessed and you already know it. Trust in yourself is the doorway to inner peace and lifelong success. So, you see how crucial trust is, as a life's practice. Giving it, being it, and harvesting the rewards of it. This is the power of trust.

Trust in your marriage is everything. It is the bedrock of a successful union. If you've been down a rocky road with your marriage and you're attempting a new and better course, a new trust must be your constant intention and vehicle forward. Broken trust is the most difficult state to rebuild, but it's not impossible. New boundaries, new commitments, higher-minded relational practices, and loving trust are the tools. All great relationships are really the spiritual ones. The deeper ones. The ones where we are able to truly let go and trust. Marriage is of the highest of these. Give your very best to each other. Why would you do anything different? Trust is the basis.

Being a trustworthy parent gives bloom to amazing children and a worthy example to follow. Trust in friendships means you can fall, be less than our best selves at times and still count on the forgiveness, laughter, uplift, and empathy of a trusted friend. Celebrate this gift. Be sure to always let others know how important they are and how much you appreciate them. This is how you cultivate and grow your garden of trusted relationships.

Trust in yourself is also cultivated and grown. It is only when we understand that we are the co-creator of our experience that we can begin to trust our higher power to guide us, our higher energies to unfold us, and trust in the fact that we receive loving assistance from spirit when we align ourselves with it. The ability for humans to really be able to let go of worry, fear, anger, jealousies, rivalries, negative judgments, etc... and instead trust and have faith, is the very key to living a free and mindful life. One that is filled with everything you need and love. Trust my friends. The more you believe and trust, the more reasons to do so will show up in your life. It's not until you decide to keep leaping forward, doing and giving your best that the miracles you seek will seek you. You are the magnet. If you deal in trust, trustworthy people will become part of your circle. You attract to yourself that which you are. If you're shady and untrustworthy in your life, guess what you can expect? All that goes with that vibe. Get it?

CTA: Today, build on your trust. Trust in yourself. Trust in your higher power to rise and succeed and trust that the best is always yet to come.

Have a great day!

MAY 23

Becoming a Light-Bearer

We are all light energy at our truest level. Our light self feels warm, inviting, accepting, and free. Our light is actually Unconditional Love. This is who we really are. Many have forgotten. Many continue to sleep in the opposite.

We must begin to recognize ourselves as both light and dark while we are here in the physical world. The darkness is contrast for us to recognize when we are off course and not using our light to stay free, heal ourselves and others.

Most have gotten trapped in the belief that our power lies in our ability to dominate, control or lord over others in some way. Many live by the lies of false power and separation from and superiority over others. Too many of us think that competition, clawing our way to the supposed top and using whatever means necessary to get there, is part and parcel to success. Shallow relationships, shady character, and no integrity. This is dealing and living separate from your light. This is the road most travel. It may seem attractive to some, but drama, tragedy, defeat, and broken relationships are all part of this road. We see it all the time. This is not success. This is the life of a taker, not a giver.

What this world really needs is not our separation, competition, disgust, judgment, and ire, it needs our light. This is the very best thing we can do to heal a dark world. A collective decision to shine. We don't have to rely on our leaders to make things better. We see how that's going. We need to decide ourselves to shift. The more of us who make the decision to become a bearer of light as our dominant energy, the more this planet will heal and rise. What we see on earth is a mix of heaven and hell; light and dark. We can tip the scales and watch in awe as our collective light penetrates the darkest of people and places. It's called conscious choice. When the majority of us make this choice, we will know peace. It starts with you and me. You are not just making this choice to heal your own dark corners; you are also doing it for everyone else. Your light is a gift to all.

CTA: Today, make the choice to give and shine your light. Become a Light-Bearer. It's your true nature and it's so much more powerful than any vote you could ever cast. It is what will truly change the world. You have a very important role to play. Give your light, rise, and shine!

Have a great day!

MAY 24

Being a Great Apprentice First

In order to be a great leader you must first become a great follower. I believe it's true that there are also born leaders. My partner Jim Pettit is that guy. Big-vision thinker with the confidence to see it through. Always been that way since I met him in sixth grade. But for the rest of us, who leading may not come naturally, I recommend becoming a great apprentice to a great leader. The trick is to feel in your heart that this person is worth following.

Is this leader a person of quality? Do they deal fairly with others with an unshakeable level of personal and professional integrity? Does this leader work from passion and bring his understudies up, or are they just looking to rise themselves? A great leader is one who wants the best for all on his team and realizes that they are there to help him in his dream, so he in turn, must help with theirs.

If you work for someone like this, give them your all, learn not only the jobs at hand until you've outgrown them from mastery, but learn the great philosophy of the leader and be a great follower of a person who leads from the heart rather than the ego. When you do this, you too will rise and before you know it, the great follower will be the great leader.

CTA: Being a great apprentice means staying open to the mentor's advice and counsel. If they are indeed worth following and learning from you must become like a partner in your mind.

Go the extra mile as your regular operating procedure. Your destiny is always found on the other side of the extra mile.

Have a great day!

MAY 25

Forgiveness

When we all begin to understand the truth that we are all part of the same spiritual source and that we all possess an ego that can keep us asleep to the fact that our true identity is that spirit and that spirit alone, we will understand that we must practice forgiveness in every interaction of our day. Including ourselves in the process.

It means that every time we are struck with a negative interaction with someone, we must recognize that they are unconscious in that moment and are acting from their lower, ego self. We also need and want forgiveness ourselves when we unconsciously do the same to someone else. It's only through self-awareness that we can learn that the act of forgiveness will keep you free from dwelling, storing, or living in the negative energy from the actions of another or those lies we tell ourselves about ourselves and others.

Forgiveness is the act of letting go. Letting go of an insult or seeming offense by another by forgiving is actually *freeing you*! It allows your mind and body to stay free of the negative energy. You know you feel better when your mind and body are free from pain and suffering, so why hold onto it any longer than you have to. The only way we can drop the negativity in our lives is forgiveness and love.

When becoming more aware that we are both spirit and ego while we are here on earth, we must first forgive ourselves for the old mental baggage we've been thinking about and carrying most of our lives. Only then can we effectively let it all go. We are all connected and the same in our truest form and we are all here to learn different lessons.

If we get this one right, the world will completely change. And to the one I think we all want to live in. So today, unburden yourself and those around you from the heavy baggage.

CTA: Call or text that person who is waiting for forgiveness or for an apology from you. Change your life right now with this one courageous action and then begin to use it as your daily tool of freedom.

Have a great day!

MAY 26

Relationships

This is the big enchilada of living a great life. Relationships are everything. We are put here on earth to experience this amazing place and live our lives to the fullest.

However, we will never be able to be our very best, live in love and gratitude and go for our goals and dreams without the help of others. Our first and most important relationship is with our higher power. Many people have a different name for this power and some even believe that it does not exist. I am not one of them.

This higher power is our true selves and we are of this power. Not separate from it, outside it, or a stranger to it. We are part of it. We know it as the energy of love. Our relationship to this higher place within us is everything we need for our life's journey. From this place we can create beautiful relationships that last our entire lives and beyond.

First and foremost, in order to create lasting, loving relationships with others, we must first love ourselves and be grateful for the fact that we were created from this highest of energy. When we are anchored in this knowing, we are free to express our deepest affections towards others, which will only attract to ourselves great and wonderful relationships. We will draw the right people into our lives to help us on our personal quests and we will be drawn to help others. It is the one true path of inner and outer success.

I have a saying that I tell my children all the time when they are questioning whether they know enough or are good enough to succeed at a new job or juncture of their lives; All other things being equal, relationships win every time. In a healthy relationship there are no givers and takers. Only givers on both sides. In your closest friendships, you know this to be true. The truth is that you can create great relationships easily and effortlessly when you yourself are grounded in your highest energy.

Let's continue this one tomorrow.

CTA: Relationships win every time. No lie!

Have a great day!

MAY 27

More on Relationships

This means that in each interaction, you are mindful and aware of what you are giving out and you choose to be open, nonjudgmental, and present for the time you are connected with another. You are there to understand, listen and be understood without the presence of ego. These are called holy interactions and they are always successful. Your intention going into any relationships must be from this place to bear any fruit. Their interests and yours must be met and harmony must be the goal. In our closest relationships, like the ones with our spouse or significant other, we must consistently meet one another's deepest needs and be aware of what they are.

All great relationships have to give up trying to control or compete with each other and let one another be able to shine their light while being supported and cheered on by the other. That's all anyone really desires. Give to each other the freedom to be yourselves and let the little go! All of it.

If you do not have this in your relationships, you're not giving or getting the best that you can and you'll have a mediocre, mundane relationship at best. In your professional life, your relationships will be everything. It's the ticket to great heights. You need to be your best, confident, non-arrogant self in order to attract high quality partners who will help you rise. You must do the same for others along the way. It's always the same motto, give what you want to see arrive in your own life.

CTA: Relationships are everything. Create and nurture your relationships today and every day and see your life become better and better. It's the best and only way to truly live a great life!

Have a great day!

MAY 28

Taking God Up on His Daily Offer

Every new day we get another opportunity to get it right. We have free will. Free will to choose our ego's demands or the life-expanding offer of our spirit. Each has their own agenda and each has immediate and long-lasting consequences for our lives and the lives we touch every day.

The Spirit's agenda only brings more life, expansion, and opportunity, while paying heed to the Ego only brings strife, conflict, blame, and a low level life experience.

We see this microcosm of our individual ego playing an overwhelming role in the macrocosm of the world. Just watch the news.

World leaders, including our own, operate predominately from the ego. Their choices, like some of our own are based on a false, individual need for power and domination over others.

This is not true leadership, nor true power. It is a "what's in it for me" mentality. It's true, they think they are doing the right thing by lording over us and telling us what is best for us, while really only looking out for themselves and "their team." This is why the world is in darkness most of the time. Because it's being led for the gain of a few and not for all. It's for an agenda of material power and not exposing us all to the true power within each of us.

The world needs to be led by those whose aim is to wake all of us up to our true individual power, so we all may *thrive*, instead of just survive. Our leaders make policy based on where their next vote or donation is coming from, rather than making "truth in living" their agenda.

We must all rise above this ego-centered game in order to end the lie of separation between all of us and our benevolent source.

CTA: Today, be part of the true solution by doing what you came here to do, spread light. Light is truth and if we each choose to shine a bit more each day, we are truly making a difference. Spread your wealth.

Have a great day!

MAY 29

Becoming a World Filled with Light

We need to become a world of light over darkness, but from a place of conscious awakening. This means we must each dedicate ourselves to "waking up" a little more each day. How we do this is a simple concept, but not always an easy one to live. If we all make this choice to shift our individual lives from the darker energies of our ego, to the consistent choice of our higher energies, we will be doing our part to take God up on his daily offer to live in and share the truth.

Our world is made up of opposites. We all know this personally. Dark and light, negative and positive, happy or depressed, winning and losing, rich and poor, fearful and courageous, love and hate, etc. It is our job and our daily purpose to choose the light, choose the positive, choose the healing energy of love. Our ego wants us to believe in and act on the opposite, lower energies. This is a certain path to mediocrity and keeps us all stuck in darkness.

When we take God up on his offer each day, to live and act in true power, we see our personal lives shift into a higher gear and we will find life energy pulsing through us on a much more consistent and powerful basis. This will be so amazing to you that you will start to spread the wealth to your friends, family, and many others. It will become the only way to fly for you. It will bring to you more riches on more levels that you can imagine and this, my friends, is the only way to bring global light to an ego-dominated world.

We are responsible to wake ourselves up. We will have help along the way on this amazing path because we will attract more of what we are giving along the way. This is the true journey of a powerful, happy, and successful life.

CTA: Today, do your part to bring about this shift. When you make this choice, you benefit all.

Have a great day!

MAY 30

The News

Tonight when you watch the news, please pay attention to the truth about the ego and its dark demands and wake up to the fact that we are being led to think, speak, and act on these demands. The news demands our constant reaction and judgment, which keeps us arguing instead of collaborating and solving. The arguing causes us to choose sides against one another and feel the hatred and punitive thoughts on a constant basis. There is war constantly raging in the background of our minds. It's being taught all over the world. We the people suffer from the insidious game of the ego. This is the world where some live in palaces while others are kept in the dark. We must leave this place and it starts with us leaving it. God has a different plan and we're all part of it. We must choose it every day to know it.

We must take God up on his offer to truly live. Give everyone you see a smile, a compliment, encouragement, and praise. Tell those close to you that you love them and appreciate their role in your life. This is the act and the art of taking up the offer. The more you do this, the better your life will become. Wake up a little more today with your own God given power.

The day we elect a leader who wants to wake us all up to our true personal power, will be the day the world begins to truly change for the best. And I will be the first one to volunteer for this person's campaign. It's not about some of us, it's about *all* of us. This is how we create heaven on earth.

CTA: Today, do your part. Shine your light.

Have a great day!

MAY 31

Sacrifice

On this Memorial Day weekend, we honor the sacrifice of all the brave men and women who have served and continue serve our great nation.

This nation was founded on an idea. An idea that we are all equal in the eyes of God and that we stand up and defend the right of Life, Liberty, and the Pursuit of Happiness. These three freedoms are truly God-given and *all* people around this globe thirst for this idea to be real for them as well.

None of these three have been easily won or secured in our short history as a nation. These freedoms have been, and continue to be fought for on a daily basis by our sons and daughters, fathers, mothers, and family. Their willingness to sacrifice their very lives for these freedoms for all of us is a testament to the spirit in all if us who long to be free of the oppression and control of the ego-centric leaders we see running many parts of the world, including our own.

Our children, fathers, mothers, grandparents, and ancestors who took up and continue to take up this challenge are sacrificing so very much for *all* of us and they deserve our undying gratitude for this service. Without you, we would not know the freedoms we have to pursue our dreams, our lives, and loving others and our God in an open society.

It is without a doubt that The Big Man upstairs wants us to pay very close attention this special weekend to how our soldiers and veterans have been and continue to be treated as less than the average US citizen, when in truth, they should be held up as examples for all of us to behold, honor, and treat with special care. Very special care.

CTA: Today, honor all those who served and sacrificed. Send them all a blessing of gratitude and love.

Have a great day!

JUNE 1

Taking On the Energy of Another

This happens every day of our lives and it happens in a split second. This works for either positive energy or negative energy.

We all do it. We walk into a room with a smile, frown, laughter, tears, radiance, or whatever drama of the moment that has captured the attention of our ego. Then, just like a magnet, others are pulled into our energy vortex and the spell is cast.

In our current society it does not take much to sway our energy up and down all day long. It is much like a roller coaster until we make the conscious decision to control our own energy, so we are not sucked in by a dramatic, usually well-meaning energy vampire. Conversely, people with great energy lift our spirit and our mood. Those are the ones we should absorb, carry forward and spread like Johnny Appleseed.

In order to learn to control our own good state of energy in the midst of vampires in our day, we must become mindful and aware of our own mindset and what it is saying to us at all times. Otherwise, we are fresh meat for whatever energy comes our way. We will easily become like those around us, adding to the swirl of gossiping, over dramatic, level ten energy. Not the way you want to live your life.

On your journey of self-discovery, you will learn how affected you have become to the whim of others energy and how often you have been swept into doing and saying the bidding of your ego and the ego of another. On a much larger scale, this is how ego-centric leaders have brainwashed their people. We must be steadfast in the protection and stewardship of our own good energy. Otherwise, it is simply up for grabs to whatever is going on around us.

Shields up! This is what I usually say when a drama around me is unfolding. This reminds me to be on guard and mindful of my place in this "story" that is being created or regurgitated. When this happens, you have the opportunity to use your light energy to shift the situation or bring a new perspective to the circle. Doesn't always work, but it keeps *you* in the right frame of mind. You won't be tethered to the hot air balloon of negativity.

CTA: Today, notice how often your energy has the potential to shift from good to bad by the energy of another. When this happens, say shields up! Remind yourself that you have the *choice* to get sucked in, shift their energy, or get the hell out of Dodge!

Have a great day!

JUNE 2

Silence Is Golden

We have become addicted to noise wherever we are in our day. From the time we wake up to the radio or alarm, then the TV while we get ready, then to the car radio with incessant commercials, music, and talk, then to work, with all the goings on of the day, then back in the car to go home, TV at dinner, TV after dinner, and at bed time. Sound like you? Sounds like most of us!

The only time we get any silence is when we sleep, and many of us leave the TV on during that time as well! I used to be one of them. The problem with all this noise and distraction in our lives, is that it never allows us to cultivate and know a place of inner peace and stillness. Any life of power and excellence must have and know this place. Without it, our minds are like a constant hum of noise, nervousness, anxiety, and whatever energy of the moment is consuming us.

Knowing inner peace is the holy grail of great living. With it, you can easily make right choices, change bad thoughts to good, live in the moment, and be present with all you do and create meaningful relationships without ego presence. It is the "ground zero" from which we need to move forward.

Cultivating inner peace is done from a daily practice of silence. We have the opportunity to do this many times during our day, when we are mindful and make it a priority. For one week, make it a goal to keep your radio off in the car, see how challenging this is for you. This will be an eye opener for most of us and we will become aware of just how noise addicted we are.

CTA: Today, choose this time of silence in your car, begin to contemplate all the good things you have in your life. Your kids, your husband or wife, an upcoming vacation. Whatever you're grateful for, this is that time to think about it and revel in some gratitude for all you have. You will be connecting to your power from home.

Have a great day!

JUNE 3

More on Practicing the Gift of Silence

After a solid week of five minutes a day in the practice in silence, you will see a difference emerging in yourself. This one week can turn into two, three, and then into a new habit. One that will keep you more balanced, self-aware, and in a state of continuous gratitude.

This will become a path for you to follow and it is sure to expand with your higher level of positive energy. A kick-start to a much more fulfilling life. Silence is where you feel the guidance and voice of the divine within. The noise we fill our day with must be released or it will be like a heavy backpack of mental chaos, one you've unwittingly gotten used to.

We all have soaked up way too much noise and we may not see the damage it causes in our thought life, relationship to self and others, and a vibration that attracts to us less than we are capable of drawing from the life force within us and all around us. The noise causes your energy to fluctuate all over the board throughout your day. It causes mental fatigue, low actions, and reactive mind states. All can be released through daily silence and higher contemplation.

We must give ourselves this gift or the world will keep you stuck and asleep in the noisy mind. Take this time! Five minutes in a dimly lit room with all electronics off. No music, no interruptions. Let others know your new goal and boundary of this special time.

This one practice will change your life and help you to know a new place of calm inner peace. This new place will help you in every area of your life. I assure you.

CTA: Today, start this challenge and give it your very best. The more diligent you become, the more you will begin to shed the garbage and let in the light. The payoff is huge. Stick with it!

Have a great day!

JUNE 4

A Family's Best Friend

My lovely wife Jan asked me to write an entry in honor of Lena, our friends' Great Dane, who recently passed.

Losing a pet it is like losing a member of the family. While they may not be with us as long, their presence in our lives has been just as meaningful and important. The great memories our children have been blessed with and the many funny stories that these beings of unconditional love have brought us are some of the best in life.

For most of us, our pets are the first ones to lovingly greet us at the door, with no expectations, other than to feel our love and freely give theirs to us in their own special way. They are there in our worst moments and our best, always willing to bring us joy, just for the asking.

They make us laugh, they tick us off at times, and they love to let us know that they too are an individual with quirks, various energies, and personalities. They are no less a family member than any of the rest. Sometimes, they are just the ones we need in our trying moments.

So on this day, we send our love to our dear friends and all who share in the love of our pets and the sheer joy they bring to our lives. While they may no longer be here in the physical, their memory and their love will be in our hearts forever. They ask nothing but to be loved just like the family member they are and they give so much back to us humans. We should always honor their roles in our lives and hold them in high regard, for they are a true bearer of light in this world.

CTA: Hug your pet and give them a blessing of love and gratitude.

Have a great day!

JUNE 5

Celebrating Others

This is a lifelong practice that must be part of our daily routine. When we interact with our friends, co-workers and family, we need to shift into a higher gear of giving. This means seeing and celebrating the very best in others and bringing out more of their good stuff by shining a light on it.

What happens when we do this is the very best stuff of life. We push the high energy buttons of those in our lives with compliments, encouragement, praise, busting their butt in a fun way and just bringing out their best by our letting them know how great they are.

This is a great practice in shifting the energy of an entire room. You do this on purpose in order to bring light to any low energy atmosphere. It changes moods, outlooks, and the entire day in most cases. Celebrating each other is our purpose.

Each of us has been given many gifts and talents. Sometimes we wonder what they are and question ourselves if we even have any, until someone else shines their light upon it for us. This automatically lifts others to a higher level on their positive energy scale and in turn, does the same for the giver. As I have mentioned before, giving and receiving are two sides of the same coin. The in and out breath of life. It's crucial for all of us.

When we choose to wake up each morning and decide to devote our day to celebrating the relationships in our lives, we have chosen greatness. This one practice of shining your light on others, bringing out their light as the result, is in fact what will change this world from dark to light. It's just the micro of the macro.

CTA: Today, decide to celebrate those in your life. Tell your children how proud you are of them. Call your best friend and remind them of a funny story you two have shared in your life. Compliment a total stranger on something they are doing or wearing. Shine your light on everyone today and spread *your* wealth!

Have a great day!

JUNE 6

True Friendship

This is a big one and it may challenge some supposed "friendships," because there are so many out there having very superficial relationships that are called best friendships.

If you are blessed to have *one* true friendship in your life, you have a real treasure and you can consider yourself rich. Very rich.

A true friend is one who knows you inside and out. Your garbage, your qualities, your fears, hopes, dreams, and defeats. One who loves you for all of it, because of it, and in spite of it. One who lifts you out of a bad head or ugly situation. One who won't wallow with you, but will help you rise back to your best self. One who apologizes to you when they have been less than their best with you and one who forgives you quickly, when you are also temporarily insane. This person is a keeper!

A true friend never competes with you. They celebrate you and your accomplishments. They revel in your success and always speak well of you when in the presence of others. A true friend does not have to be called every day to be reassured of your place in their lives. That is always a given. There is no need for envy or jealousy between true friends, because what's mine is yours. True friends share joy, laughter, pain, suffering, and victory. They are always there in your heart and they always have your best interest in mind.

A true friendship is one of constant giving and receiving of our highest self and our highest honor. A true friend never desires lording over another or feels the need to cling to their friend. A true friend gives complete freedom to the other to be themselves and express themselves. A true friend is always open to the ideas, dreams, and crazy thoughts of the other, without judgment or persecution.

A true friend is kind and thoughtful of the other and wants the best outcomes and upward movement for all.

When you think of a true friend, there will be a smile on your face and laughter in your heart. If you have a friend like this, you are *rich*.

If this does not describe your closest friends, it's time to cultivate new ones. It is also time to look at yourself to see if you are also this type of true friend. When you become this type of friend, you will begin to attract this very person into your life. You always get what you give. This includes quality friends and friendships.

CTA: Today I want you to take a hard look in the mirror and ask yourself if *you* have been this type of friend and then look outwardly and ask if your best friends meet this criteria.

There is always work to be done in growing our garden of truth. We all need to prune out the weeds in our lives, so the growth that our spirit was intended for can see the light of day.

Have a great day!

JUNE 7

"Great! You're Being Blessed!"

This phrase was spoken to me when I was going through what I considered to be the worst time in my life. I immediately paused when I heard it because my ego wanted to rail against such an opposite to what I was feeling, and yet, another deeper voice said, "wait," "pay attention," "listen." It ended up being one of the most profound statements of my life, because it was true.

Our struggles, disasters, tragedies, and what we consider to be everyday frustrations, are gifts in disguise. We as humans will only fully unwrap these gifts when we take hold of this very phrase in our lives. It's called true faith. Not just the glib, "hey, keep the faith man," but *real* faith, belief that you are being brought to something better, but you know you have some work to do on your end if you want to see the blessing.

Most will simply look at these guides as bad luck, "woe is me, I'm a victim yet again" mentality.

My friends, life is a class. You get to choose how to approach it, and how you work with it or against it. When you give up trying to control outer circumstances and begin to cooperate with and learn to read the messages life is bringing you, your life will never be seen by you the same.

You are to rise from your tragedies! You are to rise from your low circumstances and ways of living! Rising from the ashes of everyday unconscious living is where all the gold of this beautiful human journey lives. It is only by your consistent choice that you will rise. This is where you will find your real strength to overcome anything and show others the way. Anger is not strength, overreacting is weakness and holding it all and thinking you will somehow find peace this way is deciding to stay asleep and low.

You have a proper guidance system within. You must shift to its voice. You've practiced the voice of the opposite long enough. Love has its own voice and it speaks of victory over tragedy and counsels to wait before you react, because you're really being blessed.

CTA: Today, decide to live in real faith, patience, and belief in your higher guide.

Have a great day!

JUNE 8

Your Listening Skills

Being a great listener in today's world can be very challenging, due to the millions of distractions in everyday life.

We have become chronic multi-taskers in order to keep pace and get everything done on our list. The problem with living your life on a hamster wheel is that we have lost or certainly depleted our ability to stop for a few moments and truly tune in to one conversation at a time.

We have drive-by conversations with not a lot of substance or meaning. Just give me the facts, so I can check "you" off my to-do list and move on to the next item.

At the end of our lives we will realize that we didn't get it all done, because we *never* get it all done, so it is crucial that we realize that it is our relationships that are the gold we seek. This is the gold we are grateful for having cultivated at the end of our lives, both internally and externally.

Being a great listener is at the forefront of any quality relationship. Our duty on the listening end of any conversation is to tune out all other distraction and tune into the other person or persons.

Everyone is able to feel when you are half listening, in another conversation in your head about something completely different. This habit depletes the true meaning in all our interactions. We are not giving our best self at this divided moment.

Let's continue this one tomorrow.

CTA: A good listener must be completely present. Honor those you speak with and be truly present. Imagine how much you will learn!

Have a great day!

JUNE 9

Your Listening Skills *continued*

Tuning in is using the energy of your highest self. Caring, kindness and empathy are all available when you are tuned in and truly listening. You will have so much more of your power and magic to offer the other when you practice being completely present and open. You will find this process to be rich and more meaningful to both parties.

This practice is a gift for everyone involved. Giving your complete attention to another makes them feel heard and it satisfies a real need in that moment. The truth is that it usually takes no more time to have a high quality conversation, than a low level, half heard, half understood chat.

More is heard and understood at the deeper level in a present moment, tuned in conversation. More truth, more detail, and a much clearer picture of the issue. This allows for a much higher level of problem solving, quicker responses, with very effective solutions. This all comes from being present with another. This also happens to create some of the most memorable and meaningful experiences of our lives.

It is the moments of our lives that we remember and hold dear. Being a great listener is one half of that equation.

CTA: Today, tune totally in when having or initiating a conversation. Don't just listen to have a quick response, soak it in, give it some space, and allow the true moment to flourish. It is an art form in itself. One that will become the portrait of your choices. Choose to be a great listener.

Have a great day!

JUNE 10

The Art of Non-Judgment

Probably the hardest practice for all of us. Judging others, judging ourselves, situations, outward appearances, groups, cultures, and the proverbial book by its cover. Judging is right up there with the national pastime! Believe me, I've done my share!

I'm not talking about our preferences, likes, and dislikes. I'm talking about making our minds up, in a split second about someone or something, without any or little knowledge of facts or circumstances. This is the kind that cuts us off from our higher self and power.

When we harshly judge ourselves or others, we are really defining ourselves and where we are in our evolution as a spirit in human form. As far as I'm concerned, we are all in kindergarten on the scale and it's time to move up a few grades.

In my career, I have taken one look at a prospective employee, judged them, convicted them and sentenced them to no opportunity whatsoever in our organization. And as many times that I have done that, I have been proven *wrong*.

Some of the very best in my life began as one of the condemned by my ego. Once I began to see when these judgments were just lies and mirror to my own shortcomings, I began to let go of this horrid practice.

Let's continue this one tomorrow.

CTA: Remove judgment for your day. Look upon others with love and compassion.

Have a great day!

JUNE 11

The Art of Non-Judgment *continued*

Non-judgment *frees* you and the person whom you would have judged, to be open to the very best in both of you. You immediately bypass your gatekeeper and the protective fence in the other. Judgment therefore is the opposite energy of an open heart.

Everyone, and I mean everyone, has their own garbage. Their own skeletons and their own past that they would not like to have judged or prejudged. So going on that truth, we need to always allow space for another's truth to emerge. Most of the time, this needs a good amount of time.

Knowledge, understanding, compassion, and empathy are the opposite of the insidious practice of judgment. Hearsay, innuendos, half-truths, appearance, and old, worn-out stereotypes are the swords of your judge. And boy, does it love to wield that blade.

We also judge ourselves, convict ourselves, and sentence ourselves to lives of misery, anxiety, depression, and self-loathing when we decide to pay heed to the judge. This judge is in all of us. The judge gives us limited opportunities, negative outlooks, and attitudes, and it repels all possibility for loving ourselves completely while pouring it out to everyone.

Realizing that at our core, we are all from one true home, all brothers and sisters, here for a special purpose, lessons, and different life paths, we can lower our sword, get in, and find out where we share common ground and how we either fit or don't fit into each other's lives. This can only be found through non-judgment.

Instant connections, great new relationships, laughter, joy, and happiness are always readily available when we make the true and powerful choice to discard our negative inner judge.

Let's continue this one tomorrow.

CTA: Knowing that the human race is all interconnected will allow for non-judgmental thoughts and words.

Have a great day!

JUNE 12

The Art of Non-Judgment *continued*

I've seen in myself and others how destructive this practice of judging others or ourselves can be. We or they are less than, poorer or richer than, meeker than, fatter or skinnier than, and the list goes on and on. It's a cancer. A cancer that destroys your ability for a life at the top when you constantly judge yourself in these ways or outwardly criticize people and circumstances.

Let's continue this one tomorrow.

CTA: Today, I want you to meet your judge face to face. Probably for the first time. Call your judge out!

This judge never serves you although it will protest that it protects you. Use this energy to shift you into the correct mindset of loving kindness and silent blessings. When you are tempted, remember that you are of the highest order, here to make a difference. A difference for yourself and your personal growth and here to help others along their way.

Make today the last day you listen to the awful demands of your inner critic. Recognize how this voice keeps you in low energy. Rise to your higher mind. It's directed by your heart.

Have a great day!

JUNE 13

Write a Letter

Proper communication between friends, family, and co-workers is essential for understanding points of view, perceptions, and creating and keeping great relationships.

When we are in disharmony with someone in our lives and communication breaks down, the ego is ever-present and cheering you on to keep the silent war in place. Sometimes we let our ego talk us into this war for a lifetime. Grudges, misperceptions, judgments, and all the other lower energies are in the driver's seat.

During these breakdowns in harmony, our hearts and minds are closed. Closed to a solution, closed to reconciliation, and closed to communication. Except one. The letter.

I have used this practice many times during the early and middle teen years of my children. And it worked every time. Teens are especially prone to rebel and wield their ego without questioning it. But this is true of all of us.

When I was trying to guide my children to a better plan, situation, or solution or we had some blowout where both our egos were in battle, my kids would shut us off and their young power of reasoning with it. In other words, no one was talking.

I knew that the only way to reopen harmony and communication was to write them a short letter. This letter was not filled with my egos demands or need to win. This letter was always from the heart. It spoke about my love for them and my purpose as their parent and guide for this part of their lives. It said how proud I am to be part of them and them as part of me. Then I would speak about the issue from a solution-oriented standpoint that included an apology from me for being temporarily insane as well. This letter reopened their hearts with love first and then allowed the truth of the matter to be seen. The outcome was always the same. They would come to us with an apology of their own, usually some tears and a new understanding of the needs of all of us as a family. The power of a truth-filled, heart-centered letter is immense indeed.

Let's continue this one tomorrow.

CTA: A short letter, from the heart, may be all you need to mend a sore relationship.

Have a great day!

JUNE 14

Write a Letter *continued*

The letter gives the other party the opportunity to digest the thoughts and feelings of the writer without the possibility for another, face to face show down, argument or ego battle. If your letter is from the heart and you speak your truth, while desiring the best for both parties, it will open the door for harmony to re-enter the relationship and the power to move forward in some new way.

When couples fight and shut down to one another, this practice can be an invaluable tool to speak your heart, when you are not used to doing it verbally. It lets you say everything you need to say.

Keep it always from a place of love and the truth will be revealed for both of you. Even if it leads to break up, it will be a much better parting than the ego route. In the end if any relationship does not work out, you at least are not carrying forward any baggage because you were able to say everything you needed to.

CTA: Today, if you are in any ego battle that has you and another at odds with family, friends, or co-workers and you're not speaking, sit down and write the letter. Read it through many times to make sure there's no tone or ego involved. Stay with the issues and if it's someone you love and want to keep in your life, make sure to include first that you love them and no longer want this wall of negative energy between you. Keep that as the whole tone. Even through the tough parts.

Your intention must always be to have an outcome that is beneficial for both or one that leaves the door open for love.

Done the right way, you can't get it wrong. The process forward when communication somewhat resumes, is to keep that intention of harmony firmly at the forefront. It's where you always thrive and prosper.

Have a great day!

JUNE 15

The Vibe of Your Home

This is an important one to recognize, as it is something that either creates a loving, warm sanctuary or it can be a negative vortex, filled with anger, judgment, yelling and disharmony. Many live somewhere in the middle or even lower on the scale.

This is why it is a must to step back and analyze the energy of your surroundings. The place you choose to call home.

Every home has a vibe. It is more of a feeling than what you would use your five physical senses to detect. When you are in tune with your own energy, you are able to better feel the vibe of your home and what everyone in your home is bringing to the table.

If you were to describe the energy within your home, what would it be? Loving, kind, warm, or chaotic, nervous, and angry, like walking on eggshells? It's usually a mixed bag, but I assure you, there's a dominant energy that prevails.

Usually the person that has assumed the role of the head of the family creates the dominant energy of the household. If this person is usually a loving, nurturing, laughter filled force, you are blessed indeed. This energy pervades everyone in the home, including your pets and the home itself.

This is also true if you've been, or are currently living in an angry household, filled with fear, anxiety, and low energy. You feel it to your core either way. And one produces life while the other is just a nervous, joyless existence.

The good news is that once you recognize the difference in these polar opposites and you decide to become the change you want to see in your home, you will have chosen to be the light.

Your job is to shift yourself first, move yourself up the energy scale as a life choice and never let go.

CTA: Become aware of the dominant energy in your home. Is it you? How have you been contributing to the overarching vibe? You don't need to feel guilt or shame for this, for that is another trap of the ego. Just begin the loving shift upward, as you no longer feed the demands of your lower mind.

Have a great day!

JUNE 16

More On the Vibe of Your Home

When you make the life choice to improve yourself and the vibe you give off, your home will begin to shift as well. You can never go back and never give in to lower energies within your home. You must be vigilant, steadfast, and determined to bring light into your home as the dominant force. Low energy cannot and will not survive if you do this. Things will change for you and there will be some low energy vibes trying to climb back into the driver's seat, but light always wins in the end. It will become an easy choice to make as you put the time and effort in. Most give into the ego and become its voice way too easily. The thoughts of your lower mind will give way to you verbalizing it and then acting out with its disturbing tone delivering the message. This disrupts your life force of good energy for as many times per day that you allow it. When you finally realize that this energy and mindset never brings you anything good, you'll choose change. This change will be your purpose and your true path. Follow it and live in it your own unique way. This is also known as "a life well-lived."

CTA: Today, become aware of the general vibe of your home. How would you describe it? Maybe a friend whom you trust can give you an outside perspective. You will know in your heart what the truth is. Use this truth as your launching pad to positive change.

Have a great day!

JUNE 17

Likeability Wins

All other qualities being equal, likeability always wins. You can be at the top of your class, be the smartest person in the room, have all the trappings that go with what most people consider success, and still, likeability will win in the realms of career and personal relationships.

Likeability is usually a very natural energy. It is most often forged from a strong, loving family and quality friendships throughout our youth.

In many cases, however, people are raised in less than desirable circumstances and they can become fearful, guarded, closed off, and introverted. Or worse yet, they take on the negative roles and energies of the ego influences they are surrounded by and ones they associate with. This negative life conditioning contributes largely to an outer world that is limited due to the lack of personal skills and what you might call a winning personality. In other words, a bad attitude.

In cases like this it usually takes a completely different experience to show these unfortunate souls what life on the positive side looks like. In our business, we have seen many like this and we have been blessed to show them another way of living.

Part of living a life of greatness is to show others the way forward. It may be the only chance they receive to change their course. If you have this opportunity, take it on. It's a gift for you too.

Let's continue this one tomorrow.

CTA: Likeability, along with good relationships, always wins.

Have a great day!

JUNE 18

Likeability Wins *continued*

If you're in a life situation now that has lots of drama, low energy, and bad personal examples, you must seek a change of scenery and most certainly a change in energy.

If your inner voice is screaming for you to find a new job, leave a bad relationship or just seek the upward way, you need to get your house in order and put a few new tools in your box. Likeability is one of the biggest you will need. But what are the ingredients of this energy?

Likeability says the following:

I will not carry my past and spin my old script of defeat, ugly stories or fear of the future. I never need to speak of it again. When I do, I put myself back down the ladder.

I will be totally open to people and treat them like gold. For that is how I desire to be treated.

I choose to be a victor and not a victim. I am no victim.

I will easily take constructive criticism and no longer listen to my ego's demand to be offended. Being offended is a low energy response.

I will be true and truthful and give my very best. I will constantly seek to improve myself and my lot in life.

I will wear a smile as my main communication tool. This is a big one! Simple and always effective. Use it!

I will be a person of *yes* and will cooperate instead of compete. I am above no one and I am below no one. We are all equal at the level of the soul. I have nothing and no one to fear.

I will embrace change and new challenges as if they were chosen for my best and highest good. Because they are.

I will be the change that I want to see in my life and I will stay determined to remain on this upward path for my lifetime.

I choose only to see the good in others and speak about it and celebrate it in their presence. This will mirror back to me, the person I really am.

Likeability gets the job, the friends, and the good life. Every time. Likeability is simply the energy of love emanated outward in all your dealings.

CTA: Today, pack this power tool in your box of success and use it to build your day. Before you know it, you will have built a mansion you can be proud to call your life.

Have a great day!

JUNE 19

Success Is Never an Accident

What most will view as success are the outer trappings of the physical. The house, the toys, the clothes, and the cars, right? All of which is perfectly fine. The real success is in the question, "how did you treat everyone around you in getting there?"

True success and a truly successful person wants success for everyone. They share their wealth along the way because they recognize that they were propelled by others in a higher realm of success the whole way. The "pay-it-forward" mindset. Someone had to show you, correct? You must do the same and do it well.

At the end of our lives, when we look back at our place in all of this, we want to see that we were a beneficial presence, an open-hearted student, and a kind mentor to all. This is the formula for knowing success in all areas of your life. It is giving with a grateful heart. It says, "I've been given much, which inspired me to give." Everything and everyone you need to show up in your life will come from this eternal formula. What you seek, you must give.

Having the trappings and outer symbols of success are the shallowest part of this pool. It's nice to have, but it's not the real gold. The real gold is in the deeper end (your relationship to the whole journey and everyone here).

Take the deeper journey for yourself. Live from the mindset of the end of your life, backwards. Live by giving your very best, to yourself and everyone else. Don't skip a space. Everyone. Even if giving your best is your kindest goodbye.

CTA: Today, practice true success. Living by your heart is always the key.

Have a great day!

JUNE 20

The Force of Creativity

We all know this force. When we are in this life-giving mode and our attention is totally focused on creating something positive, whether it is art, photography, writing, music, building, crafting, creative problem solving, creating new relationships, or just spending time in your garden creating beauty, we are in bliss. We have left the ego in exchange for spiritual action and the art of being.

As I have said many times, we all came here to be creators ourselves, born from the most creative energy there is, Love. This is what we feel when we are in this personal creative space. Time stops for a while and you are in the midst of a beautiful moving mediation. Escaping the chatter of the mind and listening to the instructions of your soul. This is where beauty is born. Whatever you produce from this space will bring joy. Joy to you and joy to those who get to experience your song. Your music.

The best thing about the force of creativity is that we have unlimited ways to express it. The choices are all yours. Whatever you are attracted to, there is a way for you to sing your unique song through that subject. Oh, and make a prosperous life through it as well. In fact, that's what you should be doing if you're not. Happiness, fulfillment, and adventure await you on the creative path.

Let's continue this one tomorrow.

CTA: Allow time for creativity.

Have a great day!

JUNE 21

The Force of Creativity *continued*

The other side of the coin in life is what we create through our ego. This is the workshop of mediocre living and a potentially hellish life. You see, we have free will to create ourselves and our lives, but we must do it all through the higher energies of creation. We must put the love into everything we do and say. When we abide by this code, we only create greatness, happiness, awesome products, awesome outcomes, and a rich, abundant life.

Creating drama is a career path that many have chosen. No matter where they are, at work, home or even the market, they choose to sprinkle the negative in all they do. This is the death nail to creating anything meaningful. Abandon this practice at all costs. Gossip, backstabbing, revenge, poor work ethic, laziness, victim mindedness, and greed are all the lovely little creations of the ego. The more we know, the more we grow. We simply must grow past our addiction to this low energy living.

CTA: Today, create! Create everything you do and say through the lens of your higher self. The outcome of which will be a great day!

JUNE 22

Be the Other Voice In the Room

So many times in our busy lives, we get caught up in ego-centric conversations, actions and energy. These are the ones that the ego finds very juicy. They involve creating a drama first, by someone's false perception of another or a situation. Then this person decides that what their ego is telling them is absolute truth. Then they decide, usually in a split second, to spread this perception to anyone they come in contact with, or another ally in gossip town.

This type of energy expands and soon becomes the vibration in the room, home or workplace, and it's toxic. It is in fact energy pollution. This pollution makes us tired, lethargic, low, depressed, anxious, angry, and volatile. Once you have been infected with this energy, it becomes the lens you see life through.

Sometimes just for a few hours, sometimes the whole day and sometimes it is so pervasive in your life that you unwittingly become it, as your dominant energy and personality. Horrifying right? It happens every day, in so many lives, and it's cancer. Literally and figuratively.

When we see our day through this lens of the ego, we are short tempered, ready to blow at any second. We treat our loved ones and co-workers like sounding boards for endless venting and rants. If this sounds like you or your work or home atmosphere, You need a change. Either you decide to be the change and dominate the energy field with higher energies or move on.

Most people are unaware of their character and their part in the whole of life. On the ego plain, it's dog eat dog. I gotta get mine. Compete, compete, compete. Where's the love?!

We need to become the other voice in the room. The voice of truth. Saying what we need to say, but from a different place. This place is non-confrontational in its confrontations. It is kind instead of needing to be right. This voice mends instead of causing separation. This voice recognizes the ego and its insane hold on others minds and lives. The voice of truth is positive, compassionate and caring. It dissolves pain and suffering in seconds and can bring a person down from an ego rant before it affects others. This is true power.

Let's continue this one tomorrow.

CTA: Who needs drama? Not you! So why create it? Avoid gossip. Only speak the truth.

Have a great day!

JUNE 23

Be the Other Voice in the Room *continued*

Being the other voice in the room isn't always easy. In fact, it's usually the most difficult voice to be, if you're not grounded in truth yourself. Calm confidence is what you own when you are grounded in the truth. The ease in which you are able to confront the ego of another will be the very power you use to build your life. Just like Cesar Milan, The Dog Whisperer, your calm, positive, assertive energy will envelop the ego and bypass its gatekeeper every time. This puts out the fire and expands others to see the truth and shift to a higher place within themselves, instead of feeling that they lost an argument. Everyone knows truth when they hear and more importantly, feel it.

CTA: Today, assess yourself and your surroundings throughout the day. See where you are attracted to, or repelled by dramas of the ego. Are you participating or are you the other voice in the room?

Always remember that choosing the ego only allows it to continue growing in you and as part of your life. Choosing the spirit and truth gives you life. Life energy, life power, and a successful life. The choice is always yours.

Have a great day!

JUNE 24

Teaching Others How to Treat You

This is one of the most powerful lessons you need to learn and live.

So often people go through their whole lives accepting less than they deserve, including how they are treated by others. How others treat you is a direct reflection of how you feel about yourself.

When you look in the mirror, do you love what you see? Do you constantly berate yourself for one thing or another? Does your self-talk sound like a critic, constantly picking apart things you feel are flaws and faults? Are you victim minded, feeling that others are responsible for your pain and suffering or are you just the opposite, confident, self-assured, and accepting of yourself and all that comes with being you?

Both of these scenarios create the backdrop of your energy, your life experience, and how others perceive and treat you. And you are responsible. It's not necessarily your fault, but you are the teacher.

If your normal energy field screams victim, down trodden, martyr or a belief that others are somehow above or better than you, you have set the stage for a low energy life with a back seat experience. You are better and you deserve better, but it's a totally inside job to rise above and out of this mediocre mindset.

Let's continue this one tomorrow.

CTA: Treat yourself like you love yourself. Be kind to you by using positive self-talk.

Have a great day!

JUNE 25

Teaching Others How to Treat You *continued*

First and foremost, you will always be treated the way you treat yourself and others. You'll always attract to you the type of energy that you give out. Screamers attract screamers. Drama queens and kings attract drama. Hate attracts haters and misery loves company.

When you are finally fed up with poor results, low expectations and people that treat you poorly (whom you currently call friends), you are ready for a life shift. And it is not only possible, but it's a must. Hell is created right here, by you, if you allow it. Your other choice is Heaven. This experience is readily available to you, but requires will, choice, determination and above all, self-love and forgiveness, letting go of the old script in exchange for the truth of who you really are.

Unless you learn to love yourself, bless and forgive your so-called flaws and less than desirable past, you will never be able to receive the love and treatment you desire and deserve. You get what you give. Always. And if for some reason you are treated poorly after this life-giving shift, you are easily able to brush it off, not be offended, and stay in your higher self. When you become one with your higher energy in all your expressions, you will be treated as such. The red carpet will be rolled out for you wherever you go, because that is how you treat others.

CTA: Today, try on your new suit of self-confidence. Smile and give your best on purpose and with loving intention. The mirror of life will respond accordingly.

Have a great day!

JUNE 26

Seeding and Weeding

Learning to live in the present moment is all about becoming consciously aware of our thoughts, feelings, emotions, and actions in every moment. When we accept the truth that we are really the silent witness behind all of this, we will learn the value of the present moment, and how it literally creates and shapes our lives.

All our power lies in the present moment. We can do nothing about the past. So the past has no power, unless we decide to dwell in it and waste our true power lamenting over things that cannot be changed. Truly friends, this is wasting your valuable life.

The future is not here yet, and the only way we can affect our future is in the practice of present moment weeding and seeding.

This means being conscious of ourselves and our thoughts, actions, and decisions. This is all about the awareness of our own energy and what it is emitting outward in every moment. Sound difficult? It certainly is at first. Especially since most of us go through our entire lives asleep, or unconscious.

Life in the unconscious state means living as though life just happens to us. Life seems so random, unfair, and out of our control. We live our lives more in our lower ego state. From this place, the ups and downs are very frequent to us. We have no steady rudder or inner security. We rely on status and financial wealth as our marker for higher living. We feel separate from everyone else and it becomes a dog-eat-dog world. Competing and climbing over others to get ours. Politics lives and breathes in this lower realm. It's what we see leading us here in America and it leads the rest of the world. We *must* rise above this old paradigm in order to advance as a race. This happens one person at a time. Our job is to awaken. When the majority awakens and we begin to lead from this place, the world will know true power and lasting peace.

Let's continue this one tomorrow.

CTA: Be present. Live in the now!

Have a great day!

JUNE 27

Seeding and Weeding *continued*

The so-called power that guides the masses is that of selfish power. It claims to give, but it is really all about getting. Getting votes to stay in selfish power. It's how the poor never rise and it's how the selfish stay in power. We are all beginning to wake up to the fact that it's not Democrat vs. Republican or Conservative vs. Liberal. It's about the selfish dividing us in order to gain and stay in this paradigm of the ego. I believe there are good ideas on both sides and the merging of the heart with the responsible nature of order and fiscal common sense can be the answer to our division. It will only come from cooperation and collaboration. The old system of negative competition is simply outdated. True power is when we begin to help others know their own power and rise from within. We help each other uncover the real story of us. From this power we all rise and the world will be a vastly different place. We will wonder how we all got so lost.

The very best way to see positive change, both in our personal lives and in the world, is to awaken and live from our higher selves. That only means stripping away a bit of the outdated each and every day, with intention.

Let's continue this one tomorrow.

CTA: Help others. Also, collaborate with others for the greater good.

Have a great day!

JUNE 28

Seeding and Weeding *continued*

When one of us is brave enough to awaken and leave behind the old coat of the negative, we will inspire others to do the same. You will live a much smoother ride and you will want to do the same for others. It is the true purpose of all of us to rise and help others do the same.

Planting good seeds in each day and weeding your old, defeated, limited, low energy garden, will be your path to waking up and living the life you were intended to live. Remember, you do not have to see the whole staircase in order to take your first step. Your steps will be shown to you the more you seed the good and weed the outdated. The power to do this is always in the present moment. At first, you will go back and forth for a while, between your lower self and your true self. But after a while, you will begin to see steady fruit from your efforts and a smoother, happier life. From there it just gets better. Your personal garden will be lush with beauty and what you create will always benefit the world.

CTA: Today, stay in your true power as much as possible. If you fall off the wagon and enter an ego session, snap back, forgive or apologize, and move forward. True forward motion means not getting distracted, attracted to, or affected by the egos around you or your own egos demands to be right, superior or less than anyone else. Harmony, laughter, and giving your best self will keep you in the flow and in great shape to create again tomorrow. Go get it and go give it!

Have a great day!

JUNE 29

Your Sanctuary

So, one or both of you had a challenging day and you come home to your supposed safe sanctuary only to find that your ego still has a hold on your mind and energy. This is always kindling for what can turn into a bonfire.

Most often when we've engaged in, or have been in close proximity to, negative energy during our day we do not consciously attempt to shift our own energy higher before we go home. We carry this day with us like a backpack of garbage. The problem with not consciously releasing this backpack before we get home, is that we will tend to swing the backpack around the room, so everyone gets hit with some of its negative energy..

If we want to always have a safe, loving, peaceful, and positive sanctuary to come home to, we must first set the tone by our own consistent efforts to be in our higher energy. You must also let your family know that your home is meant to be a loving positive atmosphere and that everyone must do their best to add to this great energy. It may not always work at first, but everyone knowing the goal will always bring your home back to the divine sanctuary it is meant to be.

Let's continue this one tomorrow.

CTA: Check your daily baggage at the door each evening. Your home is your sanctuary. Fill it with love and peace, allowing for comfort.

Have a great day!

JUNE 30

Your Sanctuary *continued*

You see, when the dominant energy in your home is positive and this intention is agreed upon by all, your home will always be your sanctuary.

In this place, everyone in the home feels good on a regular basis, all higher energies will be the consistent vibration, including creativity, prosperity, kindness, compassion, and love in all its other beautiful forms and symbols.

Your family will become so used to this new dominant force, that if there is a temporary storm of the ego, you will all want to get back to the good life as quickly as possible, and everyone will know where that is.

A happy, positive home is crucial for you, your children, and future generations that will benefit from your decision to create and treasure a high-energy home.

You sleep better, you love more, you forgive easier, apologize quicker, and create amazing and loving memories. To create this Shangri-La, you must become intentional, present and mindful of what you carry with you and what energy you are giving in each moment. This is always the practice of true power.

We all know we should try to be our best when we come home, but the ego makes it so easy to hold onto a worthy excuse as to why everyone else in your home must feel the wrath of your day, but is that what you really want? Is that what your calm, higher self would say?

The quicker you jump off the ego train during your day, the easier it will be to stay in a higher zone. It's all about letting go of what you no longer need.

CTA: Today, bring home your best self to your family. Give them the energy you love to feel yourself. Be engaged and set some new standards for the overall energy of your home. Raising your vibe on a consistent basis will always bring others up as well. Be the change you want to see in your home and then, never let it go.

Have a great day!

JULY 1

How Hard Is it For You To Say I Love You?

So many of us have a lot of trouble with this one. Too often we hold this coveted phrase for only a select few, if we are even able to say it to them! Many would find it irrational to tell their co-workers or even longtime friends this healing sentence.

I myself have been here. I used to use this phrase only when uttered to me first, holding it back in case I didn't like what someone was doing. My love and expression of it was conditional. I'll use my love or lack of it as a weapon. I'll love you only if you're doing what I say or approve of. Get it? What I really was doing was filtering my life through judgment rather than the perfection of love itself.

I had a hard time telling my dad I loved him because guys just don't say that kind of stuff, LOL. My buddy Jim's dad passed a few years back and he had the blessing of a week or more to say all he needed to say. He said he never said these words more in his life until that week. He inspired me to not wait to say this to everyone around me, especially my dad. Now we say it every time we speak.

My friends, never never never let those closest to you wonder if you love them. You must release your love by expressing it in words as well as actions. We need to hear it. Everyone needs to hear it. Too many are starved of life force because they do not hear or feel it.

CTA: Today's practice is the most important of all practices, expressing who you really are, love. You stifle your true self and power when you're shut off to giving or receiving love. If saying these magic words is uncomfortable for you, now you know the way out. Saying it frees the real you from the bondage of the fearful ego. You need it, so give it and let it in easily. The more you say it and express it, the more you become it.

Have a great day!

JULY 2

Be a Great Audience

So many times we get so caught up in what we want to say that we forget to truly tune in and listen to another person until they are done. It's like we are already working on a reply before all the ideas and thoughts or stories of another have been fully expressed. In other words, we're not a good audience.

One of the biggest gifts we can give to another is our full attention. I have my challenges with this one, as many do. The key to this one is to be fully present for all your interactions. There is literally magic that happens in these moments, but we miss so much when we are not singularly focused.

Tuning completely in when having a conversation is *all* about being a great listener and absorber first. We as humans need and thrive on personal relationships and daily interactions. We only get so many opportunities in each day to do this, so what creates rich, meaningful moments in life is our presence in them. They become memorable.

Thoughts and feelings are fully absorbed on a whole different level, and we begin to understand our true, soulful connection to each other. This all happens first, be being a great audience.

When we feel we are truly heard and understood, we open our hearts immediately and feel comfortable in sharing more.

Let's continue this one tomorrow.

CTA: Give your full attention when speaking to others.

Have a great day!

JULY 3

Be a Great Audience *continued*

A great audience does not judge and is open to anything. A great audience loves to laugh and gives laughter and smiles quickly, easily, and enthusiastically.

A great audience is never jealous, intimidated, or boastful. A great audience is not competing for the limelight, but enhances the light of all.

The very practice of being a great listener and audience will bring all your relationships to a deeper, more meaningful level. From here, you have created a circle of love and a safety net of support for life. Give to all that which you would like to receive. It's always the same formula, my friends.

CTA: Today, practice being a great audience. Celebrate others and bring their very best out by truly tuning into the present moment. There's always gold to be had in the present when we are awake and tuned in. Always remember that your only true power is in the present. Past is gone, future isn't here yet. Creating our lives on purpose is always done by shining our light to everyone in the moment. Do your best, you'll see.

Have a great day!

JULY 4

Your Life Force

You have the power to make life work with you and on your behalf. Life is a moving force and so are you. When you fight life, you suffer.

What I mean is that in every moment we have the power to choose our response to what life brings us. Most choose to fight what is when it's uncomfortable or not what they had envisioned. You must learn to accept first instead of react first. Reaction is the norm. We're trained to react rather than consciously and mindfully respond. Reaction puts your mind at a ten immediately, where mindful acceptance keeps you calm and in a very different mind space. You're able to quickly process right minded solutions instead of widening the drama and the issue.

This is always the choice. Light or dark. You are both energies while you are here on Earth. It's the energy you feed every day that will become the backdrop of your life. Calm is light. Chaos is dark. Love is light. Judgment and blame are dark. Compassion and forgiveness are light. Hatred and revenge are dark. These are some of the energetic responses or reactions we have available in every encounter.

When you give space in those split seconds after seeing, hearing, or experiencing something that triggers your darkness, we have time to choose better. You know this. You do it from time to time. This must become your new norm. Live to give your light as your daily calling card and the backdrop of your life will shift, change, and blossom into one you've not allowed yourself to dream of. It's life's gift and it's yours to collaborate with. You're doing it anyway, just with mixed results. Those results will rise as your choices do.

CTA: So today's practice is about divine choice, free will, and your ability to create your life with the force of life, a.k.a. Love. Go get it!!

Have a great day!

JULY 5

Our Divine Guides

Everyone on this planet has been equipped with a certain genius that they alone possess. This genius, once uncovered within, will prove to be your unique gift to the world. You may even have several gifts to share, and that is what you are here to do.

As we grow up, certain people enter our lives who will have the eyes to see your genius, for they recognize something similar from within themselves. These angels of influence will tell you about your gifts in the form of praise, compliments, and positive feedback. What we may not initially see in ourselves, these special others do. They will tell you how funny or talented you are in a certain area. They are able to see a positive future for you and perhaps give you a beautiful, rich vision for your future through their lens. In these cases, this vision resonates with you on a deeper level. Your eyes have been opened to a new possibility for yourself and an exciting road forward.

In life, we will have many opinions thrown at us about what we should or could be doing, but there are but a few who influence you in a way that feels totally right to you. These are in fact divine guides, put in your path on purpose. You might call them mentors or inspirational teachers. These certain someones seem to unlock a bigger you. A you whom you did not yet know.

At my age, I can certainly look back and clearly see the influences that helped to shape me and my path forward. I am grateful even for the ones who showed me what I did not want to be. The ones, however, who hit that certain note within me that unlocked hidden talents and helped to give me the proper way of thinking about life are the ones I am most grateful for. I believe you can all name your own.

It is in the recognition of, and gratitude for, these divine guides in our life that we must do our very best to pay it forward.

Let's continue this one tomorrow.

CTA: What a true gift it is for an individual to have someone inspire him or her so much that the course of life is influenced. Be grateful if you have one of those inspirations in your life.

Have a great day!

JULY 6

Our Divine Guides *continued*

Sharing your gifts with the world means that you're helping others to rise. Taking a personal interest in those around you and giving your unique form of wisdom, compassion, understanding, and talent, just may be the kind of influence that changes someone's life. This is a very noble path that brings richness to your own soul, not reached by other means. Prospering others prospers you.

Becoming a person of positive influence always begins with how you handle your own journey. You can't give what you do not possess. If you are the type of person that seeks to constantly improve yourself from the inside out, you will influence many just by your example. You are helping to change the world. Never downplay your part. It matters.

Owning the key to your own treasures and talents by living life with gratitude for all of it, a sense of true purpose and positive intention will naturally bring forth an inner calling to be awake to the needs of others. You'll want to pay it forward. The opportunities to be a positive influence will be easily seen and heard by you and eagerly sought.

Most often you will never really know how deeply you've touched the life of another, but the simple satisfaction that you gave your very best to another is the only reward you'll need. As Mother Theresa always said, it's always between you and your higher power anyway. Give for the sake of giving.

CTA: Today, be more aware of someone in your life that could use a boost from you. So often we know we should say something positive, uplifting, and potentially life changing, but we don't. Make this practice part of your life and you'll feel your own soul enriched. Giving is also receiving. Give your very best my friends.

Have a great day!

JULY 7

Your Beneficial Presence

What is your role in your family? What is your role in your social circle? What is your role in the world? You are recognized by all of these by your unique brushstroke in the panting of life. Deciding to be a beneficial presence as part of your life's purpose, will reflect back greatness to you in all areas of your life. You have become a giver.

We as humans get so caught up in the dramas of the day and too often we literally suck this energy up and hold it as our own. We become nervous, fearful, angry, resentful, vengeful or depressed. We *become* the energy around us if we are not aware.

We are both transmitters and receivers of positive and negative energies. We are energy. So learning to harness and control yours will open the floodgates of new possibilities in your life.

Imagine that you have the power to heal yourself and others. Imagine you can begin to consciously attract new and better opportunities into your life and the lives of those around you. Imagine just for a moment that you have the power to change your life today, and then watch as your life shifts right before your eyes. This *is* the power you possess. It's called your personal field of energy. Your thoughts and choices are the dial that points to the level of life giving energy you desire. The one choice to be a beneficial presence to everything and everyone in each day, literally pushes the dial up the scale and in your favor. What you transmit is what you receive.

Always remember that if you choose to be a beneficial presence and another is trapped in an ego drama, your choice to stay in the higher, beneficial energy, will shield you from receiving and/or holding their lower transmissions. Either your energy will transmute theirs and raise them up, or they will be forced to seek a fellow energy vampire for their feeding on the negative.

Let's continue this one tomorrow.

CTA: Imagine daily that you can change the course of your life for the better. You have the power!

Have a great day!

JULY 8

Your Beneficial Presence *continued*

As Mother Teresa always extolled, be kind anyway, in the face of unkindness, be faith-filled anyway, in the face of doubt, be love in spite of hatred, and be the voice of truth in the face of darkness.

She was a woman who, in her own words, admitted to feeling a constant darkness following her. It's the darkness we all know as the ego or lower nature. She saw the darkness in others, merely as a distressing disguise, one we all have worn. She saw the light in everyone because that was her life's mission. To see and spread the truth of who we all really are. Learning to use this darkness in your own life as merely a trigger to guide you back to your heart, higher thoughts, acts, and deeds will ensure your place in the universal history books, as a truly beneficial presence. The world will thank you in many ways. You will have found your key.

CTA: Today, make the decision to be a giver. Give your best. Give compliments, smiles, hugs, laughter, forgiveness and love in all your interactions. The person handing you your morning coffee, give them a smile and a real thank you. Eye contact and sincere attention is your calling card. Laughter and lightheartedness is the vibe. Collaboration on projects instead of competing egos brings harmony and positive forward motion. You my friend, wield much power indeed. Use it for the goodness of all and your life will only be described as a beautiful, beneficial presence.

Have a great day!

JULY 9

Forgiveness

Forgiveness is the most freeing of all the energies we possess. Most think forgiveness is just an act. We say were sorry, hope for forgiveness and do our best to move forward. This is certainly true from all we have learned, and in most cases, this can be enough. However, when we begin to look at the higher purpose of forgiveness and realize how its power can literally heal one's self and an outside offender, we have harnessed an amazing, life altering magic.

Being able to change your own state of being with a thought or act happens all the time. When we are blue and a friend does a funny dance to raise your spirit, this is known as energetic transformation. The light in your friend has shone upon your darkened energy, transmuted it into the higher realm of your own spirit, and you have been temporarily healed. Get it?

When we do something or say something that physically or emotionally hurts another, you have a very important decision to make, even if you have also been hurt by this other person in some skirmish of the ego.

You can choose to *free* yourself and the other of the minutes, hours, days, months or even years of pain that is sure to be held onto, relived over and over in your minds, talked about endlessly in hatred or anger, or made worse by creating more, negative scenarios, and expanding the drama in your mind. Forgiveness is this decision.

Let's continue this one tomorrow.

CTA: Forgiveness is a key to mental freedom.

Have a great day!

JULY 10

Forgiveness *continued*

What are you still holding onto inside yourself that could be wiped clean by apology or forgiveness? When we choose to hold onto old wounds, grudges, rivalries, negative perceptions, wars, anger or hatred, we are holding onto poison. These stagnant negative energies continue to send this poison through our system because we hold onto it in our vault of offenses. We think we should, so we can stay vigilant from letting it happen again. But this is the lie. It's just poison, my friends. Nothing good comes from holding onto it. In fact, it's part of what makes you sick. Apologizing to and forgiving yourself for holding onto the poison is first priority in letting go.

Low-energy thoughts and emotions that we have made a habit of collecting, weigh us down in more ways than we have been told. The mind/body/spirit connection is absolute truth. When you begin to be guided by your higher mind you will heal and thrive.

Letting go of the poison you've held onto for way to long, let's in the light of your higher, spirit mind. It's all about dropping your ugly luggage. Forgiveness and apology keeps your hands free from ever picking it up again. These free hands can now be used for a higher purpose. Like loving everyone in your life and reaching for amazing new rungs on the ladder of life. Freed energy keeps you rising. Low, stagnant energies keep you right where you are, like sandbags on a hot air balloon. Forgiveness cuts the ropes to these sandbags.

CTA: So today, when you choose your higher tools for your day, make sure you bring forgiveness. It keeps you free to focus on how amazing you are and the many ways to give your best self away.

Have a great day in the sun!

JULY 11

The Art of Modeling

If you're not used to the practice of today's entry, deciding to take it up will be one of the most fruitful and prosperous choices of your life's journey.

I'm not talking about becoming a fashion model, although, if that's your dream, then this will also apply. I'm talking about the art of modeling the mindset, speech, and actions of someone you truly admire and aspire to be like.

During my life, there have been many whom I've admired for various reasons, including certain talents, styles, similar interests, and their massive accomplishments in one lifetime. All of these are worthy reasons to model another, but of all the aspects of others that we would like to infuse into our own journey, none will be more fruitful or prosperous to you than modeling a humble giver and a grateful receiver.

We can purchase that same suit or dress of our favorite idol. We can learn to swagger a certain way, speak with the confidence of a world leader and sing like Frank Sinatra, but the very foundation of all your goals and dreams must be that of the humble giver and receiver. This is the bedrock of true success and a success you can *never* lose.

To begin this valuable life practice, you need to start by knowing what you want the rest of your life to look like from this day forward.

Let's continue this one tomorrow.

CTA: Take time to learn who you are and the person you want to be. Then, find a mentor, and model the attributes you admire so much in him or her. Success will follow.

Have a great day!

JULY 12

The Art of Modeling *continued*

Who do you admire and why? Is it for shallow reasons like, "hey, they're rich, drive exotic cars and throw lavish parties?" Or is it for deeper reasons, like, "I love how they treat others, how they take the time to understand bigger issues and give of themselves?" One is an earthly reason to model and the other is the real gold.

There's nothing wrong with having the mansion, wanting the big life, and all the fun that goes with it, but the only worthy way of getting there and ultimately staying there is through knowing what real prosperity is.

In order to know prosperity, you must embody its very energy first. This comes from being grateful for what you already have, giving your very best self away freely, as your daily calling card, and offering constant recognition to where it all really comes from. Your higher power. This, my friends, is the formula for true success and the solid foundation to build all your dreams upon.

Whether you are a young person just starting out, going after big goals and dreams for your life, or your just decided that you're life needs an overhaul and new direction, the practice of modeling someone with this certain way of living and giving must be included as the most important ingredient. You literally become a magnet for new opportunities, great new relationships, and the good life.

CTA: Today take some time to think about who you admire and why. Question your reasons and make sure they include those who truly did it or are still doing it right. They are big givers who exhibit gratitude and a generous spirit. They share their amazing talents, spread love, and offer recognition and thanks to the benevolent stream that brings all goodness into their lives and the world. Now this is a person worth modeling. Everything after this is just gravy.

Have a great day!

JULY 13

Tuning In: More on the art of living in the present moment

When you decide to begin living life at higher levels, your first stop is the present moment. From there, you just practice staying there.

How many hours of your day is your mind in the past, reliving old scenes and scenarios? Bringing up old hurts and the famous story we continue to tell about it? Thinking what could have been, or punishing yourself over and over again for things you can never change?

How many hours a day do you spend in the future? Fearful of what might be? Expecting doom, gloom, disaster or the other shoe to drop? How many hours are you creating future scenarios that never serve you, but are actually setting you up for the failure you fear? You are creating my friends! You are projecting thoughts in the wrong direction. Your liar is spinning the tales because you aren't self-aware, mastering your mind, or living in your true power.

The key to life is being aware of who you really are and then living the rest of your life only from this truth. You are spiritual royalty on an earthly visit. You are here to grow and live in the amazing physical beauty around you, using the power of your light to guide you.

The darkness of the ego skews your vision. You will learn to use the darkness as your guide back to the light, instead of "becoming" the darkness you think is you.

Darkness is here for contrast. Use it that way. There's always a spiritual solution to every problem. The ego never solves the problems. It causes the problems that hopefully lead you back to the heart.

Let's continue this one tomorrow.

CTA: Always. Be. Present.

Have a great day!

JULY 14.

Tuning In *continued*

This next statement I want you to burn into your mind as the most important information you can use on your journey;

YOU CREATE YOUR FUTURE IN THE PRESENT. Your every thought leads to your every spoken word. Your spoken words lead to your every action. This is how you create your life. What you give your attention to, using the above formula, is how you've created your life to this point. If you're happy with these results, then you're on the right track. Keep up the great work. If you'd like to see growth, more prosperity, better relationships, new friends or experiences, you need to live intentionally in the present moment.

What does this mean? I have to start watching my every thought? I have to begin to be aware of what I'm going to say and how I say it? I have to look inside and feel if my thoughts are making me happy or mad or sad and why? I have to create space between my thoughts and my actions? *Yes!* This is called becoming self-aware. When you start to look inside at the way you speak to others, what your real motives are and become totally honest with yourself, you have begun the shift. Your intention must be all about giving your light as your exclusive calling card.

Your light self, a.k.a. your true self, a.k.a. your spirit, has its own agenda. Once you choose to live as part of the agenda, your life automatically gets better. The agenda of your light self is all about love and the understanding that we are all spirit in the human soup.

We need to trust this truth and live accordingly. Love, kindness, forgiveness, apology, prosperity, harmony, health, wealth, happiness, inner peace, outer peace and freedom, collaboration, gentleness, empathy, sympathy, growth, expansion, understanding, mercy, grace and compassion are the agenda of your light self.

Living in alignment with these higher energies is the sweet spot of life. It's known as being in Heaven's Net. You feel better here; you have much more joy and laughter here. You focus on the good in others and give your very best here. This is your inner treasure and the gold we are all seeking, we just didn't know where to look.

The present moment is the only place and time you have to make your life change. It's all about directing your thoughts instead of being held hostage to them. You are the one who decides the validity and truth of your thoughts. You have to become a master at weeding out and letting go of every thought and old belief that does not serve you. If it makes you feel good when you think it, if your heart feels right, those are the ones you speak on, give away, and project into the future. Get it?

Your thoughts are very powerful. They are energy. You have the choice in each present moment as to which energy you choose to use. Every problem or issue in your life can be solved by your light self. Too often we choose darkness as a means. Darkness begets darkness. Light heals and expands your life. The choice is always in the present. You can't relive the past, although you choose to. You need not worry about the future if you are creating with light in the present. The way forward will always be shown to you.

CTA: Today, begin your new journey as the master of your mind and the captain of your soul. Your power is, and always has been, in the present moment. Make the choice to give each one of these moments your light. Spread your wealth.

Have a great day!

JULY 15

A New Foundation for Your Marriage or Long-Term Relationship

At my age, I've known many friends that have teetered on separation, gotten separated or have gone the whole route to divorce. Many times these partners of ours have been the right ones, but the waters have been muddied by our own misperceptions, ego-centric judgments, and lack of vision for what we want our relationships to look like.

So many of us have been together so long that we still operate in high-school mode. The same thoughts, rules of engagement, and triggers, all because we just don't have a more matured view of what life could be together. We don't talk about our deepest needs because we feel the other cannot fulfill them. This of course is just another way our minds limit the possibilities.

In every healthy relationship, you must be able to get to ground zero. This means leaving behind old ways, old wounds, old judgments, and the old belief that you can't find what's needed to sustain a beautiful life together. You need to take out the garbage and never bring it back into your house. You need to start anew.

Let's continue this one tomorrow.

CTA: Only your thoughts can limit your growth.

Have a great day!

JULY 16

A New Foundation *continued*

Getting to Ground Zero can be a very rocky road at first. All the garbage that has been composting in your relationship must be let go of in order to move into brand new territory. This new territory cannot include the old stuff any longer. New vision demands new thought, spoken words to each other, and consistent action toward the vision. This loving work never ends. It doesn't end after you're comfy again or after the make-up lovin'! It persists. It continues to forgive when hurt, apologize when wrong, and improve with loving intention. These are the ingredients for lasting change. You are 100% responsible for your happiness. You must give it to each other because that's what each of you is really looking for. Acceptance of just who you are, as you stay on the road to improvement.

When people get back together to give things another try, there's always the honeymoon period all over again. This is great, but you need to set new boundaries that you can both agree to and trust. Trust in this new chapter of your relationship is crucial for its success. Trust that you both will adhere to a life in the higher realms of giving each other only your very best. Treating each other as the most important person in your life. Constant watering of the new growth you've decided to undertake.

You both must also be able to let go of your lower energies more and more along your new path. Anger, jealousy, competing to be right or making the other wrong. Finding constant common ground and things that bring you closer. These are all part and parcel of your new relationship. It can be done. I've seen it first-hand. These are mature decisions based on a mature goal.

Every relationship has its challenges. The new way to handle these challenges, especially when old triggers are pulled is to give space and understanding first, not react, but respond with a loving solution. Higher goals demand higher solutions. In all cases, that solution is the goal of lasting love. This must be your first thought and your highest priority. You both must become real. You both need to listen, really listen. You both must be committed to change. If only one is committed to growth and the other just wants to stay in high school, it will not work. It can't. Growing together in the same higher direction is the goal. It's always the little things that provide the biggest results. Do the little things every day. The ones you used to do, but got lazy. Laziness has no place in relationships. Our relationships are the true gold.

CTA: Today, if this sounds like you, have the Ground Zero conversation and find out what direction your partner sees for your life together and share yours. Design your future together instead of whatever comes. Be intentional with your words and actions, and give your very best to that special love of your life. If you are one who has gone the whole route and are now looking for a new love of your life, take this day and write down everything you need in your new relationship. Write it down I said! If you don't know what you're looking for, how will you ever know it when it comes your way? Set the course and start sailing, my friends!

Have a great day!

JULY 17

Letting Go of Anger

Letting go of anger as your sword and shield can be very challenging indeed. Especially if you grew up in an atmosphere of "it's my way or the highway!" Using anger as your mechanism of controlling your world may have given you your desired result and it's easy to defend this practice based on those results.

This practice, however, will bring back to you more to be angry about. You'll think the angrier you get, or even appear, the more control you will have. Your desired result however includes so much more than the compliance you seek. It includes the delivery of fear, uncertainty, possible vindictiveness, and loss of some kind. This actually brings you a life of conditional relationships.

The conditions you demand are not only hard to comply with, but they come at the expense of another feeling free. Everyone deserves to be free. Once your threats have no more hold on those you've attempted to control with this energy, you'll see them much less often. They'll choose freedom over the controlling way. It's a natural yearning to be free of any oppression.

Anger can be used as your reminder feeling to choose a higher response. You don't have to choose anger to solve your issue. Use it to become mindful of the aftermath it usually brings and move to your heart mind to actually solve the issue the way you yourself would want to hear it. One that offers the other soul growth over punishment and blame. Mentor others instead of telling them how lowly they are from your superior perspective. You both lose in this scenario.

With anger as your main tool of handling things in your life, you'll find yourself out of control so much more than in control. It's how energy works. It's never any different. You'll only have compliance when you're around. Stop generating fear and seek the higher way forward with all your relationships. In the end, you'll be glad you did.

CTA: Today's practice is letting go of what never works for you. Your negative energies must be viewed as contrast to the great way because they themselves never produce anything great. Ask yourself if this is true.

Have a great day!

JULY 18

Raising Your Self-Esteem

This is a big one for *all* of us. *Yes, all of us*. We all suffer or have suffered from this great *lie of the mind*.

Low self-esteem is usually an inherited thought pattern and energy. It's not a natural part of you. That's the great news. It's basically just a lie you must rise above, like all the others your ego spins to you each and every day.

The ego loves to compare you to others, and in this constant comparing, the ego also provides you with its judgment and placement of you on a ladder of misperception and false success.

You see, the ego spins the lie, we decide to believe it, and then we allow the ego to expand the lie throughout our life. If *we* do not challenge the lies, we will live our lives according to, and as the lie itself.

You are not your ego. You are the opposite, eternal force of all possibilities. Giving unconditional love and acceptance to yourself is not only the way out of self-esteem issues; it's the way out of the rest of the garbage you've collected. Guaranteed.

Let's continue this one tomorrow.

CTA: Challenge the lies you tell yourself. Accept and love who you are.

Have a great day!

JULY 19

Raising Your Self-Esteem *continued*

Shift yourself on purpose when your ego tries to grab the wheel of your mind. Love yourself, flaws and all. Know that the energy of love is the real you. When you continue to give yourself lots of love, grateful praise, and thanks for your new determined path, you are connected to the energy that will heal you and expand you. Stay there. Give that back to others now, as your gift.

You must realize that you are living a dual nature while you are here. Your negative side must be used as contrast to the right direction. Negative thoughts, opinions, self-judgment, hatred, martyrdom, lack, anger, and all the other lower energies are there to help you know and "live in the opposite," higher realm.

When your ego says you can't, you try! You keep trying! When your ego tells you that you are "less than" in some way, your new self-talk must begin to vehemently deny this and all other negative judgments and then give power to the opposite. Why would you ever talk yourself down? You must be your own champion! Not arrogantly, but with reverence for where you really come from.

It's always your responsibility to spread your light rather than your darkness. Plus, it makes us feel good. Isn't that what you're really after? Feeling good?

CTA: Today, begin to peel away the layers of lies you've given power to. Begin to think, speak and live in your favor and the favor of others. When you make this choice every day, your true self-esteem will shine like the sun.

Have a great day!

JULY 20

Be Self-Assured

When you decide to start living a life from the inside out, you'll find a great peace in knowing you are operating as your best self. You'll feel much more self-assured. This confident self will be your vehicle forward, treating each day as a new opportunity to go after what you want and need from a mental state of "can do." This is in stark contrast to living a low energy existence.

When you believe in yourself, because you now truly know yourself, your new self-assured energy will be felt by all and many new opportunities will present themselves to you. See, when your higher energies are in command, you're like a magnet for great things. Choosing to strip away your old, fearful, cautious energies for a higher place is where all you desire lives. This confidence in yourself is not arrogance. Arrogance is a tool of your ego and does not come from the place where true confidence lies.

You will be in a place where self assured means "I am below no one. And I am also above no one." This self-assured place does not compete, but collaborates, for it only wants the good of all. From this place, the world is your oyster and you'll be giving your very best away to others in the process. Shining our light is a choice worth making every day. If you do, it will become your way naturally.

CTA: Today, give of yourself in some way and be self-assured in your decisions.

Have an awesome day!

JULY 21

Integrity

Integrity is the art of fair and honest living. One who possesses this power and uses it in all areas of life will know success on many levels.

This power, as all our true power comes from our heart and its desire to give away what we ourselves desire: truth.

Integrity says, "I honor that spirit in you that I also possess and only want the best outcome for us both." This is how we grow our lives from average to great. When we decide to become a person of great integrity, we assume a great responsibility to live from the truth as our guide and captain of our ship.

From our closest friendships, marriage, workplace and service to the world, we need to be steadfast in using our personal word and outward action as a bond of trust in all. You will become known throughout society as a trusted leader whose ideas, service, and livelihood are that of a high quality individual.

Integrity always attracts others with the same mindset and character. Forming a team with this one attribute will be extremely powerful and will change many lives. Not only the people on the team, but all those around them and who deal with them. Integrity is not something taught in schools or even discussed in daily life. Integrity is usually experienced. When we see it or, more importantly, feel it, we know it from that place of truth we all have within us. It's called doing the right thing as a daily practice and life path. Much personal and spiritual success and growth come from this life skill and you will always see new fruit borne from this branch of yourself.

Integrity in our friendships means being there in good times and in difficult times. It says, I will never let you fall. I will be there for you even when it may not be convenient for me and that I will give you my very best in these times.

Integrity in marriage and intimate relationships says, "you can trust me and it is safe to give your whole heart to me." It says, "I will and can freely be myself, express myself, and love myself and you may do the same, without judgment or guilt." It says, "when we disagree, I love you still and we will find the truth and common ground together." It says "we let go of the little things in exchange for a much bigger picture." The picture of a truly uncommon and remarkable life.

In business this one attribute is the difference between ongoing, unlimited success or abject failure. It's amazing how quickly you can soar or sink in business with this one choice. Integrity is and must be a constant in our lives and it is the path of greatness and a great life.

Integrity in our families means being there and being recognized as a source of refuge in times of turbulence and challenge. It means being a leader and truth-giver, even if the truth is difficult to express. It means raising others through encouragement and praise. It means being a bearer of light. Integrity is truly just a beautiful branch of love. Its main voice is right-mindedness and right choice making. You never regret doing the right thing. You never regret giving your best. You never regret giving your love freely away. This is integrity.

CTA: Today, in all your dealings and interactions, be sure integrity is in the room. It will always guide you in the right direction and bring back to you the same. Be your very best today, my friends!

Have a great day!

JULY 22

I Got This

Whenever you are faced with a challenge, big or small, the very first phrase you need to train yourself to say is, "*I got this.*"

These three words, whether spoken out loud or in silence, will ignite your spirit to take control of the situation instead of bringing out the fear monger of your ego. This phrase, when spoken as your very first response, will become your natural way of dealing with problems.

Instead of the usual reactions of fear, dread, indecisiveness, and immobility in the face of trouble, your true self will be driving the bus and it will bring you through it every time.

How many times in our lives have we chosen the egos demand to overreact, go crazy, get steaming mad or even worse, lash out at others for something we bear some or all responsibility for. Maybe a million, like me?

Learning to respond instead of react is the way of our higher, inner strength. Never be afraid to ask for outside help if you need it, but make a life goal of saying, "I got this," and see the magic within you start to solve the issue at hand. We should never hand our power over to others if we can help ourselves rise above seeming difficulties. These difficulties are there to spur our true strength on and bring it forth. This one path of true inner strength will become our go to place as our first response.

What else this personal power will bring you is astounding. You'll start to take on more risks that will lead to a much bigger and amazing life experience. Your self-confidence will soar and those around you will begin to see a stronger, more capable you.

New and exciting opportunities will begin to come your way and you will attract a higher level of living, because *you* have taken the reins of your life. You can solve these issues yourself. You'll crush the little stuff without a whisper and the so-called big problems will become small in comparison to the new you.

Let's continue this one tomorrow.

CTA: Take control and remember the phrase, "I got this," when faced with a challenge.

Have a great day!

JULY 23

I Got This *continued*

Whatever your current challenge is, whether it's a recent break up, divorce, new job, new adventure, or the personal daily challenge of improving your life, start your day with, "I got this." Then go about your day standing a bit taller than usual, smiling all the way in your knowing that you indeed have the upper hand and higher ground of stomping out the challenges of the day.

When we practice the art of overcoming life's obstacles, we are building brand new muscles and uncovering ones we never knew we possessed. The true strength is within you! Tap into it with total assuredness and faith that you can do this yourself!

Never let your ego take control of your life, your happiness, your confidence or your push forward to a bigger and better life.

You are the captain of your ship! Take the wheel every day and steer that mother into uncharted waters in confidence. Confidence that whatever you need along the way will be there for you at the perfect time. This is the promise of the spirit, our true nature.

The magic to all of this is your attitude Take on the attitude of sure failure or defeat and you have already lost the battle. The simple phrase in this entry today will be the beginning of your new way of life. You Got This!!! You can do it if you say you can. Conversely, if you say you can't, you are also correct. Choose your inner strength and let it guide you to victory every time my friends. The choice is always there and it's always yours.

CTA: So today, go after what you want, need, and deserve. No one will give a big life to you. You are big life and your inner power is always at the ready when you give the command!

"*I got this*." Practice it, put it into your self-talk inside and out from here forward and release the magic!

Have a powerful day!!

JULY 24

Turning the Page

When we decide to take a big jump into a new chapter of our lives from a very familiar one, there will be anxiety, fear, and wondering whether we did the right thing. (All perfectly normal.)

This is especially true with a new career. And in this endeavor you must ask yourself a crucial question, "will I be happy doing this when I become good at it?" See, you're not going to be great at any new career right away! Don't get discouraged, it's all part of the process! Like going from one high school to a new one. There's a normal period of learning and social adjustment that *must* take place. It's part of it.

It's the roller coaster leaving the station and making that climb up the steep hill. You must grow in order for your new career to take root. If this is the case where you want to give it your all but you still have financial obligations that may take you off track, reverse the process at first. If you can do this new thing part time at first while you still provide from your current career, do that!

I have a friend who's one of the best waiters I know. He has become a known real estate broker while he continues to provide from his service career. It's taken some time but his many restaurant customers have become his new real estate clients. The train of success has reached his doorstep by saying a smart yes. Not putting it off, but growing without the fear of hurting your main obligations.

Let's continue this one tomorrow.

CTA: There is a learning curve in all facets of life. Don't be discouraged from trying something new. All challenges make us stronger.

Have a great day!

JULY 25

Turning the Page *continued*

My partner Jim and I created Focusmaster in 1994 when I was in the insurance business full time. I always dreamed of its success but I had a new family to care for. I didn't put it off, I said a smart yes.

This is a great way to work on your dreams. Feel secure and responsible to your most important thing, your family, but water that seed!!! Every day, water that seed! Even when it seems dead and dried up, water it. There will always be lulls, setbacks, and challenges. You must face them all with faith, action, and positive forward motion. Secure the nest but *fly*!! Let your nest be the reason for your intentional growth, not the reason to fear moving on to something new.

Small steps done in a great way will lead to big steps done in an even greater way. It's the very reason for you deciding to come here my friends. Adventure! Calculated risk! Faith, action, and patience are what you will need most. But go for it. Be smart and find the way to make it all work. It's hard to make any new career work if you're sweating the survival of your nest. There's a way. There's always a way. If you want it bad enough you will do what it takes to find it. You're better than you think. This you must keep proving to yourself.

CTA: So today's practice is in finding the way to living your dream. You must say a hearty *yes* to it every day. Even one phone call in its direction per day will open new doors. Do it. It's your adventure!!

Have a great day bringing your dream to reality.

JULY 26

Our Tone

Everyone, and I mean everyone, understands tone. When we speak, our tone is really telling the tale. We can have a smile on our face, trying to remain hidden behind our social mask, using words that are meant to sound like harmony, but our tone speaks volumes as to our true intention.

We've heard it a million times in our lives, from our parents, our friends, bosses, and of course, ourselves. When we look inward and become self-aware, we realize how much our tone creates good or alienates others in seconds.

As I have mentioned in past entries, we are like tuning forks for those around us. Our senses for true meaning behind the words and actions of others become very acute when we learn to listen to and understand ourselves first. How often have you attempted to come across to others as kind and understanding, only to be betrayed by the tone you are using to express yourself. Your tone tells *all* about your underlying motives and meaning.

When our ego is behind our speech, our tone plucks the same ego chord in those we are speaking to and they will usually respond in either silence (because they know what you are really saying), or their ego will respond you with a vengeful, snarky match to your tone. This will go back and forth, with each side going for an ego victory, instead of a peaceful, harmonious solution.

Let's continue this one tomorrow.

CTA: Master your tone. Be aware of not just what you say, but of how you say it.

Have a great day!

JULY 27

Our Tone *continued*

The famous saying, "would you rather be happy or right," is merely choosing your higher self and its truth, or your ego's demand to win this skirmish of negativity. Your tone tells the tale.

We all know this from growing up. Our moms had their tone that told us in no uncertain terms, "cut the crap!" A little tone spoke volumes! Our dad's tone had its own tune as well.

When we decide to take charge of our lives and live from a higher awareness of ourselves and our true power, we will learn how to use the higher tones that bring cooperation instead of competition. The tone of kindness over winning the argument. The tone of love and understanding over revenge and defeating the spirit of another.

We all possess both tones. Higher and lower. They both speak loudly about which side of our nature is really doing the talking. And you may think that you're slipping one under the radar of others, but I assure you, you're being perceived perfectly by your tone.

Your ego's tone will always sound domineering, nasty, snarky, above another, know it all, conceited, arrogant, unapologetic, and mean.

Your spirit or higher self will always sound accommodating, understanding, open to the ideas of others, accepting, collaborative, and kind. Wanting the best for all. You all know these tones within yourself, but it probably has never been spelled out for you that one of these creates a great life and the other creates enemies, discord, bad energy, and separation from others and more importantly, your true self.

CTA: So today, pluck only great tones from your inner guitar. You will see yourself attracting beautiful music from all those outside of you. Recognize your negative tones and the flat response you get back when you play them as well. This is a process of awakening. Awakening to the truth of what brings goodness and what brings the storms in our lives. It works either way and it works every time.

Your daily life is written like a song. It can be beautiful, sad, angry, vengeful, or many other choices. You are the songwriter. Your tone is one of the most important parts of the song.

Have a great day!

JULY 28

The Universe Favors The Bold

What a great statement. Loved it when I first heard it many years ago. It totally resonated as a truth in me and I use it every day in my daily intentions.

This statement says that if you act in faith and self confidence in all your actions, words and deeds, that the Universe will help you and reward your heartfelt efforts. This has been so true for my life that I want you all to adopt this phrase in every area of your lives. If you feel it from your heart and it feels right, but you are scared to speak or act on whatever it is, you *must* act! Say what you need to say, as the song goes. Do what you need to do and pay no attention to the small voice of your ego.

When you hear the word Universe in any motivational or spiritual phrase, you need to understand that this word means "one song." We are all part of this one song and it is just another word for Higher Self, Holy Spirit, Christ Energy, Source, God or whatever you call your higher source. It's all the same thing my friends! And we are part of it. Not separate from it and its amazing power. We are that power. Once you know this and accept it, you can use this power in everything you do or say.

Let's continue this one tomorrow.

CTA: If your actions and words are self-evident and you act with a good heart, the universe will reward you.

Have a great day!

JULY 29

The Universe Favors The Bold *continued*

This brings us back to taking bold actions in your life. It's your birthright to take bold action and live a huge life, the way you dream of it! Once you do it for the first time, stepping out of your smaller self, you'll feel empowered to do it again! That will multiply as you begin to see the fruits of your efforts. Not arrogantly moving forward, but from a higher place. One that gets what it needs, while doing it for the highest good of all. This is called living in the flow. Bold moves using the great, positive energy of your spirit.

Your ego will protest, telling you it's too risky! Stay in your safe place! Keep your mouth shut, don't take the chance! Your heart will be broken again! Whatever lies your ego tells you, be bold instead! Take the chance! Say the words and take the action. When it's what your heart needs, the right outcome will unfold. Even if the first part of the aftermath looks a bit ugly, stay the course! Let go and let God do some of the work. That's the promise of spiritually bold action!

This has proven to be one of my daily truths and I promise you my friends, you can do whatever you see as possible for yourselves.

CTA: Today, dream big, take inspired action, and be bold!

Have a big day!

JULY 30

Control or Happiness

Are you a controlling person? Would you recognize it if you were? Being controlling is a life killer. For you and everyone around you. It says, "I must control the words and behavior of another for me to be happy." Imagine the lives of those you attempt to control! A horrifying existence that brings soooo much anger, resentment, and overall low energy life for all involved.

Usually this controlling behavior is learned. A mom or dad who demanded we walk in lock step to a "certain way" in order to do what *they* thought was right for us. They meant well, but instilled in us a behavior that we carried into all your closest relationships. Our marriages, friends, children, and our business or professional life. We all know this energy and it never reaps the rewards it promises the controller. At least not long term.

Usually what happens in marriage is, one spouse is the controller and the other has agreed to be controlled. If this continues unchecked and not brought to the light of day, the controlled spouse will eventually no longer agree with this arrangement. Fights become more frequent, bickering, anger, resentment, hatred, and even violence ensues. Horror show. For both.

There are only two ways out of this controlling relationship. One is growth of both parties, through the inner work of breaking out of old roles and behaviors that never serve the relationship anyway. The second is of course, divorce or break up. Not a great second choice and one we usually do not want to choose.

If we as friends, spouses, and families want great, unlimited lives, we must give up our need to control others. Controlling people always feel they know what's best for others and are never afraid to express their judgment and conviction of others. The problem with that is, we all desire the freedom to be us, our true authentic selves. Without the need to be told our place, what to think and how to act.

Let's continue this one tomorrow.

CTA: Give up your need to control every situation. More times than not, going with the flow is the best way to live a peaceful life.

Have a great day!

JULY 31

Control or Happiness *continued*

If you find yourself being controlled by another, whether by anger, domineering personality or threat of any reason, you must take your power and your life back. You need to stand up for you! A healthy relationship is one of trust, love, non-judgment, and constant encouragement. Control has no place in this equation. None.

Declare your independence from anyone in your life you may have allowed to control you. It's your life and you need to reclaim it today!

If your controlling partner goes a bit crazy at first, you need to stay the course, let them know that this show is over and they can break up with their controlling self and grow with you or they can choose to stay in this low level hell that they too got stuck in.

Remember, you played a role in this dependent partnership, so a hand up and out of this must be extended if you want the relationship to thrive and continue. If they do not want the upward path with you, move on. You get one life as who you are. Never be a victim. Never.

CTA: So today, be brave. When you suddenly recognize you are the controller or the controlled, wake up! Break your agreement with this lowlife behavior and start the climb to a better way of living. It's there for you!!

Remember, you have choice in every moment, and choosing the higher energies will always lead you to a great life. Choosing to give up the control of others is choosing to boot your ego out the door. This is the choice of a great person and a great life!

Have a non-controlling day.

AUGUST 1

Creating a New Image

Now that you know your life has been created by your own energy, in the form of your thoughts, actions, and attention, you have most likely decided to change and improve your energy, and thus your life.

Part and parcel to seeking the upward path is the way you view yourself and how you present that self to the world. New thought needs a new image.

When you jump on the road to success, you should look the part. Updating your style is a very powerful way to show yourself and others that you are moving in a positive, new direction. If you do not consider yourself an expert in the image field, you must employ some experts. And they are there and waiting to help you totally up your game. Dressing for the life you want, not the one you got is the idea.

You need to invest in yourself first and the dividends will come quickly. Get a current hairstyle for one. If you're bald, own it and be proud. The bald head is in right now. No worries.

Update your wardrobe and ask that stylish friend of yours to help you with this new image. They have probably been chomping at the bit to help you anyway.

Carry yourself as a success at all times, because you are. Not arrogantly, but very self-assured. You are and always will be greatness. It's about time you started being it and showing it. You are above no one, but you are also below no one. Greatness is your essential nature. Own it.

Let's continue this one tomorrow.

CTA: If necessary, ask for help to improve your image to match the positive person you are becoming.

Have a great day!

AUGUST 2

Creating a New Image *continued*

Constant, never-ending improvement of our inner life will always reflect and be shown on the outside. Your body is a communication tool. It presents the you that you choose to be. What have you been communicating? Success? Lack? Anxiety? Worst-case thinking? Prosperity? Health? Well-being? It's all instantly communicated by your energy and appearance. When you feel good about yourself, you'll shine and radiate that outward. This will attract all that you deserve and have wanted. Giving and living your best includes your image.

Exercise is a huge part of the upward path. Without it, our moods are up and down, our outlook is not as positive, and we are less sharp in general. If you have no exercise regimen in your life at present, you start tomorrow! I promise you, even a couple of straight weeks of walking for an hour a day will change your life. Implement this natural healing tool of exercise immediately. Never look back! You are now a person of excellence and health and wellness are at the forefront of enjoying a great life.

CTA: Make today the day you decide to change and upgrade your image. All you need is right around you. Staying in top of your life is always the goal. Your energy, your image, and your gratitude for life will propel you to heights you've never dreamed of. It's all there. Waiting for *you* to make the moves. You'll be helped all along the way. Go get it! You deserve it.

Have a great day!

AUGUST 3

Intention

The power you have to change your life in any direction you choose will always begin with a universal power we all share. It's called the power of intention. You use this power every day, but are you directing it or are you on autopilot? Autopilot will keep you wandering the desert, while purposefully using your power of intention will deliver your dreams to your doorstep.

Intention is the power of conscious choice making and decision. This means you have finally taken the reigns of your present moments and have a solid direction for where you want your life to go.

No matter what it is, you can make it happen when you intentionally choose your thoughts, take consistent action on those thoughts, and never give up.

You are doing this every day now, but your results have most likely been scattered, less than you would like, and just unconsciously following old mind patterns. This is where most people live. Letting life happen to them rather than intentionally directing it. You own this power and have the choice in every moment as to the course of your ship.

Let's continue this one tomorrow.

CTA: Be intentional with your thoughts, words, and actions.

Have a great day!

AUGUST 4

Intention *Continued*

Every morning when you get up, give thanks first for another day of life. Then set your intentions for that day. A positive, gratitude-oriented intention would sound something like this;

Thank you for this day, another day to write the story of my life, another day to get it right and another day to give my best self away in service to you and my fellow man. I intend to succeed in all I do today and if I fall short, I will move forward, correcting course along the way. I intend to be kind, generous, and grateful in all my interactions. I intend to draw all goodness into my life and to those around me. Thank you for giving me the strength and power to live these intentions today.

Then, my friends, go about your day. These intentions, lived by you every day, will become your natural way in no time. Be persistent but be easy about it. No pressure on yourself if you slip into old scripts at first. That's normal. This is fighting the good fight. The one where everybody wins. Others will be uplifted by your energy and you are on your way to an amazing life!

A book I always recommend on this subject is Wayne Dyer's *Power of Intention*. Get this book. Digest it thoroughly a few times until you understand the concepts.

CTA: Today you begin living intentionally! Go for it. It is the journey you've always dreamed of but never knew how to get there. You are the power. Take the ride!

Have an intentionally great day!

AUGUST 5

Think and Grow Rich

This is the title to one of the most famous books on personal development. Napoleon Hill produced this masterpiece many years ago, but the truth contained in this classic is completely relevant in today's modern world. Why? Because truth is truth.

This book is not a get-rich-quick manifesto, although when you decide to implement the many truths of the book into your everyday life, you will most certainly become rich (in many ways).

The most important point I want to make about getting rich is that, in order to stay rich, you *must* uncover your inner treasure first, before you see outward manifestation of it. Oh you can get rich from other, ego means and morally corrupt means, but true wealth and prosperity are what you want. And it will never leave you.

Napoleon Hill speaks about all your inner treasure and how to not only tap into this, but how this treasure of yours must be shared outwardly in order to draw to yourself the means, the opportunities, and the right way to true prosperity. All of this is done using the higher energies of your spirit.

Some of the attributes you will be uncovering in yourself will be persistence, determination, patience, total faith in yourself, and your ability to create a success-filled life, as well as changing your beliefs that have been limiting you from your true potential. All of this and so much more are within you already. Waiting for you to wake them up and use them as your true power.

CTA: Today, download this amazing book and soak it all in.

Have a great day!

AUGUST 6

You Are Royalty

Underneath all the skin and bones, you are spiritual royalty. The closer you get to this truth as a daily intention, the more truthful this fact will become to you. You will feel it. Then soon, you will believe it, and in time, you will know it. Knowing is where you want to be my friends.

Once it's known, you'll never accept the lies again. The lies you tell yourself and the lies others tell you about yourself and others. You will know the truth by knowing yourself. Inner exploration with the intent to improve is always the practice. You are digging, you are removing what no longer belongs, and you are becoming lighter. Lighter because you are letting go of old hurts, wounds, circumstances, fears, tragedy and lots of Earth-bound inessentials, a.k.a. the stories.

You're not forgetting the lessons they taught you, you are letting go of their grip on your soul. You are letting in the light that is underneath it all. That light is you. That's the treasure we all think we will find on the outside. We think the outside treasure will cure all the pain, fear and suffering we feel on the inside, but it never will. Only for brief moments and then the luster is lost.

CTA: So today's practice is the art of letting go. Consider it like you're a sculptor, chipping away the inessential stone in order to see the beauty that Love always intended you to be. Letting go, therefore, is just agreeing with Love.

Have a great day!

AUGUST 7

It Will All Come Together

This is a very popular phrase among those who believe in themselves and their dreams. And I want you to adopt it as your own, if you're not already using it.

This is a phrase of positive power. One that has guided every great visionary to their goals, dreams and greatness.

This phrase is also known as acting in faith. Acting in the faith that come hell or high water, your dream, or something even better will arrive on your doorstep.

You are the very energy that can move mountains, and sometimes that's how it can feel on your path to greatness. However, when you keep the attitude of, "it will all come together," you are removing myriad inner obstacles that our minds will attempt to create if you are weak.

Inner garbage like doubt, fear, anxiety, and worry will always be knocking at the door. The good news is that everyone that ever lived has had to face these inner voices on his or her way to an abundant life. Your job is to stay in the attitude of gratitude for the very opportunity to create a great life, and keep this power phrase, "it will all come together" as your new mantra.

CTA: Begin your new mantra today. Stick with it and you'll begin to feel and act in accordance with the new energy it brings.

Have a great day!

AUGUST 8

Courage

Moving past the illusion of fear is the act of courage.

There is reasonable fear. That's your spirit telling you to keep your hand out of the fire and harm's way. That is natural.

There is also unreasonable fear. This is the work of your false self, or ego. This is the one that lies to you and limits you on a daily basis. Once you tune into your inner truth, your life is about to change.

Courage is an energy of your higher self. Courage says to go ahead: feel the fear and take action anyway. The power of this decision cannot be underestimated. This one choice will soon become a new pattern for you. A pattern of freedom.

Whatever the lies your lower self is spinning at any particular moment will become your window to the truth of things. Go through this window! Go past its veil of falseness and break through by saying, "I will go past this voice that lies to me. This voice offers me a mediocre life experience and I trust it no longer. This voice distorts my perception of myself and what is possible for me. It darkens my path instead of lights it. I choose to live a full life. I choose to expand instead of contract. I choose to say yes instead of no to life, and I take action in spite of this 'feeling.'"

Courage is a decision. This decision says, "I trust my higher self to guide me, protect me, and bring me to a new level of life and understanding." This is the power of courage mixed with faith. When these two energies are used by you, you will be staring your fears in the face and learning that there is nothing to fear.

Conquering and taming the voice of fear will open up new doors that you've never walked through before. Excitement, happiness, new friendships, opportunities, and prosperity in all areas of your life await you in the other side of this false energy. Your only job is to go past it instead of allowing it to immobilize you.

Once to take this courageous action, you'll be empowered to use it as a life choice. Batting this life-sucking liar back at every turn. Remember, *you* are in command of your ship! Take the wheel, make the choice, and see your true power on display!

CTA: Today, when your old false voice of fear comes knocking and telling you that you can't do or say something that will move you forward on your path to positive change, laugh! Laugh hard. Laugh in its face and feel the energy of courage welling up from your center of truth. Get to know this voice. This voice will never steer you wrong and it only delivers the good stuff.

Have a great day!

AUGUST 9

The Art of Living One Day at a Time

So many of us live in the past, reliving old wounds, continuously replaying old scenes, and adding more sorrow, guilt, shame, and thoughts of vengeance or hate to them. Or, we live in the future, where anxiety, fear of the unknown, and scary scenarios are created.

It is only in the present moment that we have the power to truly create positive new pathways, tell others how much we love them, and build a bright, prosperous future.

When we realize that we are the master creator of our lives, we will make better choices in every moment. These moments are the building blocks of our life experience and what we ultimately leave behind as our legacy.

When you wake up each morning, the first thing you must do, the first thought you must have, and the first vibration you emit, must be gratitude. This is the start to a very artful day. The art of living each moment in the present. This decision will change your life forever.

In the field of addiction and alcoholism, this one day at a time living is the hallmark of the healing process. This is what gets people past their habits and addictions with the help of those who are already seasoned in this life giving art. God Bless all those who pay it forward.

The truth is that artful living is what we all must do. Leaving the ugly parts of our past behind, blessing the past for what it taught us, and blessing it for bringing us to this pivotal life choice of living for and in the magic of the present. The future, my friends, will surely take care of itself in so many beautiful ways, once we decide to live our best in each day. Acting as if it were our last.

In this thought pattern, we love more because it's got to be done in this one day. We laugh more and create laughter, because we have to in this one day. We give more, we hug more, and we speak our truth more, because we have this one day. We forgive and forget. We lay down our swords and we come together as the connected beings we really are. Just in this day. We tell each other we love each other as we go to bed and end this day, again in gratitude for the love and beautiful moments we took part in this day.

Then, if we are blessed with tomorrow, we just do the same. This is the art of living one day at a time.

CTA: Today, follow the plan. Tomorrow, follow the plan. In no time, your life will gain loving momentum and you will begin to see the beauty you have created and a life truly worth living.

Have a great day!

AUGUST 10

Going With the Flow

There is a universal flow that is constantly moving, evolving, and expanding. And you are part of it.

Once you accept that you are an individual expression of the whole, you will begin to see the importance of your place in all if it. More as a divine mission than a happenstance experience. You have a purpose.

Whether you are in tune with your life's purpose or not, you have one. If you know it, feel it and are already expressing it through your unique way, you are very blessed indeed. You will know a great life. And you know the secret to it. It's called going with the flow.

Going with the flow means aligning yourself with your higher energies of consciousness. The flow is the living, breathing consciousness we call Love Energy, God, Jesus, Buddha, the All-Knowing, Spirit, or Our Higher Power. This energy pervades everything and it is your true self.

Going with this flow means trusting it completely. Letting it guide you with total confidence in its direction. Letting go of fear and embracing the truth. There are no worries on this path because you are aligned with real power. This power helps you and everyone you touch. We all know the flow when we feel it. It feels good. It feels right and true to us. This is the flow.

Let's continue this one tomorrow.

CTA: Find your higher power and trust in the flow. Ride the wave. Just go with it.

Have a great day!

AUGUST 11

Going With the Flow *continued*

Letting go of the lower bags that weigh us down, will help us to be in the flow more often. Once we see that this is like magic in our lives, we want to be in this flow all the time. All you desire is in this flow and is given to you, by this flow. When you are in it, your dreams come true. Most often what comes is even bigger and better than your version of your dream.

The flow is love. It is generous. It is kind and benevolent. It only gives. It only says yes and it only feels good. Sounds pretty sweet huh? It's all around you, in you and lives as you. Your job is to awaken to it and become it. Your life will be amazing.

Will you still have problems and challenges? Yes, but you will look at them from a much higher perspective and you will know what to do. You will be confident in your choices and you will act on behalf of everyone's benefit in solving them. Because everyone else is part of you and the whole.

From this place you will grow and you will expand. You will feel unlimited in your power to create with the help of the flow. The flow is your guide to a heavenly life on earth.

CTA: Today, the goal is to let go of any judgment. Let go of drama and the thoughts, words, and acts that bring it about. Stay in a loving, giving, generous space in your mind, heart, and actions. If you do this, you will have spent this day well, in the flow. Trust it.

Have a great day!

AUGUST 12

Calm Confidence

I can't begin to tell you how crucial this energy is in your life. You *must* begin cultivating it within yourself today in order to know true success and an amazing life.

The ability to be calm in the midst of the chaos, drama, and the storms of life is the very power of true security. The inner knowing and faith that whatever comes your way, you will be able to handle it and handle it well, is freedom. Freedom from fear, worry, dread, and waiting for the other shoe to drop. We all know these feelings.

I have known only a few in my life who have exhibited such a power, and I use them as an example to model after, for myself and others in my life.

Any attribute you admire in others is completely attainable by you and within you, or you wouldn't notice it. This process of modeling is really just discovering the energy of another and learning to mimic it. You learn how they think when in particular state of mind or being, and you immerse yourself in that attitude or feeling tone. Always remember that it all begins in thought, moves to feeling and then emits an energy. The energy of calm confidence is like finding a gold mine of personal power.

Inner calmness as an intention is where you begin.

Let's continue this one tomorrow.

CTA: Cultivate the calm in your mind.

Have a great day!

AUGUST 13

Calm Confidence *continued*

Your life is made up of billions of moment by moment experiences. Some great, some not. We collect these energies and are handed many that are anxious, nervous, angry, explosive and fearful. We soak them in like a sponge and they only leave us if we intentionally move past them. Some of these are unwitting gifts from our parents, siblings, friends, and other outer influences. All of which overshadow our true state of inner peace and calm. Herein lies the challenge.

Being calm is a daily cultivation in the garden of your inner life. If you even get a little better at it, your world will change. The whole key to inner peace is faith. Faith in knowing that whatever the Universe brings into your life, you have been readied to handle it. And in order to move forward, handle it you must. Your response to any issue in your life must come from this place in order to grow to new levels. You are never given things you are not ready for. So being calm or shifting to calmness after you have a reaction to a challenging situation will be your path to success and growth.

Meditation or just quiet contemplation time is a must in everyone's life. Everyone knows the value of alone time. Your task is to spend some of it cultivating inner calmness. Once you have delved into this practice for a while, you'll begin to notice its effects in your outer world. Things seem smoother, easier, and less stressful.

Inner peace is a must if we want to live in the higher energies and truly help to guide others in the right direction. If you are normally a reactionary person, going to ten in a negative expression at the first sign of trouble, this practice is a must for your transformation to a higher level of life.

Reaction is the realm of the ego. It loves to escalate a problem as its first priority. The spirit of calm has another view of the situation. A much higher view. A view of the bigger picture. This energy of the spirit says, "I must be ready for this, and I am well equipped." From this place, mountains are transmuted to mole hills in an instant. Solutions are readily at hand and clarity is in the room. We all know what the opposite looks like. Horror show.

CTA: Today, adopt the mantra of "I must be ready, and I am well equipped" whenever a challenge comes your way. Become the inner peace. Take a deep breath and say, "piece of cake." Then handle the issue from that space. You'll soon see for yourself how powerful you really are, and have always been.

Have a great day!

AUGUST 14

The Ground Zero Conversation

Recently I mentioned a couple of friends who finally came together after having what is called the Ground Zero conversation. Today I thought I should expand upon what this is and how it can free you from the negative cloud of energy between you and someone in your life.

Ground Zero is when you decide it's time to get over and bury an old relational script that you've had with someone close to you. Could be your spouse or significant other, could be a friend, a parent or sibling. Could be a co-worker or even your child. The Ground Zero conversation is when two people come together to release the pattern created by clashes of the ego. Both yours and another's. We must be brave enough to go beyond our fears and our own past mistakes, in order to get to this clearing house of negative vibes.

First let me start off by expressing that there are in fact times when you need to just walk away from an unrelenting negative relationship. Violence, addiction, infidelity, and the absence of Love are usually the reasons for an exit. If the relationship has become a one-way street, time to think about change.

In these times, you have usually said everything that needs to be said, and a lot that didn't need to be said. Time to move on.

Freedom for you in these cases still means the need for forgiveness, or you will be holding onto, and occasionally sipping from the well of negative memories.

Forgive both the other party and yourself as your declaration of freedom from the past. Never sip from the well again. Time to move up the ladder. It doesn't mean you can't be kind and have a different relationship, as in the case of divorce or separation. When children are in the mix, it's in their best interest and yours that you both be kind and civil. You're still teaching them by your example.

Let's continue this one tomorrow.

CTA: Choose to walk away from negative relationships. Doing so will give you freedom from fear, anxiety, and other negative emotions.

Have a great day!

AUGUST 15

The Ground Zero Conversation *continued*

In other times, it is our closest friendships or working relationships that need the long-delayed conversation of truth, or total ground zero.

In my personal experience, the Ground Zero conversation has saved me and freed me from continuing the facade of untrue or less than desirable relationships and replaced them with a much brighter script and truth. I assure you, there is part of the other person that wants this as well. It's only the false veil of fear that prevents you both from airing it out.

Courage and the desire for only quality, deep relationships need to be your intention and your vehicle to the other side. If you finally get to the point of either total withdrawal or the brink of war, you need to step back and ask yourself, "what do I really want? Do I know that if we could change a few things, create some new boundaries, and a new vision for this relationship, it would be awesome?" Or do you really want out? This is your very first step. What does your heart want? Not your ego, but your heart.

Unless you have a truthful answer from this place, you will never move to the next step successfully. Once you really get honest with yourself and know what you want for yourself and your life, it's time for the talk.

For those who loathe confrontation, you should first write a letter to this person, get out all you need to say in the letter. Keep it from the heart. Omit any ego language that includes personal attacks. Include a vision for how you would like to move forward in a new direction, with vivid descriptions of the better possibilities. Let the other know how much you love them and that you want better for both of you. Not just you. From this place, truth will enter and clear communication will take place when in person. The other will have the chance to digest your vision and it will be the best platform to start from. Once in the presence of this person, keep the love flowing.

If you get off track and things go a bit south, stay the course. Come back to sanity and push the higher agenda and vision. Let go of the old record, say how willing you are to start over and have a truly open and honest relationship. If at the end of the Ground Zero conversation you part in a less than desirable way, give it some space, and let nature take its course. One way or another, the truth will be revealed and the path forward will be made clear to you. You have done your best. And you should be proud of yourself for doing it the right way. The kind way and the true way.

CTA: Today, write that letter. Even if you only use it as a guideline for your in-person talk. You will have prepared yourself for what is best to say and what can be left out. Leaving the ego out of your script is my highest and best advice. Coming from the heart and using peaceful, heartfelt language will open all the doors for you. Be brave. Be truthful and keep love in the conversation at all times. The eventual outcome will be freedom, clarity, and higher living. The truth shall set you free. This is what that means.

Have a great day!

AUGUST 16

Life Is *All* About Relationships

The more you intentionally seek to create a great relationship with everyone who crosses your Earthly path, the more connected you become to the whole and the more opportunities will come to you. You are also to share and connect others with your trusted relationships when you are able to.

This is the art of paying it forward. It's the raising of all ships, not just your own. Your relationship with yourself is of the utmost importance. You must become your own best friend, love yourself completely, and honor your higher self as the most important relationship of all. Your connection to spirit is your connection to your power from home. We all have it but we don't all utilize it in our daily lives as the most practical and successful way of living. It is. This is the first relationship to concentrate on. Your inner light. The more you use it, the more you will have to give. The more you give your light, the more of it you will attract back to yourself. You'll expand. Your life expands and your sphere of influence expands. It's how it works. It works for all of us.

CTA: Today's practice is in the art of living in and sharing your light. You know how to do this. You know your light. Use it.

Have a great day!

AUGUST 17

The Morning Voice

A friend of mine asked me to talk about that morning voice that most of us share. This voice can be less than helpful in setting you up for a great day. I too have known this voice.

I had come to know this voice as Anxiety. At one point in my life it became depression, another low energy we have all tasted at one time or another. There is no shame in any of these mind states. In my case, I look back and bless the anxiety because it forced me to seek self-development as a natural way of releasing fear and low energy. For years I studied the power of the mind and listened to all the great masters of spirit and living in the higher energies of life. For this, I must thank my past struggles.

In the morning when we wake up, we are still in a half-sleep, half-awake state. Our minds can easily go one way or another. If you are going through a challenging time right now, the morning mind can get real cluttered with one big issue. When we struggle and are in a less than desirable mind state, we see the world a bit darker. We use this lens as a predictor of our day, which is the first mistake. First, recognize that you are in a bit of fog first thing in the morning and notice how this fog usually burns off after a shower, cup of coffee, and the beginning conversations of the day. It takes a bit of time to get our higher process in the driver seat during this time, so don't stress about it. Most of the time, morning worry, anxiety, and fearful predictions fade as we begin to take the actions of the day.

Anxiety is one of the worst feelings we can know as humans. It can immobilize our decision-making, cloud our perceptions about ourselves and others and spin our lives out of control. It sucks. One in three of us will know this disorder in our lifetimes. Anxiety is an energy of unreasonable fear. It usually happens to very creative people. Their active, creative mind can easily create the most fearful scenarios imaginable and when in a phase of challenge, your mind tends to believe the stories you're telling yourself. Been there. It ain't pretty.

Let's continue this one tomorrow.

CTA: For all of you who struggle with anxiety, panic attacks, depression, anger, or constant over-thinking and overreaction, my advice will always be the same; talk to a professional. Once again, there is no shame in getting better! If you had the flu, you'd go to the doctor.

Have a great day!

AUGUST 18

The Morning Voice *continued*

You must become balanced. This can take a few paths of which one or all is a great start. Trying to get past fear and anxiety on your own is very difficult because you're trying to solve the problem from the same energy that creates the problem. Outside, professional perspectives will be a great help for you.

Getting to the root of your anxious energy and cleaning out old beliefs and patterns of thought are what is offered by professional counseling. Sometimes there are cases of actual chemical imbalance in your body and medication can be very useful. No shame in that either, folks. My one caveat to this would be to always get the counseling by a loving, caring person who understands energy. Look into that for sure. Counseling is just a word. Don't ever be put off or feel like a failure. Everyone struggles, my friends. Everyone.

Getting out your old garbage will be one of the best things you will ever do for yourself. Help is all around you and the right fit for you is there. Whatever works for you and gets you to a place of balance and harmony is part of your personal journey and it's a great learning and growing experience. If I did not go through it myself, these pages would not exist. Therefore I am grateful. This will happen for you too. This struggle has been put before you in order to bring you to a higher place in your growth. Don't waste this opportunity. Take it head-on and grow!

My highest recommendation is that you first seek the inside solution. Getting to know your real self. Read, listen, and absorb the wisdom of the old and current-day masters of spiritual healing and knowledge. This is the true foundation for any real healing in your life. Adding medication for a time can be so helpful to those who are in the weeds of their minds and need a breather to absorb the counseling and let it take effect in changing your mindset to the positive.

Let's continue this one tomorrow.

CTA: Today, seek out people in your life whose balance and mindfulness you admire. Ask them. "What do you read? Whose advice do you value?" Fill your eyes and ears with the words of those who give balance to others.

Have a great day!

AUGUST 19

The Morning Voice *continued*

If your morning mindset is uncontrollably steering the day for you and you have been in a longer than normal pattern of this negative mindset, talk to someone. It will be so helpful and the steps after that will become clear. One step at a time, folks. Just speaking to a professional one time will be your intention to begin the upward path of healing and balance. You'll feel better just knowing you're taking a positive step forward.

I sincerely hope this helps you my friends. The other ingredients in a balanced life that you absolutely must include are a decent diet, exercise, quiet time or meditation, and constant absorption of positive information and learning. Your life will absolutely change. You need to always be your own best friend. Be good to yourself. Love yourself enough to get in balance and learn what that feels like. You'll never go back.

CTA: Today, if you've gone way too long in anxiety, depression, negative thought patterns and living, make some calls. Get some advice from a professional or someone you know that has come through a similar state. One step will lead to another and before you know it, you are in balance town. And it's worth it! Go get it! You deserve a great life. Give it to yourself.

Have a great day!

AUGUST 20

Doing What You Love

How much of your life is spent doing what you love to do? What would you give to change what you are doing now in exchange for something you are passionate about?

Think about it. Many of us spend most of our day doing things we couldn't care less about in exchange for a paycheck. I absolutely believe you must do whatever you need to do to support yourself and your loved ones, but while you are doing what you do, you should spend some of that time thinking about what you would really like to do and take some steps in the direction of that dream.

No matter what it is you love to do, there is someone out there making a sweet living and living their dream doing that thing. This can also be you.

Turning over stones, researching what others are doing in that field and finding someone successful in that field to model, is what your new steps would look like. It's *never* too late to chase your dreams my friends. The more you do, the more doors will open. The more doors that open, the more opportunities for bigger steps will arrive. You will be developing new skills and uncovering your hidden talents. You will be in bliss.

Just the thought of moving toward your dream is juice enough to start. One phone call a day to find out needed details will be the baby steps to bigger things. It's always about just starting. Once you start, never look back. Make two phone calls, send five emails! You'll be energized and will have something new and exciting to look forward to each day. That is what life is for! Chase your dreams and bring them into your life, as your life.

Let's continue this one tomorrow.

CTA: Make a plan and do something each day to get closer to your goal. You can do anything. Even the smallest act, such as a choice to not give up, counts.

Have a great day!

AUGUST 21

Doing What You Love *continued*

Moving in the direction of anything you want in life is all about will, determination and consistent, passion filled action. If your heart is in it and you stay self-motivated, you will succeed. The only thing you need to remember is that long term success in anything requires you to stay on the higher energies of giving, inclusion, collaboration, creativity, and wanting success for those around you, as much as you want it for yourself. It also requires integrity, honesty, and quality in all you say and do.

If your path is that of ego domination over others and a motivation that comes from selfish greed, you will not know long-term success. In fact, it will poison your dream into oblivion. Usually before you get very far.

Whatever you do, you must include the intention to benefit others in its field of energy. It should not be as much about getting as it is about giving. That is how you attain and keep success.

True success always comes when you're doing business in a conscious way. Conscious that we are all connected beings and we all desire to feel and be well. If whatever your dream is, falls in line with true principles of success, your dream is a given. Just move toward it and help will always be there for you. The right people will show up at the perfect time you need them. The finances and way forward will be shown to you and you will see your dreams come to life before your very eyes. Never doubt. Never waiver. Stay in faith and continue to move and do your very best through passionate action. When you are in the flow, if any obstacles show up, they are there to advance you forward in some way. When they come, just say to yourself, "I must be ready for this, and I know that I will overcome and move forward." This is your path to your dream and a dream life.

CTA: Today, think! Think about what you would like to see as your new life. Having an occupation that allows you to do what you love, will be like never working again. Getting paid to be in a place that is harmonious with positive energy and offers you an outlet to express your God-given talents is in fact a dream come true. Go after life like your favorite sport today. Make some moves. Shake it up and never look back! Don't you deserve a great life? That power has always been yours. Use it today.

Have a great day!

AUGUST 22

Enjoy the Ride

We are in a temporary experience here on earth. This is the place where change is all there is. A gazillion individual experiences are going on right now. Each is very different in their own way, yet in this web of divine growth we call the Universe, they are intimately connected. WE are intimately connected. We just have not figured out how to become harmoniously connected, at least not on the global stage. We are asleep to this truth.

The whole key to life is to enjoy the ride. This begins and ends with a grateful heart and mind.

We are given this time to create whatever we want. It is our blank canvass to paint a portrait of amazing experiences that will expand and grow our souls, the real us. The us that is changeless.

We cannot always choose what comes to us, so it is our job to gratefully accept what does come, even if it comes in an ugly wrapper. Your mind must be set this way in order to grow to your full spiritual and physical potential. Accept it all as if you have chosen it. From this vantage point, you will always appreciate the ride.

This place is just a stop in our eternal journey, my friends. This is the land of opposites and paradox. Some things we will never understand the reasons for why they came and went in our lives, but I assure you, there are no accidents. You are always presented with gifts. Your job is to do your best to find the gold in each experience. Sometimes we will not truly enjoy the ride we've had until much later in life, when we receive the gift of clearer sight. Wisdom.

Sometimes, lives that have been so troubled will not see the glory in it all until they cross over. It is *all* part of the eternal dance of the Universe. If I were to give one piece of solid advice from everything I write about, it would be the subject of today's entry. Enjoy this temporary ride!

Let's continue this one tomorrow.

CTA: Enjoy the ride that is called life!

Have a great day!

AUGUST 23

Enjoy the Ride *continued*

You are the master and commander of your ship. Your mind is to be used as a computer to help steer this ship. Once you take command of your mind, your ship will surely follow a steady course to smooth waters and sunnier shores. And the storms you encounter will be appreciated and embraced as your marker of new growth, opportunity, and more exciting destinations. You learn to steer your ship one right-minded choice at a time.

Becoming a wise seeker of the truth will keep you on purpose and see the beauty in every life situation. There is always the possibility of both, the worst and the best in every single interaction you have in life. It is how you choose to see it, process it and move on from it. You can always choose to enjoy the ride, or stay asleep. I recommend the *ride* baby!

CTA: Today, live it up and remember to be front and center in your part of the dance.

Have a great day!

AUGUST 24

Universal Laws

Today I would like you all to google the title of today's entry. Spend some time digesting each one and ask yourself how well you've been following these truths of life. Most likely, you're not even aware they exist.

These laws of the universe are actually spiritual truths on how to stay in the best flow that life has to offer. This includes your relationships, career, wealth, health, and true happiness. Your job is to simply know the laws and become a master of intentional creation, using them as your guide. In other words, the laws are your owner's manual for great living.

Some searches will show twelve laws but there are more. One of my favorites is called the Law of Least Effort. This comes into play when you've immersed yourself in living the laws for a while.

What happens is that you begin to get into the flow of life's goodness from your diligent practice of these truths. Your thoughts, speech, and actions must merge and align with the purpose and energetic vibration of each. The amazing benefits and blessings from this practice will become totally evident to you in short order.

The Law of Least Effort delivers effortless ease in creating the outcomes you put your intentions toward. Most often, your outcomes will be in the vein of what you've desired, but they will be even greater than you had intended and imagined. In other words, you have connected to your true self and attractive power of goodness by being in total harmony with it.

Let's continue this one tomorrow.

CTA: Search the Internet for The Universal Laws. Just become aware of them.

Have a great day!

AUGUST 25

Universal Laws *continued*

What used to feel like walking through mud to make things happen will now feel almost effortless. Yes, there are still actions to be taken and moves to be made, but you will feel more guided by the flow than by your usual ego-dominated methods of competition, striving, and struggle. You will be in passion. This is a whole different place.

The feelings we so long for as humans, such as inner peace, joy, happiness, prosperity, and harmony, are all uncovered by the practice of these spiritual laws.

These laws will not feel like the restrictive laws of man, rather, they will make you feel free. They bring your best self forward and they radiate outward as your unique, positive light.

The word "law" makes them sound ominous and demanding, but in this context, it simply means God's truths. These truths will lead you right to your own inner treasure. Once you've found it, this inner treasure will radiate from you as a reflective light from your soul. Your entire life will be filled with this light and you will have taken yourself and those around you on an amazing new journey. Life as it was meant to be lived. Happy, prosperous, deeply meaningful, and loads of laughter and fun.

CTA: Today, download and print these universal laws. Digest each one over and over until you feel the truth of each. Then go about reflecting these truths in all you think, say, and do. This is the practice. The practice that will bring you to a much higher understanding and path forward. This is the path of dreams realized and love in all its forms and symbols. You will finally have taken the reins of your own life and your creative force. This is the gift of life.

Have a great day!

AUGUST 26

A Beautiful Life

Living a beautiful life begins with your ability to notice, appreciate, and express beauty yourself. Once you have this intention as part of your daily life practice, beauty will follow you and find you wherever you go.

There is beauty in all things and all experiences. Maybe not in the forefront of our experiences, but beauty is in there.

If I said to you that there's even beauty to be found at death's door, would you believe me? It's true. Yes, there is sadness, grief, and sorrow for loss of a loved one. But this comes from a feeling that we will never see this person again. This is not the truth. It's merely a temporary illusion. Beauty in the time of loss is found when we are very present in our love for, and the way we express this love to, this special person, or even a pet. We celebrate their role in our lives and in our tears. Sadness sprinkled with tears of joy and richness not found at any other time. We are not always aware of this choice at these times. But the person who understands beauty is enriched by these experiences. This is part of the gift of our loved ones whose time to go home has come. We must be awake and present to the gift of beauty in these moments. We must develop the eyes to recognize it.

Let's continue this one tomorrow.

CTA: Notice, appreciate, and express beauty through your words and actions.

Have a great day!

AUGUST 27

A Beautiful Life *continued*

Beauty is all around us. We are only able to see it in its full grandeur when we recognize the beauty within and for ourselves. We are nature. We are part of all that we see. We ourselves are representatives of God's beauty, created to shine and share our true nature. The more you do this, the more beauty you will begin to see all around you, and especially in others. Even others you once judged as less than beautiful. You'll see with deeper eyes. You'll see past distressing disguises, into the heart of what is true.

Immersing yourself in the beauty of each moment is where you enter a higher dimension of life itself. Opening your heart and mind to what is beautiful about people and experiences in the present is where treasure is found. Milking these experiences for all you can is the way to build a beautiful life.

Once you begin a new life journey with beauty as part of your intentional thoughts, you are expanding. You are no longer living in a cloudy, dimly lit world. You are growing. You are stretching your perceptions to include the miraculous that is right in front of us. You are seeing with new eyes. This is what beauty does to us and for us. It is in our very recognition of beauty that it expands in our lives.

CTA: Today, be beautiful. Recognize it throughout your entire day. Remark on it when you see it. Praise others for their beautiful role in your life and give your beauty away freely. When you do this you become more beautiful. You only need to embody the feelings that you want to see in your life. It all starts with one beautiful thought.

Have a great day!

AUGUST 28

Your Life Quotient

How much positive life force comes through you every day? Yes, through you.

We are both spirit and physical form. The spirit part of you animates your form. It gives life to your form. The amount of energy you allow to flow through you will determine your life quotient. High or low. It's a choice we all have.

When you decide to separate from the higher, lighter side of you and become your false self, or the ego, your life force is kind of pinched off in these moments. You have turned your beautiful music down...or all the way off. You've turned your magnet to the negative, which draws all the stuff you don't really want. You suffer in some way.

A great life quotient is all about giving yourself the gift of free flowing positive energy. When you are in this state most of the time, you naturally rise in all areas of your life. You feel good. This is a Universal truth and law. You are the vehicle to your freedom from constant negative mind states, patterns, and self-sabotage. Living from the light part of you as a daily, intentional choice is how you do it. It just gets easier the more you practice. You are unlimited! You just have to keep saying yes to it, act from it, and leave behind your ego and its lies.

An amazing life quotient includes a few things. You must be committed to these daily practices in order to truly live, be happier, prosper, and know your true self.

Let's continue this one tomorrow.

CTA: Commit yourself to learn how to incorporate daily practices that will lead to a happier, more fulfilling life.

Have a great day!

AUGUST 29

Your Life Quotient *continued*

1) Live and purposely create goodness in the present moment as much as possible. Let a smile be your natural expression. Just smiling is creating goodness! Giving your light in as many present moments you can is the path. This is where all your power to change and grow resides. Stay present.

2) Stay out of the mistakes of the past, except to learn their lesson and allow them to propel you higher from the experience. The phrase "I can and I will" must be your new mantra. Give your very best and seek constant improvement. Challenge yourself to grow. Short term pain = long term gain.

3) You must become keenly self-aware. Aware of the two voices that offer their guidance. One is the false self, or ego. This voice you know as fear, anger, resentment, judgment, jealousy, worry, worst-case thinking, the martyr, and all other low, dark energy.

The other voice of love, joy, happiness, harmony, forgiveness, non-judgment, compassion, and empathy... that is the real you. Come closer to this voice as much as you can each day. Choose this voice to guide you. Give up your addiction to the ego. That's all it is. Old, ugly habits that destroy your life quotient.

4) Be grateful. Give up thoughts, speech, and attitudes of lack. Give thanks constantly for what you already have, especially if you seek to add more to any part of your life. The attitude of gratitude must be part of the new you. Gratitude is a very high energy and draws more to be grateful for into your life. Stay in gratitude. Look around you. There's much to say thank you for. Even if it was a less than pretty life lesson.

5) Let go of assumptions and judgment. Stop living from the scary scenarios that your mind creates for you. They are not truth. They are assumed truth. The truth you give credence to without all the facts. The opposite is always the other possibility. Always think, speak, and do acts of faith in your favor. Be your own best friend. Love yourself completely and grow! Always

get the facts. Let go of always pre-judging a situation and instead, give good energy, acceptance, and openness as your gift. The truth always shows up faster this way. Let things unfold without your ego's interference, judgment, and worst-case scenarios.

These are a few musts for your daily intentions and practices. As you do these, you will begin to know higher thought naturally. It will come to you. You will be guided by your true self. Solving issues gets easier. You live easier. Your life quotient has made a quantum leap.

CTA: Today, begin or continue your new path using these suggestions. They have helped me grow my life quotient tremendously and I want the very same for you my friends. Hope this helps. All the best!

Have a great day!

AUGUST 30

Consistency

Anywhere you want to go in life, and anything you want to improve in your life, is all about becoming consistent in your thoughts, words and deeds in a focused direction.

Most people give up on a new goal or dream way too easily. They chart a new course with the best of intentions and lots of enthusiasm, but then slip back into their old, comfortable habits and beliefs before their plane gets off the ground. If this sounds like you, you're in good company. Too many of us stay stuck in mediocre living when an amazing life is just on the other side of your fear and current comfort zone. Consistency must become your new best friend.

The voice of stagnation will always be telling you to stay put in your comfortable box. This is the voice you will need to challenge consistently with will, faith, determination and purpose. There is gold for all who challenge this voice every day. You must consistently move forward in spite of this voice. Within a short time, this voice will become dull to you. It will have less and less hold on you. It will be silenced by your consistency in moving on the upward path.

Let's continue this one tomorrow

CTA: Consistency in any area of your life is a huge key to positive change. It's all about starting wherever you currently are and taking new, bold steps.

Have a great day!

AUGUST 31

Consistency *continued*

If it's exercise, your body will begin to feel better in short order and then you will not want to stop. Baby steps are fine and they too are bold steps! Just be consistent in taking them. Improvement will come naturally as you begin to feel better. Better eating? Same course of action. Always celebrate your small victories. Soon they will become your big victories.

If it's improving your relationships in any part of your life, consistent, thoughtful actions, words, and promise keeping will be part of your course. All great friendships, partnerships, familial, and intimate relationships are built on consistent nurturing. Love, support, honesty, trust, kindness, compassion, apology, and forgiveness. These must be your tools of consistency in all your relationships. From here, you will be blessed with abundance in all areas of your life. Being consistent in this one area will attract all you'll ever need. Life is all about relationships my friends. Especially the one with yourself. Be consistent here too. Be as good and as true to yourself as you are with your highest relationships. Without loving and believing in yourself first, you'll have little to give anyone else. You are a gift, never forget that. Live by your light. Your light never gets it wrong.

With respect to your goals and dreams, you must be consistently improving yourself as you hone, shape, and improve your dream. Learn from the many mistakes you will make along the way. Never hold onto them, just use them for their wisdom and forward motion. It's how *everyone* grows. There's no big secret, just become ok with challenges. Blow past them with a new confidence. It's in there. Exercise your power. Bold steps bring great reward.

These are a few areas to certainly become more consistent in, and intentional about. In fact, these three areas will change everything for you. Just do it. It's how life is best lived.

CTA: Today, begin to look at your life. Where do you seek improvement and increase? What is it that you most want? You must be consistent in your thoughts of success in that area. Be consistent in taking action toward that goal. And be sure to give your love as your ticket through any door that has previously been closed to you. If you decide to live consistently in the higher vibration of love itself, the world will soon be your oyster.

Have a great day!

SEPTEMBER 1

Celebrating Even the Small Ones

Celebrating your small victories along the way is a must. If you don't take the time to notice the hand of spirit delivering what you've asked for, you will never know true happiness.

I have a friend whom I point this out to regularly. Every time I notice something great that happens to him, he replies with, "yeah but there's a lot of hurdles ahead and who knows if it will happen. I'd rather not get my hopes up only to be disappointed."

Sound familiar to you? Too many people do not know how to receive. They're great givers, but they lack one great part in their flow. Gratitude!! Gratitude is the giving of thanks for blessings just seen and the faith to give thanks in advance for future blessings that have yet to be seen. The lack of enthusiasm and celebration is like putting the brakes on what you've been asking for if you don't take a minute to say, "Wow, this is fantastic! Thank you, another cue that my full dream is on its way." It's momentum. Notice it.

Celebrate it and stop expecting disappointment in your future. That's living with the brakes on. Staying ahead of disappointment can be handled with one simple letting go method. It's called real faith. Not wishful thinking, but actual trust that if you do your part to your very best, and you continue to make yesterday's best even better today, spirit will always do its part to arrange the details for you. When you see or feel this hand in your creative life process, you'll recognize that you have the ultimate partner. God himself. Even your loved ones on the other side help you. Never doubt that.

Let's continue this one tomorrow.

CTA: Every victory, no matter how small, is worth celebrating. These victories are reminders of how far you have come and where you are going. Celebrate!

Have a great day!

SEPTEMBER 2

Celebrating Even the Small Ones *continued*

Spirit will guide you, but you must let go of believing the other voice that keeps telling you lies. This voice will always tell you, "You're going to fail, don't celebrate this, you'll jinx yourself." This voice blocks you from rising and growing as you are meant to. Eliminate it from your beliefs. You can do anything but *you* have to believe it. Small steps of noticing your blessings as they come, giving thanks as recognition, and expecting the right things to come instead of exactly what you think should come, will keep you in the fastest flow to your dream come true, or something even better. Plus, the whole journey will be brighter because you chose to believe that you never work alone.

Accept what comes as if you chose it. It's there for you to celebrate or learn from in order to move to the next level. Your circumstances are never meant to defeat you. That's the liar in your head again. Your challenges are there on purpose, to get you to grow to your amazing potential. The beauty you came here to be and give. Learn to receive with grace, ease and a thankful, present heart and mind.

CTA: Today, practice the ability to receive. Open up. Open your eyes and see what it's really all about. Love is both giving and receiving. It's what you know as going with the flow. Being good at both keeps you free and flowing with creation itself. Your world is much different here. You've found the key.

Have a great day, my friends!

SEPTEMBER 3

It's Never Too Late

So what do you *love* to do? Do you even know? If you do that's the first step to changing your course, getting rid of the old map and charting a whole new life experience.

I was in the insurance business for ten years, selling something that everyone needs but something I was less than passionate about. Loved the experience, taught me a lot about business and made many lasting friendships with some amazing people, but I knew there was more I needed and wanted for myself and my family. Boy what a run-on sentence that was! LOL.

During this time, I was steadfastly working on my true dream of Focusmaster. Always keeping the flame alive within me. I'm sure I used more company time dreaming, drawing and using their office equipment to bring me closer to my goals. Sorry Rose and Kiernan and Dave Bauer!

My point is, if you see yourself in a whole new place in your mind, you can and should move toward it. Even if you are working a 9-5 to pay your bills, you need to be taking steps, turning over stones, calling people who are in the field of your interest and finding out where you can fit into this place.

It is never too late to realize your dream! Never! We see people in their eighties going back to college for crying out loud! Simply doing it because they see it for themselves.

Become a seeker of the knowledge you need. Starting small is where everyone who has ever done anything great begins! It's all creating. Creating a new life for yourself as you see it is what life is for!

Let's continue this one tomorrow.

CTA: There are 24 hours in a day. Start your dream change with one of those hours. Put pen to paper and write down the first five actions you will take toward this new journey. Take them. These five actions will lead to five more and you are on your way!

Have a great day!

SEPTEMBER 4

It's Never Too Late *continued*

Never let where you are in this moment dictate where you want to go. YOU are the driver of your vehicle. One small decision today to begin will have you in a whole new place, if you make this same decision every day. In no time, you'll see the fruits of your new adventure.

Consistency, determination, passion, and persistence are the ingredients of change. This is the recipe of winners and you are one of them.

Any new life change begins with a thought that excites you. This is the seed you need to water and nurture every day until it blooms. Every step you take will build momentum. There will be obstacles all along the way, but remember that you have and ARE a powerful being with the inner light that is there to guide you, protect you, and assist you all along the way. You just need to believe it to achieve it.

CTA: Today, put your mind to work on what you would love to do. Write down your first five action steps and begin the journey! Remember, it's not where you are that determines where you are going. It's what you believe you can do that drives your vehicle. Believe in yourself, your true self and let no one stop your train of success!

Have a great day!

SEPTEMBER 5

Never Get Old

Getting old is a decision. Yes, we will all get physically old, but keeping your young self inside this aging shell is always the goal.

Too many of us fall into predictable, old patterns that we've seen our whole lives. Whether from parents, grandparents or television. And it's a bunch of garbage.

Your mindset and your choice to be and stay healthy and youthful is the magic behind the proverbial fountain of youth. You must constantly live your life from a young perspective. Never let the old person move in. Not in mind and not in body.

We all have that older person in our lives that has made this decision for him or herself. They could be 95 years old and look 70. They have a smile on their face and I guarantee they love and are grateful for life.

Let's continue this one tomorrow.

CTA: Becoming mentally old is a decision. Choose to live your life with a younger perspective and experience the joy of a younger you.

Have a great day!

SEPTEMBER 6

Never Get Old *continued*

I recently met a man like this in his nineties at a wedding. He was so vibrant and full of life; his outward energy immediately told the tale. I made it a point to speak to this man and get his story. I knew I would be gaining some very important wisdom. And I did.

His name was Tony. He owned his own Italian restaurant in New York City for 60 years and was beaming with pride and joy telling me his story. What a personality on this guy! Over-the-top positive attitude, in great shape, and proud that he still had all his teeth and black in his hair. We laughed like drunken pirates for twenty minutes as I heard more.

Finally I got to my main question to Tony. "What's your secret for such a vibrant, youthful life?" His answer is the advice I'm paying forward today.

He said; "I've always been happy. I wake up grateful for each day the good Lord gives me. I smile because I have a beautiful family, beautiful children and a job that I love. I always counted these blessings and loved to make others laugh and smile. That is my secret. Happiness. Simple." And he smiled at me from ear to ear.

What a presence. Simple truth and deep wisdom all wrapped in a very young spirit within an old man's shell.

I told him that he was my new hero and I hoped to be as young as he is when I'm ninety. I treated him like the gold that he was and made sure to bring over a few of our team to meet him. This was a great man. Great for no more than his inner greatness, that shined like the sun itself.

CTA: Today, and from here forward, never let an old person move into your body. Exercise, great relationships, good energy and lots of giving your best self will always keep you young. Be grateful for all you have and live life to the fullest. This is the fountain of youth.

Have a great day!

SEPTEMBER 7

Your Life Review

Having read a few books on the near-death experience, I can tell you there is a common thread to all the stories. It's called your life review.

This seems to be in the first phase of your transition back to your true home, as pure positive spirit. It's like a very vivid movie of your entire incarnation and life, in this physical world of ours.

They all say it takes only a few seconds to see and understand your entire life experience. Your thoughts, reactions, every good deed, not-so-good deed, every relationship and how it affected your path, and all the places where your soul either grew or stagnated. Your victories and when you fell short. All of it, in seconds.

They say at this stage, you have complete understanding. You see with your spiritual eyes what you may never have known while you were in human form.

You get to see how you affected others and the changes you helped, or did not help to transpire in the lives of those around you. It gives you a snapshot of your journey that lets you know how important you were to the growth of others and how you grew your own soul through the physical experience. In other words, how you did on your divine mission.

The other common thread that is in every one of these individual accounts of the transition process we call death, you are enveloped by and filled with the energy of unconditional love. Love like you've never experienced it before. Love energy that is so powerful, your human form would not be able to handle it.

Let's continue this one tomorrow.

CTA: Today, are you pleased with the way your life looks in review? Have a great day!

SEPTEMBER 8

Your Life Review *continued*

This loving force is not there to harshly judge anyone. It is not there to cast you to a fiery pit because of the choices you made. It lets you see the areas of your experience where you grew and the ones you still need to work on. In other words, unconditional love is not judgmental. Our life review is like a personal report card of our progress as a soul. This process continues on the other side in the form of helping our loved ones that are still here.

Sometimes these souls who have passed elect to return in another incarnation, sometimes as a new member of the same family. So for those of you who have lost someone way too soon, they may re-enter the physical to get some things right that did not happen for them the last time around. And this is their choice.

It is so interesting to hear the accounts of children who have briefly crossed over and the perceptions and messages they have for their families upon their return to the body. It is always the same. We are loved more than we can imagine, by a force we are part of. One that loves us so much, that it lets us see where we need to be in order to progress to higher and higher plains of spirit. It is so much different than the dogma we have been handed in so many circles of organized religion.

Love is love. Love is not a harsh judge, but unconditional forgiveness and light. This light welcomes us all back home, surrounds us and blankets us in warmth, and lovingly lets us see how far we've come. We are here to grow.

Let's continue this one tomorrow.

CTA: Live your life with purpose. Don't just go through the steps. No one likes a zombie.

Have a great day!

SEPTEMBER 9

Your Life Review *continued*

For those of you who have recently lost a loved one, please take comfort that this is simply the next step in their spiritual evolution, and while your heart is broken from this seeming separation, your loved one has a new role as what we call an angel. If they left too soon according to our time schedule, they may have spiritually chosen to move beyond the physical to be a larger force for you and God, in the higher realm of spirit.

You will most certainly be reunited again in the wink of an eye. Hold to that truth and that promise for the rest of your life. We will all be reunited with our loved ones in the spirit realm. They are with you all the time my friends. We simply do not have the eyes to see them. This experience of temporary separation is also there for our souls growth. Know this and let it happen. Broken hearts do heal. It takes time and it may never be quite the same while you are here, but total healing will happen upon your spiritual reunion.

My main point of today's entry is about realizing that you too will someday have this life review and from this point on, you should intentionally go through life, seeking and living on a higher path, making the changes in yourself that you've been putting off.

Love more, laugh more, and believe in yourself more. Care more, take more risks, and live and love life to the fullest. Your loved ones from the other side are helping you in ways you cannot know right now. That too, is part of the plan.

When you finally get to see the movie that was your physical experience, make sure it's one that you'll be happy to see. A blockbuster success!

CTA: Live today on purpose.

Have a great day!

SEPTEMBER 10

Your Time on Earth Is All about Change

Everything changes, including you, in many ways. All of which you have a big say in how it is perceived and how you process through it. The real you is changeless and timeless. The real you is eternal light. If you choose to perceive and process all Earthly change through the wisdom of the changeless, you will live a very rich and meaningful journey.

Why? Because looking at your life as beautiful growth, instead of the chaos that the world wants you to be part of, will adjust your perspective to see the real reasons for everything. You'll be a student of life through your very unique perspective, your light perspective. It is a very different journey indeed. Love is your guide instead of fear. Faith is your key to new and exciting change, and patience is your best friend because you know that it is all unfolding in perfect order. You are in tune with the your higher nature and eternal compass. You get it right from this place. You never need to fear change: you welcome and embrace it. It's for you. It's all for you.

CTA: Today, practice going beyond the fear of change, shifting your perspective to the positive within, and never taking your eyes off of the light. Darkness stagnates and causes fear. Light guides. It's always just a choice.

Have a great day!

SEPTEMBER 11

The Great Unknown

We come here to experience the great unknown. How we choose to think about it all will become the portrait of our lives.

Going through life with a faithless fear of the unknown will prove to be a bumpy ride indeed. Always worrying about the future, stuck in the mistakes and loss of the past and an overall nervousness about life itself. This is the trap of your ego. If you pay attention to it, feed it with its favorite foods, like anger, resentment, judgment, anxious thoughts, and self-created scenarios in your mind, you will travel a road that is always focused on the negative what-ifs. This lower-minded path knows no peace. You are so much more than this mindset has trapped you in. You can and must do better for yourself. The time to begin to rise is always in the now.

Living from the level of your soul, or true nature, is the other road and it is much less traveled. This road however, has everything you love and need on it. Fun, laughter, positive adventure, inner peace, prosperity, harmony, joy, beauty, and true meaning.

This road will ask for your complete faith, especially in the darker times. It will ask that you love yourself completely and forgive yourself for past mistakes. It will ask you what you want and then go about delivering it to your doorstep. Working with and in spirit, will be a much different road indeed.

At first it will look like the foggy picture for a while, but as you continue to think, act, and speak only on your life's new intentions, you will end up in the sun more often, and then you become the sun, the light that can never be eclipsed by the darkness again.

No matter what you face in the great unknown, your new inner confidence and faith will transform you into a person of true power, eagerly seeking the blessing of the great unknown, instead of dreading it. You will anticipate and expect only the best to meet you at every turn, and you will have unwavering faith that you are now guided instead of flying blind. A very different perspective on the unknown indeed.

Everything I write about really boils down to accepting your true inheritance that lies waiting within you. Knowing that you yourself are spirit, able to create any experience you desire, with total assistance from above. Your mindset must be consistently on this road in order to meet and become your true self. My friends, it's the only road worth taking. The other road is a mediocre ride at best, and a tragically unnecessary one at worst.

CTA: Today, end your fear of the unknown. Embrace your true, powerful nature, and begin your new journey with the truth that you are here absolutely on purpose, with a divine mission. Love yourself enough to create and live a great, amazing life on the road of the great unknown. You deserve it.

Have a great day!

SEPTEMBER 12

Your Legacy

This year is the big 5-0 for me and many of my awesome friends. So, for my friends turning half a century old, science has just confirmed that fifty is the new twenty. Well, my science, LOL.

What this great era in life seems to bring, is the gift of wisdom. When we get to look back on our lives from this vantage point, we can see where our road has shaped us through both adversity and love. We get to see how we responded to things then, and how we hopefully have grown and learned to be more guided by a higher knowing and purpose.

Never regret your past, my friends. It may not have been all rainbows and unicorns, but it has brought to you a very unique perspective, and probably just what you came here to learn and experience.

The gift of fifty also brings with it a very natural inner desire to live the rest of your life with more purpose and a more generous spirit. This is called the legacy building phase of the human experience, or the afternoon of our lives. I believe it is in our DNA.

This desire tells us to leave behind a beautiful, permanent imprint on this temporary visit. What this imprint looks like is up to you, and it will be your legacy.

Family, friends, and Mother Earth will hold your memory in great stead, when you decide to live the rest of your life intentionally creating a beautiful legacy. This is also a great reason to live well and give well. In other words, what do you want to be remembered for?

Let's continue this one tomorrow.

CTA: What do you want to be remembered for? Are you living your life with purpose in order to achieve that?

Have a great day!

SEPTEMBER 13

Your Legacy *continued*

Do you want to be remembered as overbearing, domineering, angry at the world, fearful, anxious, punishing, judgmental, violent, unforgiving, envious, greedy, lying, cheating, lacking, or less than you could have been? I think not. But these are some of the lower choices on the menu of our human experience that we get caught up in, and sometimes live our entire lives from.

The way to create a lasting, loving legacy is to simply give your best from this point forward. Discard the distasteful part of the menu and only serve the healthy, life-giving selections. These menu items are the ones everyone loves and needs. You already know what they are, you just need to keep them in focus and become the very energy of each.

Love in all things includes the energies (gifts) of compassion, understanding, forgiveness, happiness, joy, laughter, intimacy, grace, empathy, peace, kindness, generosity, prosperity, great health and well-being, creativity, optimism, support, guidance, goals and dreams, passion, purpose, a grateful heart, and a mastered mind.

These are all the ingredients for an amazing legacy. Your legacy leaves beautiful light behind as your memory. This light will be so bright that it will continue to guide others forward in their own journeys. It is part of our purpose to prosper each other in such a way. Living in this mind state helps to guide your every thought and decision and brings to *you*, a life well lived.

So today, wherever you are on your personal journey, choose to look at the legacy you are building right now. If it's a bit off-course, no worries. You have the power to redirect your path at any time. That time is *always* in the present moment. This very moment, where *all* your power lies. Choosing to live from the perspective of leaving a beautiful imprint on this temporary trip is not only worthwhile, but it is the very path of true living and a beautiful life.

CTA: Give what you want to be remembered for and discard the unnecessary.

Have a great day!

SEPTEMBER 14

Fond Memories

In dedication to my friend Paul Christopher, who recently passed, this page is about our life's diary that we all call memories.

What a gift it is to have the ability to recall our fondest memories in a split second. If your mind is right, and you feel you have to visit the past, always make it a nice trip. Concentrate and reflect on the great ones as much as possible.

In our individual journeys here, we are blessed with a general tribe of fellow travelers. The ones we love and appreciate are never forgotten. Their part in your life, whether small or large, has shaped us or altered our experience in some way. These are the moments we recall, can recite a particular story about, and recall how we felt about this fellow traveler. Just hearing a name from your tribe will bring that story or stories to the forefront of your mind instantly. When I heard of Paul's passing, it was a sad moment indeed. My diary's memory of Paul came in that instant, like I was watching his particular clips in my life's movie. I know you can all pull up your own laughter filled, crazy fun clips from your mind too. Here's a few of mine. Sharing yours may help in the healing, so don't hesitate. It brings great meaning to you and his memory to do so.

I grew up with Paul in Spiegletown. He was a great kid, a cool kid, from my younger perspective. We always had fun playing backyard football at Steve Dugan's house and he always had a lot of great guys as friends. Many we share. Paul was the guy that everybody loved. He was a true Burgh guy. He was a staple at every monument party, bonfire, Bill Finkel's famous house parties, and all the rest of the great 70's and 80's gatherings. Paul was part of our Spring Break trip to Daytona Beach in 1983, LOL. We shared a room with about 8 other guys. We had a freakin' blast! Paul was a big part of that blast. He always brought his smile to the party. This is evidenced by the many pictures on Facebook this week.

These are just some of my personal fond memories of Paul. While he played a smaller role in my path, it was always a great one. He was everyone's friend. If I were to assign Paul a purpose for his visit here, it would have been all about being an awesome friend. He knew and played his role well. He brought joy to others lives and I hope he knows how much his contribution to our tribe is appreciated. His spirit served us all well. Thank you, buddy. From all of us, God Bless you with your new wings as you watch over all of us from our real home. God Bless your family as well.

CTA: Celebrate your friends every day by giving them your very best.

Have a great day!

SEPTEMBER 15

Our Temporary Ride

We come into this physical world with divine amnesia, God's gift of not letting us remember where we're really from for a while so we can fully embrace our three-dimensional human experience.

The problem for us as humans is that we also forget that we still carry with us our power from home. This power is what we should be using to create the coolest, most amazing three-dimensional ride we can imagine while we are here on this temporary adventure.

Knowing this truth, we can begin to reconnect to our true inner power and shift our lives into high gear for the time we have left on the ride. Never waste a minute, my friends!

Part of our human self, we created. It's the part of us that does not believe it is eternal; therefore it goes about life believing it is separate from others, rather than connected to and part of the whole.

This side is our lower nature, or ego. Your lower self believes that its nature must rule and dominate others. It believes that anger, violence, competition, and control are the reality we must stay in. But we don't have to.

The ego fears death and makes you fear life. It makes most of us stay in our little safe boxes and simply hope to get to the end of our lives in one piece. Nervous, afraid, less than or more than others. These are the dictates of our false self. I like to call this side of us the liar. Never listen to the advice of this side of you and you'll find yourself flying with the eagles instead of continuing to keep company with the crows.

Let's continue this one tomorrow.

CTA: Never waste a moment of your time. It is such a valuable asset.

Have a great day!

SEPTEMBER 16

Our Temporary Ride *continued*

I can't express enough how truly great you are. Consider it like this; you are a Superman or woman who came to this new place with powers you forgot about. As you decide to live your life with total faith that you in fact possess these powers, you will uncover and begin to remember where you really come from. It is your divine inheritance and we are *all* meant to uncover it while we are here. Part of my purpose here is just to remind you. You can do or become anything you see and believe you can. Your job is the belief part.

Choosing to uncover your power and talents and sharing them with the world will create just what you are here to do or be. Move in that direction, friends. Start today.

I believe we choose to come here. We all have divine missions and purposes. Many we will not fully understand until we go home. Some we will see easily and understand fully during the ride. This sustains and fulfills you and those around you.

I also believe we get to come here with a particular tribe.

I believe we choose our parents and our children choose us. What a cool concept! When I first heard it myself, I loved it. All of these are gifts of eternal life. You are all part of my tribe and I am part of yours, even if we do not really know each other very well. We are here in this particular space and time for a reason. I believe the reason is always to move closer to our true selves, in the quest to create a beautiful, peaceful, co existent heaven in the physical world. Hope that's true. We are like spiritual pioneers in a human dimension. Many of you just forgot that you still have wings. Maybe they're a bit clipped at the moment, but I assure you, you can fly.

CTA: Today, dust off the wings you forgot you had. They are there under the pain and suffering you hold onto. Shed the past, stop worrying about the future and choose to live in the truth of who you really are. Grab your wings and believe in yourself! You are a spirit on a temporary ride. Don't make too much about everything. Just love it all, appreciate it all, and give your heart away freely to everyone you come into contact with. Your wings will begin to spread and soon you'll be up there with the rest of the eagles on the ride of your life!

Have a great day!

SEPTEMBER 17

Wink of An Eye

These are the words spoken so many times throughout my life by my dad. As I reflect on my big 5-0, I reflect on the truth of that statement for myself and all of us.

My mom's birthday was yesterday and there's no doubt that on that day in 1964, I was trying to get the hell out of that "womba" to be a birthday gift for her. LOL.

But it would come a day later. As it turns out, she was the gift for me. As were my beautiful wife Jan, my amazing children, my best friends, my incredible sisters, my loving, supportive dad, and all of you.

I sit here typing on my cell phone in true gratitude for a life of amazing gifts and experiences, many with the readers of my entries. You have all graced my life with your presence and today I say a heartfelt thank you. I am moved to tears by all the birthday wishes and I surely feel the love behind all of them. These first fifty have certainly come and gone in the wink of an eye, but I have so many treasures from all of them.

I am a man who knows how truly blessed he is. God has given me so much I can never repay. I do my very best to spread his truth, so that others may wake up to their own blessed lives. You are all very blessed as well. Always count them and you'll know it first-hand.

As I move ahead into the future, I look forward to the very best that is surely yet to come. We have all been given an inner flame to nurture and grow. It is our true self, calling for us to live. Live life to the fullest. Never waste a minute of the precious gift we have all been given. It is only through our gratitude for all of our experiences, even the ones in the crappy wrapper, that we truly recognize this gift.

CTA: Today, my heart is overflowing with gratitude for the role you have all played in my journey. It means more than you'll ever know to me to have a tribe of such awesome friends. You are all great. Thank you so much. And always pay heed to the fact that it's all in a wink of an eye. Give love to all as the calling card of your life. You will live a life full of meaning and a legacy of love that is sure to be passed on.

Have a great day! Love you all.

SEPTEMBER 18

The Endless Stream

Life is indeed an endless stream. It is the eternal dance of the soul. You are the dancer.

It is only through the thought that all life here comes to an end that we give meaning and purpose to our earthly experience. Feeling this knowing within us should be a pull to give more of our true selves and grow through our eternal nature while we have the opportunity. That opportunity is in every moment. The present moment.

Learning to live more from your eternal nature is the stream that brings a life well lived right to your doorstep. This stream is always flowing and desires only to bring you the very best. Your experience up to now has most likely been one of hitting the rocks on either side of the stream, more than a smooth, beautiful ride in the middle of the flowing waters.

We have so much more control over our individual stream than we've been told. You just didn't realize that you can choose to live as part of the stream. You are indeed part of the stream. And yes, hitting the rocks on either side has taught you some valuable lessons, but this is only *one* way to learn.

Let's continue this one tomorrow.

CTA: Go with the flow, letting the stream of life carry you without resistance.

Have a great day!

SEPTEMBER 19

The Endless Stream *continued*

Being part of the endless stream means that you possess this incredible flow of power and beauty. Your daily choice to commune with it and become it in all your interactions brings you to know it. Really know it. Not some ethereal, made-up power, but the energy that creates worlds and the one that created you.

This force will become your daily, go-to energy and the one that raises you, protects you and most certainly, guides you. Making it your new life choice to seek this self-power and practice it every day will transform your very existence and the existence of those who feel your new light.

We get into trouble on our journey down the stream when we decide to paddle against the current. This is when your ego has the oars. You move against the stream, instead of letting it carry you. You don't trust the stream, which makes you feel alone and powerless. You avoid the stream and decide to sit on the shore, stuck in fear, worry, anger, or sadness. Jumping in the boat and trusting it to take you to better places is your answer.

Throwing away the oars may take some time, willpower, determined actions, and faith, but that's what brings the real beauty back into focus and then radiating from you as your new calling card. Give yourself the gift of change. Change after all, is all there is here on earth. We can choose to flow with it or fight against it, by not accepting what is, and deciding to build from there instead of staying immobilized.

My friends, life is meant to be lived. Really lived. Not half speed or in constant fear of the dreaded "what ifs," but courageously, spontaneously, and with an eye on the incredible beauty of the endless stream that you are. Knowing that your true self is eternal should give you the confidence to just get out there and knock life out of the park! Start by being good to yourself and choosing to rise.

Deciding to spend your life on the shore and occasionally dipping your toes in the stream is like choosing crumbs when you have an endless supply of the most delicious gourmet dishes right in front you. Time to do some fine dining, my friends.

CTA: Today, begin to trust the stream to work things out for you. Give your problems over to the stream and put your oars down. When you're tempted to grasp them and perhaps argue, fight, quit, or judge yourself or someone else, say no! Not this time. This time I choose to let go and be carried instead. With diligent, daily practice, you will just become the stream. Flow baby... flow.

Have a great day!

SEPTEMBER 20

Patience

Patience? Oh yeah... this is the one we all have big trouble with. Especially dreamers and doers. We see a big vision for ourselves and we want it all now. Today's "instant gratification" society is used to getting it fast or else! But everything, and I mean everything, worth having takes time and a lot of patience.

If you accept the fact that every dream has a gestation period, you can relax in knowing that there are steps we must all take to get to our goals and dreams. We've all heard that it's about the journey and not the destination, but impatience and trying to jump ahead are energy killers.

We will never enjoy each step if we are trying to constantly jump over the joys and lessons that are there for us along the way. And trust me, there are many. The key to practicing patience is to do it in every area of our lives. Small things done in a great way always add up to big dreams accomplished in a great way. And *always* remember that you never get it done. When you reach your goal, there's always another in the distance. That's the fun and adventure in the journey. The real treasure of life. So today, when you're tempted to jump out of the car and tear that other driver a new one, give yourself some space between the usual thought and the usual impatient *reaction* and respond instead with a deep breath and some patience. Remember, impatience only disrupts our own good energy in exchange for something we always regret, whether said or done. Everything is unfolding for you in perfect order, my friends. Enjoy the ride in style and in patience.

CTA: Practice patience to your best ability. Breathe and let go of negative reactions when they are still small in your mind. Trust that you are not working alone. Relax and give thanks for the fulfillment of living in the process of bringing your dreams to reality.

Have a great day!

SEPTEMBER 21

The Attitude of Gratitude

An attitude of gratitude is the energy that lets us see, feel, and know all the blessings of our lives. It starts by giving thanks for all we have and even for blessings hoped for. If we practice this attitude from the beginning of our day to the end, giving a silent or spoken word of thanks each time we are grateful for a kind word, a great piece of news or the smile on the face of our children or something that makes us laugh, we consciously realize how truly blessed we are. This attitude of gratitude is the energy that attracts more goodness and blessings into our lives.

When you practice gratitude each day, within no time, it becomes your new normal and you'll find yourself, and those who feel your good energy, happy and uplifted. It's the best way we have to truly appreciate our lives and those in it and only produces more of the good stuff. Live your entire life in gratitude for all that you are and all those seemingly tough times that have brought you to a new level of love and understanding.

CTA: What are you grateful for today? Count the ways and you'll realize you already live a blessed life.

Have a great day!

SEPTEMBER 22

More About Gratitude

If I could only give you one practice to lead you to your inner treasure, it would be gratitude. But why is this mindset of gratitude so crucial to knowing a beautiful life? Because you are noticing your blessings.

This simple decision puts your very being on a spiritual elevator and brings you right to the top floor, your heart space. It's a direct connection to home. It says, "I acknowledge the hand of spirit in this moment and I am thankful to know that I never work alone." Whether you've just received some amazing news or you are in front of a sick loved one, gratitude both asks for the spirit's hand in any situation or gives thanks for what this divine hand has just brought you.

The more you use this mindset as a practice, the more the door to truth will open for you. You'll begin to see what most are still missing. Miracles happen to you every day and in every moment if you have the eyes to see. We all possess these eyes, not just a select few... all of us. That means no matter how darkened your doorstep may feel to you right now, the hand of the eternal is always there waiting for your asking. You're no longer saying please, you're saying thank you in advance for the answers I know are forthcoming.

Feel the difference in those two? One is filled with faith and the other is filled with the overall energy of fear. It's a shift to the language of that which gives unconditionally. Yes, this hand is always giving you what you are asking for, so watch your thoughts, speech, and actions. You're always asking. Look around you; are you happy with what you've created? Or would you like to rise past some of these? You must begin to ask in the positive because that's what the eternal is. It's love.

Love always says yes. It's the most positive force there is. If you're not giving thanks in advance for the good stuff you want to enter your life, then you're just focused on the same. Even if you make it a new practice to simply say, "thank you for all my blessings, the ones I now am able to see and the beautiful ones I trust you will bring" and go about giving love your unique way, as your new, improved calling card, everything will begin to change for you. Direct your life with spirit or you'll languish in the normal when you could be bathing in the sun. It's just a shift that takes practicing life in a certain direction. For some, it's just a tweak to the right, for others it will take a lot of will and faith-filled determination. Never doubt this path, just enter where you are and trust.

CTA: Today, when even a friend makes you laugh, recognize it as a gift. Didn't it raise you to a new floor within? Silently give thanks for noticing on a different level. You're giving thanks to your new life partner and the friend who just gave you a gift.

Have a grateful day!

SEPTEMBER 23

True Greatness

If you look back in history, every truly great person was great because they somehow changed people's lives for the better. They weren't great because they were rich and successful. The rich and successful part came as a result of whatever they did for humanity. When this country banded together during World War II, the country was in harmony and after the war, the harmony lasted for quite some time because true greatness was present. We became a hardworking, American Dream society. One that collectively picked itself up and created better lives for itself and others. This was not a society of dependent victims; these folks had the natural do-it-ourselves mentality.

Today, unfortunately, we have a society of victims and entitlement. In my humble opinion, these people are being completely robbed of ever knowing their true greatness. The gift of overcoming the obstacles that were meant for growth and their subsequent *victory*. They never get the chance to know their own victorious self because they are handed a supposed easier road. This is a dream-killing trap that only creates a mediocre, dependent existence and low energy life.

I believe *everyone* who cannot care for him or herself should be cared for by all of us. But the rest, we are robbing them. True leadership is when we inspire greatness from within. Not from us vs. them, but us vs. ourselves. We need to get back to being great. Creating again. The American Dream. Jimmy Hendrix said it best I think; "When the power of love exceeds the love of power, we will have a great world." Finding your greatness is an inside job. Once you take that journey and uncover it, you need to share it with the world. That, my friends, is your true purpose. The big man upstairs made us all to be great. Strip away the inessentials and you will find the great person you were always meant to be.

CTA: Today, live from the inside out. Practice being your great self instead of letting the outside dictate your day.

Literally, have a great day my friends!

Have a grateful day!

SEPTEMBER 24

The Leftovers

Why is it that so often we treat strangers with more loving kindness, attention, and generosity than we do those closest to us? I see it all the time. We give our best all day long and our family gets the leftovers. The negative story of the day, the bemoaning of the workplace drama, the bad mood because of traffic, and all the rest that we all know is our leftovers.

My favorite is when a friend calls during this regurgitation process and the leftovers suddenly disappear while on the phone laughing and giving a temporary best to the friend. Then of course once the call is over, back to the mood of madness. This spreading of leftovers on your family sets the tone and the energy within your home.

We've all done this. If it's your normal routine, you must recognize what you're really doing. Venting with your closest is fine, but the energy that usually continues from it will carry forth into the evening which usually brings a new drama into your home. This mindset is the culprit. It's like having dirty glasses on. You can't see the truth of the beautiful present moment in front of you because you're still in the past within your mindset.

When you come home, it should be your sanctuary. It should be your respite from the day. This sacred site is where you must do your best work. Give your best love and be most present. They are your treasure and you're tarnishing it with your negative mindset. The truth is that if left unchecked, it will infect everyone and they will carry it forward too. It's how households become negative.

CTA: Awareness is the practice here today, my friends. Awareness of your mind and where it is at all times. It is either serving you or it's sinking you. It's only in daily practice of awareness that you will pull back the curtain of your life and be able to release all the stuff that never works for you. The present is always sunny if you decide to be there on purpose.

Have a great day!

SEPTEMBER 25

The Gift of Reconciliation

I am working on a very creative project right now, which always puts me in a very special plane of thought. This place is open. Open to correct thought and truth.

During this time of contemplation, I was thinking of two of my closest friends who had been in a sort of Cold War of the ego for a long time. Sometimes we wondered if true harmony would ever return to their otherwise-loving friendship.

A Cold War of the ego is when there is pain and suffering believed to be caused outside ourselves by another and then carried as truth for long periods of time. Many times for life.

The only way to cure your own pain and have any true reconciliation is to end the story. The story is all the evidence you have gathered, catalogued, and stored in your file of pain and anger. This is the vault that causes disease, anxiety, and a low energy life, if we do not empty it and blow the door off for good.

Giving up the story can be very difficult. Your ego loves holding onto it. Chewing on it, enjoying it as an occasional meal and regurgitating it to anyone with ears. This, my friends, is poison. Every time you relive your story, you are drinking poison. This poison affects all your relationships, not just the one whom you are battling. It affects your marriage, your children's perceptions of how to deal with life and it ripples outward into the universe, only to bring back to you, more of the same.

I stand before you today a very proud man. Proud of two friends who have had the Ground Zero conversation of truth. This means airing out all the garbage; and I mean garbage. Letting go of it in order to empty the ugly vault and letting in the love, peace, and harmony that creates all great possibilities.

When you empty this ugly vault, you must now be the witness. The witness of all your old thoughts, trying to get back into the driver seat and re-create the war in some other fashion. Once the olive branch is given, take it! Be grateful for the chance to empty your poison for good and be steadfast in your conviction to lead a newer and higher relationship. This is what I have just seen and I am very happy and proud indeed. They have both come such a long way and now, the possibilities are endless.

CTA: If this sounds like your story, you can change it. Forgive and forgive fully. Accept the apologies from each other and watch your balloon of life energy rise. It will take you away from so many other ugly things as well. Make that call, go see that person, and clear out the dusty vault of your ego.

Have a great day!

SEPTEMBER 26

More On "Great! You're Being Blessed!"

These words were spoken to me when I was going through a very turbulent time in my life, and I wanted to share with you why they were and *are* so powerful to me. They are my go-to words today, when struggles come.

No matter what you're facing, you are constantly being blessed. Your job is to retrain your focus from what is temporary, to what is eternal. It is also your job to realize that spirit is constantly guiding you and wants you to pay attention to the lessons and blessings in each moment while you are in the midst of a struggle or life challenge. You need to become the witness once again.

Struggles are the catalyst to growth and unfolding of your next level of life. Being totally present and looking for the hidden and unhidden blessings must now become your focal point.

Did you ever notice how much closer you become with family and friends when you are in a struggle. The deeper the struggle, the bigger the lessons and blessings (which are the same thing).

We need to grow out of an old place in our hearts and minds, into a new place, where higher knowledge and wisdom exist. The gift of Life produces this growth with us, through us, and most importantly, as us. Our cooperation and trust in this force is the highest and best way through any struggle. It is also the richest pathway to reopen our hearts and minds after the struggle has passed.

When we learn the lesson, and I mean truly learn the lesson from any challenge, we must always act in accordance with that newer, higher knowledge. This way, we help ourselves up the ladder and we share this way with others who may be going through what you have already come through. Paying it forward is always part of being a prosperous person. Giving is receiving.

Let's continue this one tomorrow.

CTA: Be present and know that difficult times are opportunities to grow.

Have a great day!

SEPTEMBER 27

"Great! You're Being Blessed!" *continued*

The goal of human life is to recognize that we are not separate from what is known as God or Spirit or The Universe. We are part of it. Able to create anything and improve any area of our lives. When we come to this knowing and we trust in it, we can be more relaxed and aware through any storm.

Being awake and aware to our duty during these storms of life is where the gold is found. You'll recognize rich blessings, like a swarm of your closest friends there to aid you in any way they can. More hugs and love. Deeper and more meaningful conversations. The coming together of family and relatives. New thoughts, people, and guidance forward will enter your path and so much more. You *need* to be focused on these blessings during your trials.

The higher path counsels that gratitude for these blessings will be your rock and then on the other side, you will have truly grown and are now equipped to pay it forward.

Never let your focus dwell in the pain. Feel it, let it take its course, let it open you up to your most vulnerable, but if you choose faith, trust, and higher awareness through it all, you are a Champion! And you can expect to be further blessed in so many ways.

Counting your blessings is not just a quick spiritual catchphrase, it's meant to be a real practice. This practice always pays huge dividends. You will see.

Take each challenge as what it really is. It's an opportunity to get closer and closer to your true self and your true power.

It is never meant to defeat you, it is there *for* you as a challenge to rise again and grow. This you must do.

Never give up and never give in to the victim mindset. Get back up and move forward in your new faith that you are not separate from true power, but you are indeed part of it.

At the end of your life, you will be able to say that you did your best. Your best for yourself and all those you've touched through your own personal growth and journey.

CTA: Today, if you are in the midst of a storm, give thanks. I know that may be hard, but it shifts your mindset to the power of your spirit and your connection to all that is eternal. You are this power. Stay in it no matter what you face and you will always come through a better you.

Have a great day!

SEPTEMBER 28

You Have Music to Play

This is an absolute Truth. You came forth into the physical world with a purpose. You had an agreement with your higher self to come here to do and be something special. It's more about remembering what that is than it is about finding it.

In order for you to remember your purpose, you must first recognize what you are attracted to. Whatever you dream of doing, get closer to it. The closer you come, the more memory you will have of what it is you are here to do.

Yes, of course, you will do many, many things in life, but there is an area where you will shine like no other. In order to uncover your purpose, you must first get rid of all the junk that is covering it up.

Most of us have our treasure buried under a heap of negative garbage. Your treasure is surely under there and you are the only one that can get to it. You have the only key.

Think of it like this, the baggage that we hold onto, including fear, anger, frustration, victim mindedness, jealousy, envy, greed, martyrdom, hatred, lack, and loss, are like a low, out-of-frequency radio channel. You can't quite make out the song because it's mostly just static and noise.

Our job is to clean up our own frequency in order to clearly hear the song. Our song.

What will happen as you go about this noble task is that the release of the need or desire to see life through these old lenses. Did you ever notice that once you have become one of these negative energies like anger, it is so easy to pepper your entire day, and everyone in it, with all it's equally negative cohorts? It's *all* just an old pair of glasses you no longer need to see life through. Your true 20/20 vision will return to you by shedding your need for, and attachment to, these old glasses. This you must do.

CTA: Do your very best to see with rosy lenses today.

Have a great day!

SEPTEMBER 29

Overreaction: The art of stressful living

We've been trained by each other to overreact to just about everything in life. Even the so-called reality shows give us this as their lesson. High drama sells best.

Therein lies the issue. We've been trained to believe it's just part of life, when in truth, it's just a bad habit. What does overreaction bring to your life but stress, anxiety, anger, worry, and fear? We're practicing the art of life in the wrong direction.

Even those who call themselves our civic leaders feed us more. They feed us what's wrong with everything instead of leading us to what's right. Overreaction is your ego taking you in the direction of needing to apologize in some way, but most will not do this either. The ego hates to admit it's wrong even when all the evidence is in. How many times have you assumed a story to be 100% true in your mind and then reacted with the fury of anger, revenge, punishing words, and aggressive expression, only to discover you were wrong?

The ego will make you immediately defend your bad behavior instead of apologizing. The drama now widens, when the fire could have been put out early. The other is now offended, kicking their own ego into action and the drama is in full swing. Sound familiar? How wide you let the fire burn depends on how awake and mindful you are to where this is now heading. Most will let the city burn before they take responsibility for their overreaction. Apology is the water to the fire, and forgiveness is the act of understanding and freedom for both parties.

Let's continue this one tomorrow.

CTA: Think about your own life. Are there apologies you need to give? Or maybe forgiveness?

Have a great day!

SEPTEMBER 30

Overreaction: The art of stressful living *continued*

We are no longer taught by our leaders to take responsibility for or own minds, words and actions, when in truth, we are completely responsible for all. Overreaction is being irresponsible with your energy.

Your body, mind and overall offering is in temporary chaos when in a reactive state. It's no good for you. It's no good for any part of you. If your current life situation is mostly about this vibe, you need to learn about calm, confident response. This is a completely different approach to life and it draws a completely different response from life.

When you are in harmony with the positive, positive happens in return. Those who use overreaction are attempting to solve a problem with anger or intimidation. Very effective for sure in some cases, but the destruction it leaves in our lives is staggering. With diligent practice, the calm confident approach brings more permanent harmony, health, and a well-lived journey.

How do you yourself feel when someone comes to you in a reactive state and unloads their negative guns on you to get you to comply with their wishes? Most likely you either respond in kind with your own guns, or you're at least doing it in your head, having a silent war raging through your entire being.

This, my friends, is what we do to each other. We bring down the whole energy around us to the basement. Everyone suffers in this vortex. The answer is to seek the higher path of mindful response. I'm not saying it will always work, but in most cases your ability to stay in your higher realm will always bring a better result. Your own energy is what you're guarding. Your mind is what you're guarding. When your ego is in the driver's seat, you can expect to see yourself in the mirror of another's response. Their face will look somewhat like yours. They will be nervous, angry, and constricted, which is fertile ground for a widened war.

So today's practice is in calming your inner beast to a point where its counsel comes second to the voice of your spirit. Most drive their entire lives with the ego in the driver's seat.

CTA: Today, tame that voice that causes so much trouble and live in the light. Jump in, the water's much warmer.

Have a great day!

OCTOBER 1

Saying Goodbye to Reaction

One of the very best spiritual practices we can ever do for ourselves and everyone around us is non-reaction. Many might think it uncaring if you don't go to a ten with them when a challenge enters the room, when you are actually leading the energy.

Calm confidence is the alternative to angry, fearful, or nervous reaction. It's choosing a higher response. You have the ability to achieve this level of the mind. It's just conscious practice my friends. It's choosing faith in a higher hand, your partner in all of this Earthly stuff. It's your true power.

You should be confident. Not arrogant. Calm, resourceful, positive, problem-solving confidence. "I can" energy instead of constricted, negative reaction. Television trains us to be reactive. Our nervous parents or negative people surrounding us spread this energy. You possess the key to ending this underlying nervous vibration within you. It takes time, sometimes outside help, spiritual mentors like higher-minded friends, and a host of other positive self-improvement gurus. They help to change the lenses in your perception glasses. You learn to see life and yourself in a different light. Non-reaction is a huge door opener to inner peace and confident forward motion.

CTA: So today's practice is in the art of non-reaction. Your inner speech must be that you can handle this differently this time. Give space before you let your ego fly its flag. Go ahead and fake it 'til you make it for a bit. You have to be able to act it in order for your being to feel it. It will challenge you greatly if your normal reaction is dug in like most. It's like trying on a whole new style of dress. In short order you'll feel great in your new duds. Go get it!!!

Have a great day!

OCTOBER 2

Truth

This is the big one. This is the one to consistently strive toward if you want to rise to your highest potential in this human adventure.

What is truth? Truth is knowing who you really are. Plain and simple. You are a God. You have the amazing ability to literally create your experience as a spirit in human clothing. The spirit within you is a singular piece of the truth of all that is. I am that, you are that, everything you see is that. God is everything, and we are part of God, get it?

On earth, we are dual-natured. We are both spirit and ego, positive and negative, opposites in one human form. We learn and grow our souls from this contrast. In order to live an amazing, positive, prosperous human experience, we must live from our spirit. Realizing that the ego or negative polarity to spirit is our false self, the angry one, the fearful one, the one that whispers that you are not good enough, pretty enough, smart enough, and all the other lies, will begin to become your guidepost back to your true self, or spirit, instead of you becoming the negative reactionary that is your ego.

Just knowing that we have a true self and false self is an awakening for most. I know it was for me. The big secret is that you simply must live from your true nature as much as possible. This attracts to you that very energy and then you will see the true power you possess. It is amazing, and it's yours. Tapping into it on purpose is the gift that keeps on giving. To yourself and others.

Your True Nature consists of, but is not limited to, the following (in tomorrow's entry). Live these truths in your every thought, interaction and deed. Give these energies of love away freely and generously. This is your true purpose for being here. The more we all practice living the art of love, the less we will see of the horrors we witness on this planet every day. You must do your part.

Let's continue this one tomorrow.

CTA: Live in truth. Always be honest to who you are.

Have a great day!

OCTOBER 3

Truth *continued*

Truths of who you really are include these energies and spiritual actions.

Love

Kindness

Easy forgiveness

Easy apologies

Inner peace

Calm confidence

Generosity

Laughter

Empathy

Compassion

Uplifting others

Creativity

Collaboration

Sharing

Joy

Unwavering Faith

Awareness

Inspiration

Peace

Strength

Daring

Adventure

Positive Attitude

Optimism

Prosperity

True Wealth

Mentoring

Humor

Praise

Worthiness

Friendship

Trustworthiness

Accepting others as they are

CTA: Today and for the rest of your days, your job is to give these away as only you can. You have a truly unique way of giving these, so simply share your truth. Not your ego's version of the truth. Give and live only by your true nature, the God within you. Your divine destination awaits you, my friends, and what a ride it will be.

Have a great day!

OCTOBER 4

True Communication

If we wish to have true communication with another, we must come from a place of the heart, rather than the judgment of the ego.

The ego always has its own agenda. Attempting to solve issues with someone, or even attempting to understand one's plight, has to be balanced with compassion, forgiveness and a desire to give instead of the desire to tear down another, especially when we love another.

The old paradigm or belief that your anger, disappointment, judgment, or holier-than-thou place you speak from, actually helps to heal another, comes from an old, worn-out position that is grounded in the ego mind alone. Unless you choose to see things through the true lens of spiritual connection to one another, you're not giving your very best. Your ego is in the driver's seat.

True communication comes from the desire to heal, not to punish. Yes, you can bring a serious, necessary discussion to the table as a result of being angry or disappointed at another in your life, but when it comes to the discussion itself, you must do your very best to keep these emotions in check during that important conversation.

Putting yourself in their shoes for a time will help to open your heart to the possibility that your position may be somewhat skewed toward the desire to punish rather than find common, loving ground from which to rebuild.

Healing or helping another move forward after they've made a mistake or shown bad judgment will require your will to see life through their particular place in their journey. No, they may not be where you are. They too are struggling with things just like you, only in a different way. We are all here to learn and teach particular lessons. Some we may never understand or agree with, but that is not our place to cast a judgment that hurts instead of heals. In other words, a one-size solution does not fit all.

Let's continue this one tomorrow.

CTA: Be empathetic and compassionate in your communication with others.

Have a great day!

OCTOBER 5

True Communication *continued*

So often, we get past some struggle in our own life only to judge another in their struggle that we know nothing about. The lens of negative judgment as a main tool of solving issues only leads to broken relationships and closed communication.

If they are in your life, do your best to love them. They are there to learn from you and to teach *you* something about yourself. You may not love what they do, and there are in fact times to close the door on some relationships, but the ones that you value, or have some issues with, must be guided by your higher self in order to be constructive instead of destructive. There is a way, and it's called the way of the heart.

The heart will tell you to be compassionate and forgiving, because that is exactly what you would want from someone you love if you were in his or her shoes.

The heart wants to heal and grow relationships. The ego just wants to be right or superior to another in some way.

The heart will lead the relationship to its highest potential, while the ego simply wants to bring shame and guilt upon another as the main tool of trying to teach.

Most often these methods lead more to causing self-esteem issues and closing others off to their higher purpose. Remember that those you love may take what you say to heart for the rest of their lives. They may not be mindful enough to know that your opinion of them should never define them. Imagine you keeping your self-image in a negative place from taking on someone else's opinion of you as fact for your whole life. Maybe you're doing that right now. My friends, *never* let yourself be defined by the negative opinions of others. It's a life trap. *You* define yourself and your life. Don't give anyone else that power.

When you put others in a box by your opinion of who they are, you do them a great disservice at the very least, and create a potentially stigmatized life at the worst. Your words can harm or heal. Healing is your natural state.

Let's continue this one tomorrow

CTA: Practice the fine art of understanding; remove judgment.

Have a great day!

OCTOBER 6

True Communication *continued*

One of life's main lessons you must learn and practice is that we are all trying to get it right in our own way. If you love someone, you must do your very best to lift them rather than lower them. You can be very honest and constructive without the ego's demand to persecute them in the process. Choosing to persecute, as a rule, will only bring back to you a circumstance for you to feel the same judgment. Maybe not in the exact same way, but in the same vein. What goes around comes around. That's why you always need to give only what you want to see show up in your own life. Judgment and punishment are two that I bet you do not want.

The overarching lesson to learn from today's entry is that each of us struggles with certain ego-centric demons, whether it's the angst of youth and early life decision making, an addiction, low self-esteem, anger issues, anxiety and depression, or any of the rest of the challenges of the human experience. It is only through the knowledge and truth that we all face similar challenges that we will learn to forgive instead of judge, heal instead of harm, and love instead of hate.

Helping another rise always helps you to rise. Conversely, being punitive or judgmental as a regular practice, only keeps you separate from others, including your true self and higher spiritual planes. The good life.

CTA: Today, if you've chosen to punish or judge without putting on your glasses of compassion and trying to understand the plight of another, bring peace and love back in the room by a heartfelt apology, a loving hug, and the understanding that you, too, have faced or someday may face the same situation. When we choose to give our best self to a tough situation and seek to understand, we will always find true communication in the room and a loving solution to move forward from. It *always* comes back to love, my friends. Give that.

Have a great day!

OCTOBER 7

Giving Thanks In Advance: The ultimate act of faith

When you decide to co-create your life with your higher self, or spirit, you will constantly be practicing acts of faith as the higher path to your goals and dreams.

Saying thank you for your end result in advance solidifies it in your mind and the mind of the benevolent source that brings all dreams to life. You never do it alone. Your dreams are always brought to you through your persistent belief in them, and your belief in your own ability to manifest them from thought to physical reality. It's how *everything* works.

What you attract into your life is always based on your thoughts. What thoughts are you most consistently thinking? Are they positive and self-assured? Or are they lower in energy, self-doubting, feeling less than, discouraged, and defeated? It's very common, but you hold the key to shifting your life into a much higher gear. You need to change your pattern: your thought pattern, your pattern of actions, and your usual mantras of doom and gloom, in the form of your outward speech to others.

Your pattern displays your inner beliefs about yourself and your life's path. We are ALL creators my friends. We all have the power to change our old, negative, powerless pattern into a force of amazing health, wealth, and happiness. You just need the road map.

From the standpoint of our higher selves, we are all the same. We come from the same home, which is not here. We all go home in the end. What we decide to do here is our own choice. Choosing to live at the highest levels can become your life's message. Giving thanks to God in advance of your new life's unfolding, is acting in faith that you will be lead to it and it will be lead to you. His power, your body. Trust.

Let's continue this one tomorrow.

CTA: Have an attitude of gratitude.

Have a great day!

OCTOBER 8

Giving Thanks in Advance *continued*

Shed the doubt and get into the flow of your power. It's very real. It's not magic, although the miracles that you begin to recognize in your life every day will seem very magical indeed. You've always possessed the wand. You just have to use it every day as your new calling card.

What if I said that I took a brief trip to the future, say a year from now. And you started today to live your life spreading good news only. Spreading laughter instead of gossip. Speaking of health instead of illness. Speaking about your goals instead of past failures and moving in faith that you are a beautiful part of the whole, instead of separate and alone? What if you decided to try new things and meet new people? Bought some new clothes and updated your image? What if you became a giver instead of a taker? What if you decided to love everyone the best you can, instead of judge their journey, which you really know nothing about. What if you decided to start today loving yourself completely, instead of loathing part or all of you. What if?

I just came back from next year and I'm happy to report, *you* are amazing! You have many new friends, you are so much happier. You can truly see you've changed! I'm so proud of you, and so are your family and friends!

You accepted life's most difficult challenge and you've succeeded in finding your true self. Your true power and independence! You've taken the reigns and you know your true self-worth. You are a beautiful piece of universe, not a lowly human trying to get by.

Live your life from this truth. You are so much more than you believe yourself to be. Wake up and live, my friends. Get in the driver's seat and never let go of the wheel. Today is your day. Seek all the wisdom you can get your hands on and start peeling away the lies you tell yourself. You are no longer a victim. You've decided to be the winner you are. God is *for* you. What does that leave out? Your power is yours for the taking. Start today and never stop your intentional growth. A year from now you will be an entirely new person and your new surroundings will validate it.

CTA: Today, give your old record the boot. When you are no longer afraid to let go of the past, and you choose to give thanks for the blessings to come, you will have entered the flow. Have faith, speak to it and go after your dreams, knowing that it's only a matter of time now.

Have a great day!

OCTOBER 9

Acts of Faith

Life is all about the title of this entry today. The more we practice this art, the more positive life energy will come through us to help us build an amazing life.

What is an act of faith? Any movement forward in your life toward something you want or dream about will include many obstacles and challenges. Acts of faith are the way through.

Taking acts of faith is the art of positive actions, based on the knowing that you are helped by spirit. Trusting in spirit to guide your path and bring to you the necessary people, skills and experiences you need, in order to reach your desired goal.

This is also called the art of co-creation, consciously choosing to live in the higher energies of spirit in all your endeavors and relationships. Success lives here.

Always remember that challenges come to you as a gift to sharpen your sword and your soul, a.k.a. growth.

Having a bigger life requires you to grow big. If you take this conscious path toward your dreams, once you get them, you'll be able to make anything happen. You will have learned the formula for true and lasting success. Love, career, friendships, and an exciting journey are all found by using this formula.

If you're fearful of taking any action in life that you know will help you toward your dream, take it anyway. Feel the fear and then use it as your trigger to act. Always remember that acting brave is always the precursor to actually becoming brave. It's simply about practicing anything you want to be better at. Making decisions and acting on them is no different. The more you do it, the better you get. Never back down from a seeming obstacle. Blow through it, go around it, or figure it out. But never let it stop you. Acting in faith toward your dream is a totally spiritual practice. It brings the spice to your life.

CTA: Today, make a move, shake it up, and move forward. You are watched over, guided, and protected. Once you choose to do it this certain way, you will be attracting all you need. Success is imminent. What you focus your attention on always grows, so make sure your attention is always focused on the good stuff.

Have a great day!

OCTOBER 10

The Gift of Complete Attention

One of the greatest gifts we can give to others is our complete attention. In creating new relationships or our relationships with our family and friends, looking a person in the eyes while talking to them connects you at a much deeper level. It lets the other person know you care and that they are completely heard.

The eyes are truly the window to the soul and when eye contact and presence of attention are one, it removes all barriers and lets in a whole new level of communication and understanding. The ego, your social mask and gatekeeper is no longer a factor in that moment. This is how strong connections and beautiful, trusting relationships are formed.

CTA: Try it today and see the difference it makes in all your personal interactions.

Have a great day!

OCTOBER 11

Drama

Drama is always created by overreaction to a situation and then that energy is spread like a toxic wave. The way to freedom from drama is to respond rather than react. Creating space between the overreaction of yourself or someone else is where a different energy can be brought to the situation.

If you overreact to someone else's drama, you've given up your power to change the energy of the situation to a calm, peaceful place. You see this done all the time by the Dog Whisperer, who totally changes a barking pit bull by his calm, peaceful energy. Usually in seconds. We all have barking pit bulls in our lives. They are there so we can learn not to fight fire with fire, but to help bring others out of the fire with a higher energy of love, understanding, or compassion.

It's like being a people whisperer. It's therefore responding rather than counter reaction that brings peace to a fiery situation.

CTA: Be your very best at responding today. It is better to be silent many times when your ego is screaming to react.

Have a great day!

OCTOBER 12

Clarity

Clarity of mind comes when we learn to recognize the voice of our true selves versus the voice of the ego. Spirit will always be the voice of truth, which includes the energies of Love, Faith, Compassion, Loyalty, Gratitude, Purpose, Charity, Friendship, and Belief in yourself and your talents. The Ego is that other voice that tells us we are not worthy, we're ugly, we can't possibly do this or that, hatred, jealousy, gossip, fear, and doubt. We all hear both sides in our daily lives. The key to a fulfilling, fun, and rich life is to recognize and live by your higher energy and tame that dark voice by consistently practicing the good stuff.

Remember, we always get back what we give. Give your best self and you'll enjoy a glorious life.

CTA: Practice some needed silence today. Just be for a while. In this space you bring forth Clarity.

Have a great day!

OCTOBER 13

Body Language

Body language is a telltale sign about our state of mind, our energy, and what vibe we are giving out to the world. Do you walk with hunched shoulders or a wear a face that says, "life is a struggle and I'm surviving?" Once you ask yourself what energy you're giving out to others, you'll be in the present moment, noticing your posture, your scowl, smile, or how you're thinking in that moment.

This is where we hold our true power to change. Ask yourself, "what do I want to project, so that I am open and welcoming rather than closed and disinterested?" Your body language shows on the outside what you are living on the inside. Change your thoughts, change your body language, and you'll change your life. One small choice in this direction every day will become a huge change in a short period of time. Go get it today!

CTA: Become aware of your own body language today. Recognize what it's saying in comparison to your honest thoughts within. Many times we are projecting aggressive body language while speaking calmly. Another will always read your vibe not so much from your words, but your body language and tone.

Have a great day!

OCTOBER 14

Passion

Passion is the fuel that brings dreams to reality. No matter what you're passionate about, there's a way to create your life and your livelihood around it. The most successful entrepreneurs in the world attribute their success in large part to the passion they have for what they do.

Passion is also an energy in itself, welling up from within and giving the feeling of creativity, ideas, excitement, and joy for one of your naturally favorite things to do. Modeling the successful actions of someone who has found great reward in the area of your passion is a great way to get started in creating your successful life. Learn everything you can about that person and their journey and then bring your very own style and energy to the table. As they say, do what you love for your livelihood and you'll never work a day in your life. Don't put any limits on what you can accomplish. You are an unlimited, goal-seeking being by your very nature. Go after your dreams every day and live the life you deserve.

CTA: What are you passionate about? If you said not much or nothing, you must begin the exploration. Ask your spirit what it loves to do. The answer will come as you do your part to get out there and explore. Start that today.

Have a great day!

OCTOBER 15

A Practice In Gratitude

Raising our positive vibe will always bring us more of the good stuff into our lives. Like attracts like. Positive attracts positive.

Gratitude for all that you are, all that you have, and all the blessings to come is the perfect vibration to live your life within. It simply brings your life into focus and expands your awareness of truth.

I have a simple practice that keeps me in a good freeing tone and energy. From this place my day is created and the same good feeling is given away as a beacon for others to rise and feel good too. Adopting this daily practice will raise your life to a new level and The Universe will keep sending you more good stuff to share. Your cooperation with the flow of positive energy means you have become a conduit and channel for the betterment of the whole. This is where a magical life becomes your everyday reality.

The practice goes like this; upon waking up every day, give a silent thank you for a new day to raise your spirit and the spirit of others. Then go through your day intentionally recognizing each good thing that occurs. Starting with your conversations, interactions, and each opportunity life gives you to shine your unique form of light.

Each moment either gives you blessings or the opportunity to bless another. For each of these moments, become aware while you are in the midst of it. Be the silent witness behind your expression of giving. Then simply give a silent thank you each and every time.

What happens when you take up this new practice in being grateful will be a momentum. You'll begin to notice more and more gifts to be grateful for, either in giving or receiving. Both actions are gifts to you.

Then at the end of your day, when you've loved your family up and your head hits the pillow, look back on your day and give thanks one more time, even for any struggle that has taught you something. It's all for you. Your job is to work with this energy and become aligned with it through your awareness and gratitude for it all. Your life will change. You'll never go back.

CTA: Today, count each blessing by giving each one your awareness, love, and recognition. This is the way you enter and stay in the positive flow of life. Greatness awaits you today. Jump in. The water's warm.

Have a great day!

OCTOBER 16

Inner Peace

Inner peace is the golden ticket we all need to cultivate in our lives. It is that place within us that is undisturbed by outer events. It is our inner anchor in life's many turbulent storms.

We are all born with this still pond inside us, but the world and its million distractions and attention-grabbers steer us away from knowing such a place. We need a time of silence each day that is strictly devoted to calmness and quiet. Even a few minutes a day will lead to this natural place of inner healing and solace.

Much is said about meditation and its effects on our overall health and well-being, but many feel this practice is too weird, difficult, or unnecessary in our fast-paced, dog-eat-dog world. In fact, meditation is the practice of getting reacquainted with the calm, non-reactive space within us that assures us that the three-alarm things of the outer world will not overtake and sweep us into its negative vortex.

Inner peace, therefore, becomes a refuge of faith, that whatever the storm of the day presents to us, we always have that calm port within us that also becomes the calm port for others. Remember that the energy you present when trouble occurs will be a dominant force in the overall perception of those around you. You need to become the peace you want to see and have in your own life. The only way you obtain that inner peace is to uncover it with the very practice of it. It's a beautiful day to do just that. Tell your boss that I gave you the rest of the day off to practice some peace. In fact, take the week off! LOL.

CTA: Set aside some much needed alone time today. Create a peaceful spot for this. Ask for no interruptions and give yourself this beautiful gift.

Have a great day!

OCTOBER 17

The Gift of Laughter

Laughter is truly the best natural medicine. We've all heard it, but how often do we intentionally create it for one another? We are all blessed to have funny people in our lives and they naturally attract others because of their humor.

A chuckle is one thing, but a huge belly laugh is enough to totally change the very physiology of the mind and the body. Laughter actually makes us healthier.

If you or someone you know is going through a tough time, you need to inject some laughter into the day on purpose. If you are one who possesses a naturally crazy, demented sense of humor, you are meant to use that to benefit those around you. You are a healer. Give it away as much as possible. Not just to those you know, but anyone you come into contact with.

This energy of humor alone can transform the darkness of this world to light. In our business we have always used laughter to create an awesome, positive work atmosphere that literally spreads into everything we do. We love to hire funny, positive-minded people because we know they will lift our day and the days of our customers. It works every time it's used. Every time. When you brighten someone's day with a good hearty laugh, everyone benefits.

CTA: Today, make sure laughter is at the top of your daily intentions. Create it, spread it, and live by it. It is one of the greatest blessings of life.

Have a great day!

OCTOBER 18

Talent

Everyone on this planet is blessed with at least one special talent that they need to discover and nurture. If you don't know yours, you need to start with what you are naturally attracted to. Whether it's music, sports, art, or even things like inventing a new product for whatever you're into, you really need to further uncover and express this talent in your own unique way.

It is part of our life's plan to utilize our God-given talents to expand and grow in something we love to do. In our business we purposely try to bring out and expose the special talents of each of our team members in order to place that person in an area where they naturally flourish. They feel good about themselves and in no time, new talents are discovered that they didn't even know they had. It's one of the great joys of life.

It's never too late to steer your life toward new territory, doing something you love. Many people bury their talents in exchange for the safety of an hourly wage and a job that is lifeless to them. If this is you and you dream of doing something more, something bigger than ever before using your talent, do it! Even if you start on the side of your current career.

Sometimes it's good to enlist a partner with talents that complement yours. We call that a mastermind group in our business. Gathering different talents and heading for the same goal. The key to expanding your talent and taking it to an exciting new level is to do a bit of it every day. It will grow! And so will you.

Never bury your talents and die with your music left inside you. Remember the time will pass anyway. You can do it. Go 200 feet at a time and you will reach your destination. Happiness is not the destination; happiness is the way we get there. Do what you love and watch your world expand.

CTA: Do one thing today to start in that direction.

Have a great day!

OCTOBER 19

The Magic of Life Is Found In the Ordinary

When you live your life from a conscious state, awake and expecting great things to happen, you'll always see the magic in the seemingly ordinary moments of the day. If you go through life in an unconscious state, which is unfortunately the norm, you will surely miss most of what life is trying to give you. When you do harken back to the best times of your life to this point, it will be *moments* you recall. Not days, but those special moments of laughter, the birth of your children, special vacations, funny things you did with your best friends, etc.

These were all snippets of time when we recognized the greatness of these moments. We need to be aware that we helped to create these moments and that's what we do each and every day in the ordinary course of our lives. Instead of looking at life through the lens of happenstance or coincidence, we should immerse ourselves in each moment, each interaction, and relationships throughout our day. We should be conscious and present long enough to create special moments, going deeper than usual in gratitude for these interactions. Give your best in those moments and include compliments, praise, and laughter on purpose.

When we choose to add these positive energies to the ordinary, moments become memorable and extraordinary instead of flat and mundane. You should control and create your daily experience in presence, which is where your true power is. Magic is truly in the ordinary when we *decide* to make it extraordinary. So today, practice being present in all your interactions and create and spread the good stuff. What you give out will always come back to you multiplied.

CTA: Give your best today and create some great memories.

Have a great day!

OCTOBER 20

Perception

This is the one that gets us all in trouble if we are not mindful and self-aware. As we all know, everyone has a very unique and individual way we perceive our world and the millions of experiences we will have in our lifetime, so this one area of life we need to get right. It will be the deciding factor of whether we have a great life or one filled with drama, strife, and constant misperception.

It is our very thoughts and beliefs that create our unique life experience, so we have to go inside ourselves every day in order to know just what our pattern of thoughts and beliefs are. Most of us will never embark on this crucial journey. Mostly because it can be painful to admit that it's us who may be the problem instead of the world outside that is doing it to us. My friends, it is always how we perceive the world that causes us pleasure or pain. Everyday life offers us a chance to look at ourselves and how we process our lives through the lens of perception. If you find you are a constant complainer or judge of everyone and everything, you are the problem.

The good news is that when we decide to take 100% responsibility for ourselves, our thoughts, and our actions based on those thoughts, we can change those negative perceptions and thus, change our whole experience of this one life we have. It can be the biggest challenge of your life to take complete responsibility for your life's expression and perceptions when your ego demands that it's everyone else that's the cause of your pain, anger, fear, envy and the rest of the lower energies. But I promise you, *it is worth it*!

If you decide to take this journey inside, you will need to be strong, honest, and willful. You must be able to forgive yourself first for past decisions and then never need to look back. Your past is your past and it has no bearing on new decisions and directions. Most of our perceptions come from childhood conditioning and surrounding perceptions of others that we simply absorbed as truth. Question your thoughts and perceptions constantly! Chances are you are telling yourself a lie about 75% of the time. Ask yourself if what you are perceiving is 100% true or just a negative judgment or old belief.

Self-development author Byron Katie has great books on what she calls "The Work." It gives you great tools to help you change your negative perceptions into ones that will surely serve you rather than sink you. I highly recommend her books as a guide in your journey of self-discovery and truth.

CTA: Today, watch your mind and listen to what it says in each interaction with those around you. Notice what its demands upon you are and give yourself some space between thought and outer actions and you will start to see how your perceptions create your reality. As the famous saying goes, no one said it would be easy, just that it would be worth it. You can do it for sure! Go get it!

Have a great day!

OCTOBER 21

Vision

In life, most people will let the wind decide where they go until they wonder how they got to where they are. In many cases it's not as pretty as they would like. It is virtually guaranteed that if this is sounds like you, you either never had a clear vision of what you wanted for yourself or it got lost along the way.

The good news is that it's never too late to create a new vision for yourself and your relationship to those around you. You need to start with some quiet contemplation and using the theater of your mind to create an exciting new movie of you and the life of your dreams. This vision must include seeing yourself in a truly positive light, realizing that *you* are the vehicle of change and you can most assuredly steer your vehicle to a beautiful new place. As the saying goes, you must first become the change you want to see in your life.

This means envisioning yourself saying and doing right-minded things, becoming a person of great character and integrity, and attracting to yourself the kind of people into your life that you are proud to call friends. This is the path of power and it always leads to great things. You'll need to see yourself as no longer part of the traditional complaining, competitive, ego-dominated world, but as a light that others can count on and absorb.

This is true of your closest relationships, whether it's your marriage you want to improve or a friendship that had gone cold. If you can create this new vision for any part of your life first in your heart and mind, you will then need to share it with the ones you want to include in this vision. If it is a heartfelt vision and you want it with a burning desire, the others will either come along or they won't. In either case, you will use these findings to help steer your new ship forward. It's the surest way to get and stay unstuck and flowing toward your dream life.

It is true that some may not want or even understand your new journey but it's your journey. Those who were meant to be there will be there. It is absolutely essential that this new vision should be as big and grand as you can make it. No detail should be left out. It's like creating an exciting business plan for your life. I promise you that there are no limitations to this process or in life. Only those that we lie to ourselves about.

Make this vision so exciting that it propels you into positive action each day. In order to see your destination, you have to know where it is and what it looks like. Plan it like a beautiful vacation and then go about getting there. All the right people and assistance will appear for you when you decide to never let go of the vision and always move forward. Life is meant to be lived to the fullest or you are simply wasting time and letting the wind blow you where *it* wants instead of you taking the wheel and going where *you* want. The world is your oyster when you stick to a positive vision of your life. Today, be an awesome creator of a great day and then simply repeat that intention every day. You will see what you envisioned for yourself coming clearly into view in no time.

CTA: Today, spend half an hour in contemplation and begin to envision the life you would love to have. Then begin thinking about it, speaking about it as if it is inevitable and taking positive actions in its direction. This is the creative process. You are the creator. Get going.

Have a great day!

OCTOBER 22

Compassion

This is the energy that comes straight from the heart. It's the one that allows us to imagine what we would feel like in someone else's shoes. Sometimes we are placed in situations on purpose in order to recognize the all-important face of compassion. For many, it's not an easy emotion. So many have been raised in homes where they were not afforded such a vital human need themselves, so their hearts were hardened and subsequently closed. This is fertile ground for the ego to take hold and tell us that here is nothing we need to do and that we are separate from our true source and those around us. But the truth is the exact opposite.

In order to get what we need from the outside world, we need to expose ourselves each day and give the gift of compassion to others. Simply taking an interest in the struggle of another and giving your special brand of love will be a gift for both of you. So many have been given so much and it is up to them give back to the closed off, unconscious and lost, in the form of wisdom, talent, kindness, prosperity, and compassion.

Giving is so much more than just money. A simple encouraging conversation with someone could change their day and even the course of their life. We need to teach others to fish instead of just giving the fish. Teaching someone how to lift him or herself is the biggest act of compassion we can give. It says that we took the time to give of our inner treasure so that the one struggling may also rise, but with the wisdom and talent they have been taught. Compassion is therefore the paying forward that we hear so much about. Giving your attention, time, and gifts is giving your very best.

CTA: Today, if you know someone who is going through a tough time, offer true compassion. Give them a call and spread your love.

Have a great day!

OCTOBER 23

Harmony

The energy of harmony is very special indeed. It says that different collective energies can come together as one in order to peacefully coexist, live, dream, create, and work together as a conscious team. We are all in tune to this energy. It's created when we trust, respect, and value the differences we each bring to the table. Harmony demands that we leave our egos at the door and open ourselves to the very best of our collaborative and creative selves.

You can also experience harmony with nature on your own. Who doesn't like being outside on a beautiful day with nothing to do but be grateful for that day? That's harmony. We all feel it and we should all create it every chance we get. It needs to first be an intention and then the subtle action of harmonious speech and conscious listening.

Laughter is the fastest way I know to create a harmonious atmosphere. It's instantaneous. Harmony at home is absolutely crucial to maintain balance in your life. If you're constantly bickering, sniping, and gossiping at home, you are completely disconnected from harmony. Home is the most important place to create and practice it. Who wants to come home to a house filled with negative energy?

Always remember that in each moment, we get to choose our thoughts, speech, and actions. Harmony says to hug your spouse instead of complaining about your day. Harmony says to appreciate what we love about each other instead of noticing the human flaws. It says to outwardly express the greatness of one another on a regular basis, especially our families and friends.

In the end my friends, it's a narrow path home. One that few will take on in a purposeful way. It is everything we all want, but we are 100% responsible to create it. *You* sculpt your life.

CTA: Today, intentionally create harmony at home and at work. Create laughter, collaborate instead of competing, and express gratitude to all those who bring joy to your life. If you do this your day will have been purposeful and awesome. Go get it! You are the master painter of your life.

Have a great day!

OCTOBER 24

Your New Core Beliefs

One of the most important pieces of life information you must know and become aware of is that you are a being of energy beneath your physical, outer shell. The real you is in fact the ghost within the machine.

This ghost, a.k.a. your spirit, is the one who's animating and using your earthly machine for your temporary visit here. While we are here, we are all dual-natured beings. Both positive and negative. Opposites within one form.

We are made up of many different feeling energies. Ones we like and ones that make us feel less than our best. Sometimes, much less. We are really like an energy ladder. Learning to take control of this ladder, intentionally rise, and stay on the higher rungs is the gold we are all really seeking.

At the very bottom of the ladder, we have our more earthly or primal energies. These serve to protect us in some ways and get us in trouble in many other ways. Some of these would be described by us as lower states if mind, like anger, disappointment, hatred, competition, fear, disharmony, nervousness, anxiety, martyrdom, self-pity, and many others in the realm of what's known as ego consciousness. The ego side of us tells us lies about ourselves and everyone else. You know this voice. We all do. It's here to give us contrast. Not to believe it's actually us. It's not.

Moving up the ladder, however, we begin to find higher energies of the spirit. These would include love in all its forms and symbols. Heart-centered energies. The ones that make you feel good; joy, happiness, trust, inner peace, calm confidence, giving, receiving, prospering, feelings of health, wealth, and beauty. This is our true voice. Our voice from home. This is the eternal voice of truth and all knowing. You have total access to it because you are part of it. Not separate and outside of it. Getting to know all your energies will allow you to use the lower ones as your internal alarm to wake back up and shine instead. This is the noble practice. Make it part of your daily intention to awaken a bit more.

CTA: Spread your light on purpose today. It's what we all need.

Have a great day!

OCTOBER 25

Dis-ease

We know all about the things that play a part in causing human illness. Mostly we concentrate on food, manmade toxins (redundant), lack of exercise, and heredity.

In truth, my friends, we must focus on mind first. Your mind must be mastered by you in order to steer your body's proper function. Your mind must be mastered by your spirit (heart/soul) in order for you to know optimal overall health. See, a faith filled, grateful, confident, calm mindset is fertile ground for success on all levels, especially your health.

If you're like most, you're taking your cues and counsel from fear and doubt. These two culprits of many of our moments of dis-ease will actually build up resistance in your mind and body. This resistance slows down and blocks your life force from flowing as it was intended. Everything here is designed to bring us back to our light. Some wait until they go all the way home before they see it again. They get snagged in a low-energy existence.

I say you don't have to wait to live in the light. The more you begin to repair your mindset by throwing out fear and doubt as old mechanics with outdated tools, the more light you let back into your mind's eye. This will be an uncomfortable new viewpoint to you at first, but it becomes much clearer. It will be like glasses sent from heaven. They are. Put them on. Never take them off.

Let's continue this one tomorrow.

CTA: Move away from dis-ease into a state of ease by training yourself to think positive, healing thoughts.

Have a great day!

OCTOBER 26

Dis-ease *continued*

We see so many who are trapped in the illness mindset. They bemoan their every ache, pain, and new symptom of the latest woe as their daily talking points. You can count on it. This was most likely a habit they grew up with or have fallen under the spell of influences around them.

We as humans love to chat. It's how we connect, but there are two levels of conversation with very different effects on our mindset and life flow. Yes, negative and positive. Of course we can talk about circumstances we perceive as negative! Healing through connection is a must. The friction in your flow comes into play when you begin to implement your woes as part of *who you are* rather than a bump you're in the process of overcoming through faith-filled thoughts, spoken word, and actions. It's not ignoring your pain, it's speaking spirit (faith) into it. Weave a new story of who you are instead of the ailment talk show.

If you've become very attached to this story, it will take time to get comfortable with your new way, but aren't you worth it? You hold yourself in a negative vibe with this old habit. It blocks perfect healing, happiness, and higher health. Your mind is where it all begins.

CTA: Today, wake up to your negative conversations. Aren't they filled with that low energy you actually want to rid yourself of? They feed each other. Your self-talk, spoken word attitude and how you project it affects your health. Reversal of habit begins today. See how hard it is *not* to talk about this comfortable sidekick. Your eyes will begin to open to how you may be sabotaging your health, wealth, and happiness. You can do it.

Have a great day!

OCTOBER 27

Inspiration

The very meaning of this life-giving word is "in spirit." When we see, feel or hear another's extraordinary action or words, it resonates in the deepest part of our true selves, our soul. Inspiration tells us that anything is possible and we too have this power.

We are all naturally tuned to the energy of inspiration and we can experience it every day once we become more aware of our own higher energies. Our journeys have been blessed with the inspiration of others who do extraordinary things in their own way. When we are inspired by another, we too become better if we add these experiences to our innermost selves. You'll find yourself being lighter, more capable, and in tune with your best self when you are inspired. This is your spirit saying go for it! You can do it too! The more you live your life from this place, the more blessed your journey will be.

Inspiration is in fact living from the spirit rather than your lower, can't do it, why bother, victim mindset. The high-energy cocktail of inspiration followed by inspired action is the energy that brings your dreams to life. Without it, you won't have enough gas to get you out of your driveway, much less realize a goal or dream. Inspiring others is done very naturally when you begin to live from this place. In many cases, you won't even be aware you're doing it unless you hear from another that your way has affected their lives in some beautiful way. Living an inspired life requires you to love who you are and the certain, unique way that you do it.

I am inspired every day by my family, my friends, and by total strangers whom I witness doing the right thing. I am inspired by others I see on Facebook, choosing to say something great about their kids, their spouse, or their outlook on a positive life. I must admit that Focusmaster would probably not be in existence if it were not for the inspiration of the movie *Rocky*, which I saw at twelve years old. Nor would I be part of The Old Daley Inn if it were not for the inspiration and vision of my best friends and partners.

When you are in tune to your spirit, inspiration is present at all times. It brings immense joy, energy, and greatness along with it as a constant. We can all be an inspiration to others when we intend to spread it as much as possible. If you've been inspired by anyone in your life, tell them and then try to pay it forward by being your very best.

CTA: Go through this day filled with gratitude for all those who have helped you along by their inspiration. Feel the energy that creates a great life and spread your wealth.

Have a great day!

OCTOBER 28

Encouragement

This is the one gift that you can give away, totally free of charge, and it can change the very course of someone's life.

So many have grown up in homes that offered very little, if any, encouragement. When this happens, there can be deep self-esteem and confidence issues. It is through the encouragement and praise of others that these issues can be healed. We have all encouraged people from time to time, but making the act of encouragement a daily tool in your high-energy journey will be a gift to both the recipient and *you*. Don't you feel great when you know you've shifted someone from a place of despair and fear to a place of personal empowerment?

Encouragement practiced regularly keeps you in your higher awareness and power as a byproduct. You'll feel the energy you created in the other person. We are like tuning forks for the energy of others. What we witness and are exposed to when in the company of another is where they are in their energy. We naturally feel when someone is low and needs some lovin'. It's in both best interests to be lifted and you have the power to do just that.

So today, notice everyone's energy that surrounds you. Try and feel it instead of using your other senses. If someone is out of sorts, give them the gift of encouragement. If you look back in your history, I'll bet you certainly remember the moments when you were encouraged and then succeeded in some way as a result. Even if it were to be freed of a bad head.

CTA: Free some friends today with your power.

Have a great day!

OCTOBER 29

Seek and Ye Shall Find

What the heck does that really mean?

We've heard it said a million times in our lives, but to know what this means and understand it, really know it, will give you a bigger life than you've ever imagined for yourself. The seeking that's referred to is the truth about who you really are and what your purpose is here on earth. I know, seems like pretty heavy stuff right? It's not. It's in fact the best, most life-giving journey that we are all meant to take. Maybe it won't happen in this lifetime for many, but the ones with the ears that are right now tuned into what I'm saying and find it attracts them, they are the ones; *you* are the one who is ready to go further with your life.

So here's the way it happened for me. I heard the type of words I write every day and wanted more. I became a seeker. Seeking out anything I could find on the art of living a great life. I listened to audio books from all the great masters and simply took their advice. I mean really took it and acted on it. It just becomes easier the more you live it. It's like anything else you do in life that you want to learn or get better at. Living life in a higher energy as much as possible only brings one thing...a great, fun life. Seeking will become knowing.

First you must get to know your higher self by using your lower self as your guide. You know when your energy feels like garbage and your mind is creating ugly, scary scenarios. You need to use that darkness to remind you that your spirit, your light side, is the other choice. When you begin deciding daily to tip your scales to your best self as much as possible, you're consciously choosing light over dark. Making this daily decision will form a new habit of intention and subsequently success on a much higher level in all areas of your life. It's not magic, although many times it will feel that way.

It is simply claiming our true inheritance while still here. The treasure you seek is more of the real you. Living intentionally from this treasure trove of greatness is truly the only way to fly. It's simple, my friends. Don't complicate it. Become a seeker and learn more about who you really are and were meant to be. It works like you've just read life's little instruction manual for an awesome life. Just read it, learn it, practice it every day, and you will become it. Life is not meant to be mundane or mediocre. It's meant to be lived to the fullest. That's our job! So punch in, for God's sake! Get to work on a bigger, better you.

CTA: Download a new book today on spiritual growth. Remember, good thoughts in, good energy out.

Have a great day!

OCTOBER 30

Going to Ten

This is a famous phrase in our organization. We usually use it when one of us is temporarily insane. It means that some drama of the ego has captured one of us and we do our very best to bring them from a negative high of *ten* down to a *zero* as quickly as possible, for their wellbeing as well as for the rest of us. We do our best to operate in a drama-free zone. Like any other organization and in our home life, we need to do the same if we want to live a great life. Drama is just the folly of the ego, expressing itself in outer speech and action. It brings nothing good to our lives and it infects those around us.

If we have a constant, daily goal and intention to live as ego-free as possible, we will find our lives begin to smooth out and get easier. It will be easier to accept ourselves and those around us. When we realize that each of us possess a dark side and a light side, we must do our very best to live from the light side while recognizing, understanding and forgiving, that we are *all* a bit lost to this knowing. This makes it easier to forgive and understand when a person's ego has them in its negative grip and is at a *ten*.

The cure to this for all parties concerned is to understand that we all fight this battle and everyone needs to shine their light on the friend or family member that's at the *ten*, so they can get back to their *zero* as quickly as possible. Remember, if you try to fix them using your ego or equal negative energy, that is what will expand! Fire with Fire in these cases only makes a bigger fire.

It's through this awareness that we need to shift from our egos way of living and *giving* our true selves. Our spirit always knows the way, always has a perfect answer to our issues, and will only guide us in a great direction. Our job is to get to know our true self better by shedding the stuff we don't need. It's more like chiseling away the stone we don't need to reveal our true sculpture.

CTA: Today, practice staying in gratitude so you don't climb the ego scale to *ten*. Have some fun and stay at *zero*, or even better, go to *ten* on the positive side. It's there! And it's just a choice away.

Have a great day!

OCTOBER 31

Your Energy

I write about life mostly from the perspective of our many internal energies and I think that's the very best way to explain it. Once I understood this myself and began to live more from the higher vibe, my life just got better and better all the way around. My marriage, friendships, and business became more abundant and fulfilled.

I want you to think about your personal energy as a radio. In the lower end of the dial you have 88.1 and it goes all the way up to 107.5.

When we are living from the lower frequencies, the songs in our lives are sad, depressing, angry, jealous, envious, lacking, and fearful of the unknown. So many of us live from this station or a bit up the dial.

Just up the dial, at say, 95.5, things are a lot better, but they are still unpredictable and roller coaster like at best. You are singing a good tune a lot of the time, but bad songs can easily disrupt you and send you back to 88.1 in seconds.

In order for us to live at a great, higher frequency most of the time, we simply *must* practice being at the higher frequency as a constant. This will be difficult and probably the most challenging life change you can choose, but the payoff is indescribable. It is so worth it!

In order for you to gain momentum and move up the dial, you must first declare to yourself , "I am going to make this journey up the dial part of my life's work and it will only bring to me the life I want and deserve." Once you declare this for yourself, the real work begins. Never sway from this goal, never give up, and never give in to your ego's demand to stay stuck in a mediocre life. Mediocrity is only found on the lower stations.

Living life at 107.5 is always on your mind, in your thoughts, words, and actions. Living in this frequency brings all the beauty of life. Great new friendships based in honesty and trust. Dealings and business done with fairness and integrity. Happiness on a daily basis is the vehicle you move forward in. Fun and laughter are part and parcel to your everyday life. Great marriage, great relationships with your children, fun adventures, financial and personal prosperity, and dreams come true. All of this is found in the higher stations.

Once you realize where your personal energy has been living on this radio of life, you'll begin to understand why you've been constantly attracting what you've been giving out as your frequency to the world. You attract to yourself what's held in the frequency you are living and giving. Who you choose to become will decide what kind of life and circumstances you will bring to yourself. It's a totally inside job, people! And it never fails you. Up or down the dial is *your* choice and *your* responsibility.

CTA: From today forward, declare that you will only choose to move up the dial, for yourself and for others. Giving your higher station outwardly gives light, beautiful, attractive energy to the world and without question, it will return to you tenfold in so many exciting and unexpected ways.

Have a great day!

NOVEMBER 1

The Art of Giving

As I have mentioned in prior entries, anything you like to do in life can become an art form. One that is creative, thoughtful, and done with all your heart. Giving is certainly no exception. In fact, it's the highest form of beauty there is.

When we think of giving, it's usually thought of as money or a physical gift of some sort. There are so many ways to give and you are already doing it in many areas of your life. Your smile, your encouragement, heartfelt advice, hugs, laughter, sharing your joy, raising the spirits of a friend, mentoring others, and so much more!

When you express yourself in any way you are giving. What we need to become conscious of is what we're giving! And it matters a great deal.

All of the areas of giving mentioned above will always return the same to you, multiplied! This is the in and out breath of a great life. Giving and receiving are really two sides of the same coin. In other words, you always get what you give.

Becoming an artist of the soul is what you want. It brings the very best out of you and then back to your front door. If we are mixing our darker colors into our daily canvass, you can be sure that they will also return to you!

The path of a great artist of giving demands that you consciously choose your colors in every moment and each interaction. When you learn to give some space between your thoughts and your deeds, you will become the artist of your life. Choosing to give your light away freely instead of the shallow offerings of your ego. This always produces a canvass of beauty and appreciation.

CTA: Today, practice the Art of Giving. Give only your light to your family, friends, and anyone in your path. You'll find great joy in this practice and it only leads to more of the same.

Have a great day!

NOVEMBER 2

The Mind/Body Connection

We are learning so much more about how our thoughts, words, and actions affect our overall health and well-being. Science is only now beginning to agree with what spiritual masters have been saying for centuries.

Living a life of inner power insists that we must learn to love ourselves first. Health and well-being will automatically improve. This is a wild thought for many but consider that our body's cells totally respond to our moods. When we are depressed, angry, jealous, vengeful, or any other of our lower energies for a period of time, we are ten times more likely to get sick in some way. Illness or non-well-being is an outer condition of some inner turmoil.

If you have friends or family who revel in what I call, "The Ailment Talk Show," you'll begin to see how people hold themselves in a vibrational match to illness. They sit around a table and compare whose illness or injury is worse. Full-blown sagas on their tale of woe. This repeated record player of negative health has become a horrible habit of so many people. They have no clue that they are indeed affecting their health.

Health is a huge part of our overall well-being. We can see in others this pattern they've unwittingly chosen and how often they continue to get sick. In between their next illness or injury, they continue to talk about their last episode to whomever will lend them an ear. Horror show for both parties.

The person of power considers an illness or injury a mistake that will surely correct itself and thus, will spend no time in martyr town. They speak only of health, happiness and overall well-being. Think I'm crazy? It's been proven that a mind geared toward health actually produces more of it. Mind/body is for real and living a right-minded, positive life will improve everything around you as well as your innards!

CTA: Today, if you recognize yourself in this entry, jump off the set of the Ailment Talk Show for good. Recognize that this only holds you in a low pattern. It will take time to form a new habit of positive speech about your health, but it's a must for a great life. Add any exercise to your daily routine and train your mind to see you in this new, healthy light. It's just another choice my friends! Choose wellness.

Have a positive, self-loving day.

NOVEMBER 3

Space

This one is extremely important in your life. It's a practice that pays huge dividends.

When I talk about space, I mean the room you need to give yourself between your thoughts and your spoken word, as well as the space you need to give yourself between a seemingly negative occurrence and your reaction to it.

If we give ourselves a few more seconds before we speak out our latest thought, we can take these precious seconds to remember to choose to speak from our higher voice instead of the ever present ego. I assure you they are totally different voices. And either one is at your disposal.

The spoken word of the ego has a whole different tone to it and we all recognize it when we hear it. Sometimes though, it is hard for us to hear it in ourselves. We have bought into the ego full time in our lives and it is true, we have both ego and spirit while we are here in the physical. However we have and must use the power and spoken word of our higher selves much more often if we are to enjoy a big, exciting, and fulfilling life.

When it comes to giving space between an outer, seeming negative occurrence, it's an absolute must! When we learn to respond mindfully instead of react or over react, we give ourselves the gift of calm, problem solving or faster acceptance of what is. From this spacious, calmer mind, we can better hear our higher, inner voice, which always gives us a better answer. A better answer that serves us instead of widens a tense situation. A better answer that chooses forgiveness over revenge. And a better answer that expands us to a higher level of understanding and living.

You see, space is the invisible power that is here to help us create a beautiful, harmonious life. When we remember to give space throughout or thoughts and life, we will make much higher choices that deliver so much more joy, happiness, and fulfillment.

You have this power. You only need to choose it every day. Silence will help you find this calm, confident self within you. It's there and it takes a bit of time to find it, but it's yours for the asking.

CTA: Today, remember to give yourself and others the gift of space. Your relationships will grow, your light will shine, and your world will change with this one choice.

Have a great day!

NOVEMBER 4

Your Imagination

We are *all* creators of our world and I believe we can all agree that everyone's worlds are different. Although we tend to flock together with like-minded people, even those worlds are very unique.

We have all been blessed with the power of imagination. This power, when intentionally steered to a positive, creative destination, will create a wonderful, amazing, and purposeful life. However if we are not the commander of this power, it can create havoc, chaos, enemies, and a low life existence.

Our free will grants us the choice to create beauty or hell depending on how you control your imagination. So often we give up this power to whatever thought or scenario we are believing in the moment. Left unchecked and unquestioned, our minds can create horrifying stories of what might happen in our lives and we spend our lives paying heed to the lies we imagine.

We need to break free of these negative imaginings if we are to live a great life. We have the power in every moment to imagine a scenario one way or the other. Too many times we have chosen the scary stories our ego tells us are true. If we fall into the pattern of believing everything we think in this negative possibility, then that is the world we will create for ourselves. Too afraid to move forward, too afraid of making proper decisions and never checking in with what our true power has to say in the matter.

Let's continue this one tomorrow.

CTA: Tame your imagination. Live in the now!

Have a great day!

NOVEMBER 5

Your Imagination *continued*

We need to begin using the power of our positive imaginations to create a beautiful new story that will become your life. Each and every day we must wake up and decide to tell a new, exciting story of where we are heading. We need to tell the story of all our victories, our dreams and positive goals. When we choose the story we tell instead of playing our old, worn out record of woe, we will begin to imagine and thus create a new record to spin.

We need to spend time in quiet solitude, writing down the details of our new life. What does it look like? What do you look like in it? Where do I want to go and who do I want to be around in this new land? These are all potentially life-changing questions. When we finally decide to design our lives instead of letting the winds blow us around with no compass, we will have taken the wheel for the first time.

Your imagination has great power but you *must* be its master in order to harness it. You need to draw it, write it down in great detail and then believe that you *will* accomplish it! Any new dream of life as you want it will take time to create, but time is the gift we've been given to do just that.

CTA: Today, take the wheel back from your imagination. Let the inner liar know that you've decided to reclaim your life. Banish any scenarios the liar tells you. You know the liar, we all have one in our heads and it spins tales of dread, sorrow, being less than, not having the skills, being too fat or too something that is not the truth. Rise up and claim your true imagination. The one that imagines greatness, beautiful relationships, victory, and love in all things. This is what our imagination was intended for.

Keep the faith that you have all you need within you to imagine your way to an awesome life. I promise you that you do indeed.

Have a great day!

NOVEMBER 6

Overwhelmed?

Becoming overwhelmed is usually about the inability to say no, taking too much on at once, and feeling it all has to be done yesterday. Your time management skills, prioritizing, and the ability to ask for and welcome outside help are the bridge over troubled water.

If you constantly believe that you are the only one who can do it, your plate will constantly be overflowing, as will your negative emotions. In this mind state you'll be emitting harried, nervous, and even aggressive energy, the kind that brings more of what you don't want into your experience. The kind that makes others want to run from you instead of work with you. You're on the hamster wheel.

A list is always the answer. If you leave it all up to your mind to make an internal list, your mind will tend to group it together into a big package of stress. You'll spread this negative energy around like a wildfire, shooting in every direction and blaming everyone else for your suffering when what you really need is the list. Then, delegate from a different energy altogether. Yes, your three-alarm fire bell will get the attention but it will not be the best vehicle for the job.

The words, "I need your help," when delivered in the tone of one friend to another, is much more effective than words like blame, guilt, martyrdom, and anger. They just draw a short-term, disgruntled band-aid for the bigger picture that really needs to be addressed. When your energy is scattered, so will be your world.

CTA: So today's practice is about getting organized, prioritizing projects, and asking for the help you need in a way that draws others to the cause. It's all in the approach. Life is all in the approach. Use your best and the best will come running to you.

Have a great day!

NOVEMBER 7

Expect the Best

This is an absolute must in your life! If you're not already doing this, today is a big day of change for you.

Positive expectation sends out a completely different energy and attracts much different things, people and opportunities to you than always expecting either average or, more often, the *worst*!

If you are a person who always expects the worst and dwells on the worst-case scenarios that your ego constantly spins, you are in a low vibrational pattern and you are attracting negativity, low energy circumstances, and low energy people into your life experience.

You must begin to be acutely aware of the vibe you send out all the time. Be aware of your thoughts and expectations, for they will drive your speech, your actions, and your expectations. This is how you create your life!

Making a daily habit of expecting the best automatically puts your mind in a positive state. Being in this state, you will be easy in your day, happier, more productive, and grateful. This emanates from you as an energy that those around you will see and, more importantly, *feel*. They will like to be around you, work with you, and harmonize with such a great energy. This is where you begin to attract all the good stuff.

When I say good stuff, I mean better relationships and more opportunities to do different things. You'll open up and become more creative in this positive state. A higher quality of people will begin to enter your circle and you're off on a new, higher life experience. All having started with your new habit of expecting the best.

Never settle for less than you deserve. You are a powerful creator in either direction, positive *or* negative. It's all about the state your mind is in and what you do with those thoughts. *Always* choose thoughts that serve you rather than sink you. This is the path of greatness. It's always your choice.

CTA: Today begins your new favorite habit, expecting the best. This, like all other practices, will take time. If you have to fake it 'til you make it, do that. You are rewiring your mind to a higher frequency and awareness. It's a habit that reaps huge rewards on so many levels!

Have a great day!

NOVEMBER 8

Compassion and Understanding

These two go hand-in-hand, as you all know. When we choose to be compassionate, we are choosing the opposite of our judgmental self.

We see ourselves through the eyes of someone else's pain and suffering. In other words, we have either been in their shoes or we are imagining ourselves in their shoes. What it must me like to be in such a place.

When we see or know of someone in our lives who is suffering in some way, the choice to go into the situation for them, instead of avoiding it, is a practice of your higher self. It says I care enough to try and ease your pain. And perhaps you can share with them a victory of yours after having gone through a similar situation.

Compassion is a heart-centered energy that heals both you and its recipient. In that moment, you are both benefiting from your act. This is how we go about raising the energy of the planet to a new place. It's one small act at a time from all of us.

Awareness of all the higher tools in your toolbox will help you to use them effectively in helping others to move forward and at the same time, cutting your old sandbags of low energy tools. Judgment of others is just one of those sandbags you cut, especially with the use of the tool of Compassion.

CTA: Today, when you see someone in some ugly place you have already visited, tell them about your path out of it. Tell them about the good stuff that awaits them on the other side of it. Give them a new vision to focus on.

Do this and *you* will also Have a great day!

NOVEMBER 9

The Art of Real Living

As I have said many times, any outward act can become an art form with enough practice, patience, creativity, and will. But any and all art forms begin on the inside. Your life and how you choose to live it is the ultimate expression of an art form.

When we finally decide that our old, worn-out, negative expressions of our ego no longer serve us and we need to change course, we are at the leading edge of a new life.

This is a very courageous decision, as it will involve challenges along the way. Most of all, our old way of thinking will be challenged first.

We are all products of our surroundings. From birth, we arrive with a blank slate of spirit, inside our new human form. Onto this, we have a bunch of outside influence added to us. Perceptions, attitudes, outlooks, behaviors and judgments. Many of them complete lies. Well-meaning in most cases, but lies nonetheless.

The only way forward, truly forward, is the road less traveled; the road of our true selves. We have to uncover what has always been there.

How you dig for this treasure of yours is the highest of all practices and it just happens to be your main purpose for being here. Learning to hear and recognize your inner voice is the path of greatness.

We must relearn to be our authentic self. How to start? I guess the way I started is the way I will suggest. It is by learning the wisdom of the ages. It has always been there, but has been overshadowed by our earthly egos and conditioning. We truly need to unlearn some things in order to let the truth of you come out of hiding. You are there! I assure you.

Let's continue this one tomorrow.

CTA: Choose to live the life you want. Life is all about choices.

Have a great day!

NOVEMBER 10

The Art of Real Living *continued*

I am going to list my top five personal development books to get you started. One important point you need to know and do; you will need to read each book more than once. The things you miss or do not quite understand in the first read-through will become clear in the re-reading or listening of the books. This is key to absorb the wisdom. So here they are:

1) Wayne Dyer, *Your Erroneous Zones*

2) Eckhart Tolle, *The Power of Now*

3) Wayne Dyer, *Change Your Thoughts, Change Your Life*

4) Don Miguel Ruiz, *The Four Agreements*

5) Byron Katie, *The Work*

There are so many others, but you will begin to see the common thread of wisdom in all these awesome books. I find listening to them on audio is the best way for me. But whatever works for you is your way in.

CTA: Today, buy or download these in order. Spend lots of time on each book. Quiet contemplation of the words in each book and how they pertain to your life, is the practice. Practicing outward actions described in each book is also powerful work.

You and you alone are the magician of your life. Learn some new tricks of truth. Your truth.

Have a great day!

NOVEMBER 11

Turning Your Mountains Back Into Mole Hills

Most of the mountains in your life are really mole hills. We can see this truth when we look back in our lives and we are either surprised how small an issue really was or we realize we needed to learn the lesson from the mountain. Both of which you could have conquered with a calm, confident self instead of blowing the roof off your emotional house.

Calm confidence is the ability and knowing that you can handle whatever comes your way. You've made it 'til now, haven't you? Many, many mountains have been climbed, gone around, or ground to dust in your life to this point. You'd think we'd all have a confident, self-assured demeanor by now. But it's not that way for most.

The reason for this is that we continue to operate on old, outdated thoughts and processes for solving the issues of our lives. How can we expect to be a better problem solver if we continue to choose overreaction as part of our process? It's insanity.

When we want to grow in any area of our lives, we need to consistently improve our life process. This means better knowledge, practice, and persistent action. If we choose our same old methods, we will only get the same old meager results.

Let's continue this one tomorrow.

CTA: Step back to evaluate uncomfortable situations. If you engage, decide not to overreact. Free yourself from the cycle of drama.

Have a great day!

NOVEMBER 12

Turning Your Mountains Back Into Mole Hills *continued*

Our emotional life is so crucial to living in balance. That's why it is imperative to know ourselves intimately and how we process the events, upsets, and seeming failures that are part of life.

Once we go inside and become the silent watcher of our usual processes, we will immediately know where we need to improve. Whether it's nervousness, anxiety, low self-esteem, anger, fear, or whatever, your ability to identify your usual negative patterns will be your doorway to positive change.

The mountains in our lives are merely experiences we attract to ourselves based on the thoughts, actions, and energy we give out as ourselves.

Once we balance our own ship, the outside stuff will take care of itself. Anything that comes to you when your balanced is a lesson you are to learn or one that someone close to you must learn and you are there to help that person through it with your new growth. Paying it forward, so to speak.

When you finally decide to up your life game and gain the knowledge and wisdom your true self already knows, your mountains will all be molehills compared to your old way of processing life. You will be a super computer rather than a calculator. It's just what happens.

CTA: Today, set out to up your game. The journey inward is the only way to begin. If you bypass it for some quick tips route, you will have learned a few parlor tricks instead of knowing your true power.

The only way we live a consistently better life, one that is filled with growth, meaning and purpose is to know our true, confident, generous, prosperous, loving self. After that, it's all gravy.

Have a great day!

NOVEMBER 13

Focus

This one always determines what you draw into your life. In other words, what you continually focus your attention on grows. This can be great or it can keep you in a less than desirable life pattern.

We are energy. The energy we give off comes back to us. Once we accept this truth, it's time to change our focus, be aware of what we are putting it on and stay vigilant in using this power to draw what you want, not what you don't want.

Most people talk, act, and complain about all the things they don't want and it's amazing to them why they keep attracting more to complain about into their lives.

Endless stories of woe, illness, bad luck, lack, and low energy. All drawn and attracted to them by their inner beliefs, thoughts, outer actions, and speech. This forms your energy and becomes your life.

When you take 100% responsibility for your life and begin to let go of your old patterns of negative thoughts and you quit bringing this mess to the party of your present life, your focus will be your tool of change.

Most do not realize they are focused on the negative. They will say, "what are you talking about, I'm just saying it like it is!" Therein lies the issue. You need to be thinking, believing and speaking only on your successes, loves, purpose, and goals. This is the focus of a person of power and the mindset of a winner. You create your reality!

This focus must be constant! Never veer off course into your old self-defeating script. That must be declared dead, gone, and buried.

This new focus must be the new you. Live it, own it, and love your way to new heights.

Once you begin anew, you will start to notice how much better you feel, how people now respond to you differently, and myriad new opportunities you are drawing.

Your rewards are all based on the way you approach life and what you're focused on. Always focus on the positive, act in faith, and give your very best in every moment. This way of living will bring back to you an amazing, prosperous, laughter-filled life. Guaranteed.

CTA: Today, notice what you're focused on. Is it an ugly perception or the beautiful day? Is it a loving thought or a thought of revenge? The choice of what we focus our attention on is always ours. Choose to steer your life with the wheel of positive focus.

Have a great day!

NOVEMBER 14

More on Your Process

Constantly improving and growing is what makes life worth living and it's what we are here to do.

One of the areas of growth that is essential for happiness is learning to let go of negative mind baggage that our ego loves to collect.

At the end of a normal workday for most, we have most likely collected some of this mind baggage from myriad interactions of the day.

Our ego will want to expand this baggage when we get home, spin some of our own perceptions into it by re-judging it, talking about it with anyone who loves a juicy negative tale, and the next thing you know, you feel like garbage, only worse! Worse because you didn't let it go much sooner and now you took it home.

The practice of non-attachment is what you need to do. Do not become attached to the negative stories, energy or people we all have in our lives. This means veering away from the social circle of doom and gloom, raising others out of it intentionally if you can, and letting any and all ego related interactions go through you rather than stick to you and your mind.

This requires a shift from your normal unaware mindset, where you normally just suck it all in and then slowly process it within yourself. This is where our collection of negative drama lives. Sometimes for our entire lives. You *must* learn to reprocess the crap out of you as quickly as it comes at you.

You will begin to notice that the negative people in your life will not be as enthusiastic about sharing the doom and gloom with you because you are no longer an attractive sounding board for it. Once again, it comes down to your conscious choice and your awareness of the deeper truth of things.

Unpacking your backpack of negativity during your day will allow you to arrive home with your best self, unscathed and intact. This is the path of a powerful person and a mindset of the big picture.

CTA: Today, let any and all drama that comes your way go through you instead of sticking to you. Let it all roll off of you. In these moments you have chosen the high road and you'll be so glad you took it!

Have a great day!

NOVEMBER 15

Love

Love is the highest of all energy. Yes, we attach the meaning of love to people, places and things, but it is the very energy of love that created all of it, including you.

Being in the wedding business, I hear a lot about this subject. I get to hear promises of it, what love means, what love is and is not. When it comes down to it, I believe love is a force. A force of creativity, a force of peace and well-being, a force of forgiveness and truly a force of freedom.

Love is the eternal force of being. You can never fully disconnect from it, because you *are* it. There are many other names for it. God, Jesus, Buddha, nature, higher self, source energy, and many more. But these are all names and labels for the same thing, the all-pervading force of Love.

This force heals, it nurtures, it helps us to grow, realize our dreams and gives life to everything you see. Love is life itself.

When we are in touch with this force and we intentionally use this power in every area of our lives, we prosper. We thrive and we live this experience to the fullest. When we pass it along to others, we give life energy itself. We rise and others rise.

It is the most natural path we can live from.

We were all born from this power and we will all return home to it someday. Shedding the old coat of the ego and its opposing views.

Let's continue this one tomorrow.

CTA: All you need is love. (Did you just sing the Beatles tune?)

Have a great day!

NOVEMBER 16

Love *continued*

When we begin to tune into our natural power and realize its true strength in, and as, our lives, we begin to see the value of shedding the ego while we are still here. This stripping away of the dark energy within us, will release the treasure we have all been seeking.

This treasure fills us with all the inner goodness that keeps us in a higher plain of living and feeling great, and it attracts to us all the outer symbols of love itself. These include amazing relationships, marriages, parenting, success, calm confidence, prosperity, wellness, laughter, joy, happiness, and inner peace. It's a constant knowing that you are really a part of the eternal, placed here to grow for a while.

When it all comes down to it, this one force is where you need to live. When we stray from it, we struggle, we fight, we fail. The good news is that Love is always there, luring you back to your best and highest self. Seek it when you're lost. It always brings you home.

CTA: Today and moving forward, realize that you are a piece of this very force that created you and the Universe. You have and own this power. When you use it, amazing things happen. You are not separate from what most of us call God, we are of this power. Just like taking a hand full of water from the ocean. Is this water any less the ocean now that part of it is in your hands? Use your power to create good. And use this power to create an amazing life.

Have a great day!

NOVEMBER 17

Consciousness

If this is a term that is somewhat new to you, it does not surprise me. Of course you may have heard it many times and just brushed it off as some old hippie term from the sixties. However, once you begin to delve into the higher realm, you'll soon realize the true power of this word.

Most of us live our lives in an unconscious state, never going deeper than what others tell us we are, or are not, or even worse, we live our entire lives in an earthbound state of ego. This is not life. This is being asleep. Asleep to the truth.

Consciousness is our natural state. It is a much higher state of awareness. Awareness of who we are, our purpose for being here, and the true state of aliveness. This is the awakened state of knowing the truth and living your life from this truth.

When you are conscious, you see the world and everything in it from a higher perspective. You are able to see the light in everyone and you can easily recognize when they are caught up in the negative swirl of the ego. From this place, you are able to truly help others and yourself.

Once you begin to delve deeper into who you really are and the divine power you possess, you are waking up. Waking up from a potentially terrible dream that you helped to create. This new awareness will be scary at first because your ego will then want to punish and judge *you* for all the pain you've caused yourself and others. This, my friends, is just another trap of the ego, designed to keep you stuck in guilt and shame. You see, the ego is always playing both judge and jury. "Someone must be blamed!"

First and foremost, you need to understand that we all have wallowed in the negative from time to time. Some of us have chosen our lower energies as a life path. That path only leads to one place, a hellish existence marred with broken relationships, poverty, lack, and limitation. This is not life and this is not what was intended for you.

Let's continue this one tomorrow.

CTA: Always live your life with intention and purpose. I can't say this enough.

Have a great day!

NOVEMBER 18

Consciousness *continued*

Waking up is a natural process that takes time and it takes your cooperation in order to be realized.

Sometimes we are pushed into awakening by a less than desirable method, like tragedy or death of someone close to us. This seemingly negative occurrence breaks open our hearts and we instinctively seek the light because we feel so much darkness. This is only one way to awaken. We can also choose to wake up. This is the path we were meant for.

Becoming conscious is the very best choice you can make. It gives you life energy that you never knew you had, but was always there. This power within has been waiting for *you*. Waiting for you to hear its still small voice in the midst of the darkness of an ego-dominated world. This voice is your true self.

There are many paths to the truth, but the wisdom of the ages is how I entered. This wisdom is readily available and waiting for your consumption of it. All that I speak about, I first had to seek. I had to empty the cup of what I thought I knew and refill it with wisdom.

Up until that point, I was lost and did not know I was lost. I thought I had it pretty much figured out. I lived my life from a selfish, human perspective. Competing, judging, gossiping, hating, and being less than I was capable of. Yes I was loving, kind, and having fun, but there was such a mixed bag of energy flying out of me, that my experiences and outcomes were like a roller coaster. Anxiety, depression, and fear were a *normal* part of my life. I'm sure you can relate.

Just because these lower energies are *normal* in our world does not mean they are *natural*. They are not. These are the energies that will fall away when you choose the upward path. These are slowly peeled away from the true you, as you become conscious of yourself and your daily life choices.

Let's continue this one tomorrow.

CTA: Break free from the norm to a higher frequency where you can truly engage in life.

Have a great day!

NOVEMBER 19

Consciousness *continued*

Consciousness is living life in a state of knowing rather than guessing and searching. The true self always knows what's right and will surely lead you on the right course. Gaining wisdom in order to help yourself awaken is the first order of business.

You need to know about energy. You need to know about the Universal Laws of nature, which you are part of. And you need to know that you are here for an absolute purpose. It is your job to chip away the falsities of your lower, mind created, earth bound self and master your higher energies. I know this may sound like a lot of work, and it is. But aren't you worth it?

You will be awakened from your lower self upon your passing back to your natural home, but we *all* possess the power to do this while we are here. This is part of the overarching plan I believe. To awaken this planet. As you will see on the news each day, we are in desperate need of awakened souls. We are certainly not being lead there by the powers that be. Far from it. All you see on the nightly news is simply unconscious leaders using the ego for selfish personal gain at the expense of the whole. We *must* wake up to the games and lies of the ego on a personal level in order to create a world lead by a higher energy. Spirit.

CTA: Today, seek the wisdom of the ages. Go to the book store, go to iTunes or wherever you shop for literature. I recommend anything from the following authors as I have mentioned before, Wayne Dyer, Eckhart Tolle, Deepak Chopra, Mike Dooley, Don Miguel Ruiz, John Assaraf, Byron Katie, Joel Osteen, and many others in the personal development section. Immerse yourself in higher learning and watch your life change as you change. It will be a whole new ride, my friends!

Have a great day!

NOVEMBER 20

Celebrate Your Victories

Now that you've decided to go for what you want in life, you'll be hitting some bumps along the way as you climb the ladder of success. There will be many challenges and seeming obstacles. Remember always that these are just there to sharpen your will, your resolve, and your game.

Also on this higher path you will experience small victories. These are there also to sharpen you in the area of your confidence. It is extremely important to not only notice these victories, but to inwardly give thanks and gratitude as well as outwardly celebrate in some way. This increases the vibration of success for you and will draw more of it into your life.

Complaining, looking at only the potential pitfalls and challenges will do the same if that's what you focus on most often. Your thoughts, energy, and what you act on will be the general asking for your life experiences. What you are in your vibe is what you will attract. This is very important for you to know.

Celebrating any and all victories can include a great phone call from a customer, praise for the way you acted somewhere, the life direction you have chosen, new friends you have made, the promotion you received and the billions of other blessings that come into your life. Never take them for granted. Living in the present moment will allow you to see how blessed you really are.

Gratitude is the energy you expel when you celebrate your victories. The more you do it, the more of them you can expect to arrive in your life. Gratitude is therefore the real lesson of today's entry. Always exude it and you'll be doing a lot of celebrating.

CTA: Be on the watch for all things to be grateful for today. When you notice one, say thank you either outwardly or in your heart mind. The more you count your blessings, the more of them to notice will show up.

Have a great day!

NOVEMBER 21

Mercy

Mercy is an energy and a decision that comes from your higher self and is crucial for living in harmony with everyone in your life.

Mercy is love, forgiveness, and understanding all wrapped up in one divine gesture. This gesture is used when another is caught up in the swirl of stress, anger, overreaction, and any of the other lower energies of the ego.

During these times, if you are not present in your higher energies, your own ego will want to judge this person in some negative fashion or worse yet, lash out at them for what you would consider a fault or flaw in them. This of course is where all suffering, arguments, and strife come alive. One ego resonating with another only expands the ego and its many ugly faces.

Mercy is when you've intentionally chosen to slide right past your own ego-centric inclinations to react to others reactions, into your higher gear of understanding. Understanding first that we all share in the insanity of the ego and that we too would love some mercy during our own times of temporary insanity. In other words, you choose to help the other let out what they need to let out, not judge it, but instead try to pull the other out of this horrible head they are in. Or at the very least, not go into reactive speech of our own.

Remember this very important fact for the rest of your life; you can never help someone out of a negative state of mind by being negative yourself. You must be on a higher plain of awareness to affect any shift in another's energy.

There will be times when you just need to walk away from a situation because another has themselves so whipped up in a heady drama, that they just need time to calm down and process themselves out of the negative. Stepping away with a silent blessing that they find their way back is also merciful. You're not judging because you know you've been there and still go there from time to time yourself.

Let's continue this one tomorrow.

CTA: Before stepping into a situation, decide whether your presence will be helpful or hurtful. Try to sense why you want to engage. If it will bring a positive helpful outcome for all parties, go for it. However, if it is to stroke your own ego, back away.

Have a great day!

NOVEMBER 22

Mercy *continued*

It is so very easy to judge others when they are stuck in an ego-centric moment; however the higher ground for you is to stay in a giving energy. From this place and this place only, will you be able to forgive any lashes you've received during the others temporary insanity and welcome them back into your heart. All done from your choice to be merciful instead of the ego's first choice, which is to punish.

The ego loves to punish others for their shortcomings. It does this through its favorite tools of making others feel guilt or shame in some way. This choice just teaches the other to do the same when you are low. And it goes on and on. So is the way of the world. We can and must do better.

The key to life is always awareness. Awareness that we all share in the collective spirit, and while we are on earth, we all share in the insanity of the Ego. It is only through shedding light on the insanity and its unnecessary place in our lives, that we will collectively awaken and shift the planet towards heaven on earth. Mercy therefore, is an amazing tool of awakening that you must practice each and every day. This is your part. Play it.

CTA: Today, when you are in the presence of another's ego-centric moment, stay in your giving mode. Offer mercy instead of judgment or give the other the space they need to return home.

Have a great day!

NOVEMBER 23

Notice How You Feel Today

God gives us all a huge opportunity today.

Today on this national day of gratitude, we get a front row seat to feeling our higher power at its best. And guess what? You're choosing it. Be aware of how you're becoming gratitude without thinking about it. This is the real you that I write about every day.

This you is more open and loving right? More joyful, giving, allowing of others, and aware of beauty in the present moment right? We hug, we kiss, and we feel good. Really good. That, my friend, is your power. The gift that keeps on giving.

Today we are in our natural state. The one from our true home. The unconditional love within all of us. This is what we embody today and must do our very best to embody everyday as our part to raise all.

Today is a great day. The day that all you have to be grateful for comes into focus. Be awake today. Be present in all of it. Milk each beautiful moment for all its gold. Take a look at what you've created through love and forgiveness. Take this day as a chance to focus on what you love about everyone around you instead of their less than best selves (that we all possess).

Give your best today and let others know how much you love and appreciate their unique role in your life. Even if it came in an ugly wrapper that guided you in a better direction. (We all have those "guides" LOL.)

Be good to them too. They've been in your life for very good reasons. Hopefully you've recognized why. It's there.

Celebrate those who have gone home before us, for they are still with us and want to feel our joy. Give it to them. They are one of your guides now. Let their love in.

CTA: Today, I wish you all much love, prosperity, and happiness. When you begin to live your life in this natural giving state, every day will feel like Thanksgiving. Isn't that what we're all really after?

God bless you all.

Have a great day!

NOVEMBER 24

Positive Energy

Once you accept that everything you see, feel, taste, and hear, including us, is all energy, vibrating at different frequencies, you are at the doorstep of a new understanding and a new life.

Quantum physicists and modern science now agree with what all the ancient mystics, philosophers and spiritual masters have been teaching for centuries, and it's time for you to pay attention.

We are all part of this web of cosmic energy. Some call it spirit, some call it the energy of unconditional love, and some call it the energy matrix or source energy. Most of you will call it God.

When we finally realize that we are all talking about the same thing, we can move past the labels to find our place in this web of infinite possibilities and use our own power that is a piece of this amazing force. And we are supposed to do just that.

They say that God helps those who help themselves, but so many have no idea how to do this, even though the answer has been within us all along. It's our own energy! This is the key you have been looking for. You just have to get yourself in tune with the right side of energy or spirit or whatever label fits your belief system.

Being a positive person means taking 100% responsibility for your own energy system and using it for the benefit of the whole.

CTA: Be mindful of your words and actions, as they determine your physical state of positivity or negativity. Always err on the side of positivity.

Let's continue this one tomorrow

Have a great day!

NOVEMBER 25

Positive Energy *continued*

Your own energy always begins with your thoughts and beliefs. How you view the world and what side of the scale of positive and negative you normally live in. Your inner speech, your outer speech. Your choice of whether to act and how. How you give or don't give. How you treat yourself and others. This is what your energy is emitting.

Your choice of only the energies of your higher self is what attracts all goodness into your life. In other words, choosing Love as your way.

All of your higher, positive energies are simply subsets of the most positive energy there is, which is love.

Kindness, caring, empathy, faith, hope, gratitude, prosperity, wealth, generosity, wisdom, serenity, creativity, sharing, laughter, joy, forgiveness, happiness, and more. These are the choices that bring to you the inner peace and security, prosperity, fulfillment, contentment and satisfaction that we all long for.

It's when we choose the energies of the earthly plane and man's lower knowledge that we attract the negative into our experience. Hatred, fear, doubt, greed, competition, gossip, self-loathing, ugly deeds and decisions, are just some of the negative or lower energies we all possess.

Most people have no idea that these are the very energies that drive their daily experiences, outcomes and their life path. Time to wake up, folks! You can choose.

Let's continue this one tomorrow.

CTA: By choosing positive thoughts and self-talk, you will attract more positive into your life.

Have a great day!

NOVEMBER 26

Positive Energy *continued*

We are both energy receivers and energy transmitters to a universe that says yes to us. You simply must know what your own energy is asking of this benevolent source.

The things we speak about, do, and contemplate are what we are asking for, so it is imperative to know yourself well. Inside and out. If you have not understood why you get what you get, now you know.

Most people think that positive-minded people have their heads in the sand, or that they are wearing rose colored glasses that do nothing but hide them from the reality of life. The truth my friends, is that we all create our own reality by choice. You are either making conscious choices, where you direct your life path by the positive energies I've listed above, or you are living unconsciously, simply letting the wind blow you around by your emotions and reactions to them. One gives life while the other is a conglomeration of mixed experiences. Most of them not so good.

My advice today is to get to know yourself well. Are you choosing the direction of your life and the energy you use to get there? Or are you living in an old paradigm of limiting beliefs and low energy? When you can honestly assess yourself and what you have been emitting as your personal energy signal, you are at the doorstep of a new understanding. One that can take you places you've never been!

CTA: Today, spend some alone time in your Lab of change and choice. Look at the decisions you've made and the path you've been on. Choose to seek the higher road in all your thoughts, actions, and deeds. You are the change you seek. You just may not have realized your role until now. Helping yourself is the true path to helping the world.

Have a great day!

NOVEMBER 27

Practical Spirituality

I was with some of my closest friends last night, some whom I haven't seen in a while, and the subject of my daily entries came up. I was told that people were wondering what is up with Marty and these entries? Is he a preacher or something? I had to laugh because I know how this must seem weird or "religious" to some people.

My personal journey into self-improvement, higher living, and true success actually began when I was twenty-three years old, with my introduction to Anthony Robbins, the famous life coach and motivational speaker. These concepts that he taught were like a magnet to me, making perfect sense.

Over the years I learned about other authors who shared a common thread. The common thread was the truth. The truth that we are much more than meets the eye. The truth that we are really the ghost in the machine we call our body and that our soul or spirit is the real us. Living from this truth and tapping into the power of the spirit is how we are able to expand, grow and create an amazing life. These authors lead me to a new mindset that serves me rather than sinks me. A new mindset that has brought great success to all areas of my life and it is my great pleasure to share with you what has brought me such light, fulfillment, and happiness to my journey.

What I write about every day is the practical daily use of spirituality. When most people hear the word spirituality, they immediately think organized religion, hellfire, damnation, and all the other dogma that has driven us away from even speaking about spirit as a way of living. Believe me, I was one.

Let's continue this one tomorrow.

CTA: Spirituality does not always pertain to religion. For some, it is just a state of mind.

Have a great day!

NOVEMBER 28

Practical Spirituality *continued*

This book was intended, first and foremost, for my children. I wanted them to know what I know and what has worked so well for me in my life. I thought I should share it with my friends on Facebook and give this book away to you first, as a gift. This gift is for everyone, but not everyone will understand it, care about it or even read it, and that's totally ok. I am truly grateful for those who find value in these words and the thought that they may in some way help you to move forward into a great new life.

Some of the subjects I write about will totally resonate with something that is currently going on in your life. If this entry helps you, it was meant just for you. Others may challenge what you thought you knew as truth. For those who feel drawn to these words, it is your time to hear them. It is your time to break out of old patterns of thought and raise your level of awareness. Practical use of our higher energies in everyday situations is the path you have been searching for and if my words are a catalyst of transformation for you, I am grateful.

Religion and spirituality share common threads. Spirituality however says, follow your own heart, your own path from the heart, and the truth that you hear from it. Most religions teach these truths, but fall short sometimes in helping us to use it practically in our daily lives.

It is my sincere hope that the book I am writing will offer you some value. It is part of my purpose, as is all our purpose, to spread the Love. This is my attempt in doing just that. Your inner guide is waiting for you to wake up and join the living. When you do, happiness, loving relationships, fun, and truth are what come from this wellspring. Let it out. It's the real you.

CTA: Be still and listen to your heart today. If your answer does not come immediately, give the gift of space and time a chance. It will show up. Look and listen for it without being attached to the issue. Faith is the way.

Have a great day!

NOVEMBER 29

Resistance

Resistance is the name for what we feel when we are not accepting the present moment.

Self-mastery includes the art of allowing the present moment to take place without the energy of resistance or judgment. If we are in the midst of a struggle, whether it's a disagreement or some negative outburst or energy of another, our own acceptance of what is taking place, is the calm, confident energy that keeps us in balance and able to either help the situation by accepting energy or having the wisdom to walk away.

No matter which one you choose, you will have stayed in your higher energy, being unaffected by the ego of another or your own.

The ability to stay in tune with your higher self during a struggle is a spiritual practice that reaps huge rewards. This practice, like all others, begins with self-awareness.

Notice how you feel on the inside when you find yourself in a negative conversation or momentary struggle. It's like a constriction in your heart and solar plexus area, right? That's the feeling of resistance. If you let it fester for long, your own ego will jump into the pool of negativity.

Learning to stay peaceful when outside forces are turbulent is staying in power. From this place you will find quick answers to internal questions and right choices to handle the outside situation. You have the amazing power to transmute the negative into positive when in this power.

Let's continue this one tomorrow.

CTA: When engaged in an uncomfortable conversation or situation, find your peaceful place. It will take practice. But with practice comes mastery. You will be a black belt of calm in no time.

Have a great day!

NOVEMBER 30

Resistance *continued*

The daily practice of positive living will eventually transform you into one of those people who only attract the good stuff. The good friends, the good job, the good life. It all starts with you.

Resistance is like putting the brakes on the flow of goodness into your life. If you find that you know this feeling far too often in your life, you must change.

Change can include more resistance in your life at first, because you have finally decided to clean up your own house and leave behind much of the old ego-centric you. Others in your circle may protest and not understand your change. You may need to leave some toxic relationships behind. This, my friends, is all temporary resistance. Don't ever let that stop you. Learn that initial discomfort always gives way to personal growth. It's the only way we push out of our old cocoon of the past in exchange for some wings.

CTA: Today, feel the resistance and know that to stay in calm confidence and higher energy is the name of the game. Let this be your beacon of light that guides you past defeating old habits and toxic relationships. Nurture the light in all areas of your life and resistance will become a brake petal you no longer need. You'll be flying in the flow.

Have a great day!

DECEMBER 1

Soul Language

Internally we all know the two voices within us. Most have never given any true awareness to them. We've been running our lives mostly on autopilot, letting outside circumstances dictate our moods, mindset and attitude toward the world. Most times we find ourselves having a roller coaster life experience when we allow the outer to control the inner. This must change for you if you desire an awesome life.

Learning to speak and understand soul language will be your magic wand to create a whole new world for yourself and those around you.

We all understand soul language, but may never have been consciously aware of how it creates all goodness in our lives. When we finally become awakened to it and its power, we will want to speak it fluently and as our native tongue. Learning to let go of our other voice, the ego, will be your doorway to higher understanding and a new way of living.

The more we speak to each other from our soul voice, the more truth will enter our lives. Both yours and the people you speak this language with.

Soul language is voice of loving kindness, praise, compliments, soulful advice, positive expectation, faith, and hope. It says I can and you can do it. This voice knows no limitations and always speaks of obstacles as opportunities to climb even higher. This voice promises greatness and this voice delivers all you need and desire in your life. It's the voice of cooperation with others. It speaks in a higher vibration and tone that our heart understands immediately, and it opens us up to truth and love. Every time.

You know when you are speaking from this place. It's rich and has substance. It is meaningful and has purpose. You are in giving mode and what you receive in return is the same. We enrich each other when we speak it and we all rise. Our jobs are to simply learn that this is the only language we need to speak. And this is the practice of a powerful person.

Let's continue this one tomorrow.

CTA: Speak to others with your soul voice. Be true to who you are. Doing so will allow more peace and harmony in your life.

Have a great day!

DECEMBER 2

Soul Language *continued*

When you decide to awaken to your life's purpose, you have chosen to help this planet and everyone on it. We are all connected at the level of the soul, so when we speak the language of our ego, we have disconnected from our true energy and power. We have temporarily broken our magic wand.

The good news is that once we recognize how we pinch off our power, we will make the choice to get back to our true language. Your powerless ego cannot speak this language and would rather you not either. It has a much lower agenda.

Your soulful contribution matters a great deal. If we want to see the world change, we must change. One at a time.

Peace in the world requires us to speak this language of truth. We are all seeing and hearing what the egos crazy language is in this world. It's nuts and we need to transform it. The very best thing we can do as individuals is to end our own ego games and learn that this voice only destroys. When we take up this challenge, we always benefit. We grow and others grow by our example.

CTA: Today, go through the day thinking and speaking your very best soul language. Give compliments, humor, praise, hugs, passion, empathy, kindness, and love. Make this your dominant intention and look back at your day when you go to bed tonight. Your own soul will have been filled with gratitude. Gratitude for a day well spent.

Have a great day!

DECEMBER 3

The Anxious Mind

Anxiety is one of the worst feelings and states of mind we as humans can have. So many of us know this all too well. If you've been suffering way too long in silence, today is your day to act. Seek professional assistance.

You need to get rid of this awful voice that seems to have a say in every area of your life. This is the voice of unreasonable fear and it steals your joy and your true potential. There are many ways to conquer this nervous dictator and its part of your purpose to let it go for good.

My first recommendation is talking to a pro. Never think of counseling as failure, weakness, or something only crazy people need. We all need it. Unfortunately we usually do nothing and let it rule our thoughts, actions, or inactions and our relationships. To remove this potentially immobilizing pattern from your life will be like being released from a prison you once thought protected you. You'll learn to finally be calm and still in mind and body. You'll be able to expand your life like never before and every relationship will get better, most importantly, the one with yourself. Releasing the old garbage is crucial and a professional ear and guidance will help to bring you out of these dark woods forever.

CTA: So today's practice is just for you. Take action!! Seek and ye shall find. I know this dreaded voice. The only reason I am able to write these words to you now, is because I did the same. Go get your life back.

Have a great day in peace.

DECEMBER 4

The Power of Optimism

The sheer power of this energy cannot be underestimated, and it is an absolute MUST if you are to ever reach your true potential and realize your dreams.

There are many who believe that positive thought, optimism, and a daily countenance of cheerfulness are just sticking your head in the sand to the ugly realities of life. They think it's more like ignoring or just looking away from negativity. Actually it's the blessing of faith in motion. Faith that no matter how ugly things get, that you are loved, protected and stretched to a higher knowing as a result of these challenges. This is the path where optimism lives and sustains.

My friends, whatever you focus your attention on in life will become your reality. There are billions of realities going on right now as you read this entry. *Everyone* has a unique perspective on the world and it is an absolute choice as to which lens you view it from.

Just because you believed something yesterday, does not mean you must hold onto that belief. Especially when these beliefs do not serve us but most often sink us. You are absolutely, positively, 110% capable of shifting your focus from the lens that destroys to the lens that creates life. It is always up to you.

I know there are those who will start spouting off about all the proof in your life that says it sucks and then you die. If you are in this camp, you certainly can expect just that to arrive at your doorstep on a regular basis. This is because *you* are the creator. You bring to yourself that which you think on, focus on, constantly complain about and then, the actions you perform with this low energy, will return to you in various forms and circumstances. If you want to see positive change, *you* must become the change.

Changing your perspective is a lifelong practice of growth. It includes leaving behind old, worn out habitual mind states, attitudes and beliefs. You must become detached from the past, live in the present, with a positive, faith filled belief in your future. You must begin speaking and acting on this intention and soon, it will become you. A new you. The true you.

Burn the old skeletons of supposed failure. They are gone. Stop digging them up over and over. This only keeps you stuck in neutral or dying inside. Release negativity through positive acts and new habits. Become the super you!

Let's continue this one tomorrow.

CTA: Your focus becomes your reality. Focus on what matters.

Have a great day!

DECEMBER 5

The Power of Optimism *continued*

This one life you have, as who you are, is an amazing gift. Think of it like you're on an amazing vacation to the physical world. Here we feel solid and there's solid beauty all around us. We are in the land of paradox and seeming opposites. We get to create whatever we want with our free will. You can create an amazing life for yourself no matter what your past looked like or who your parents were.

Everyone was meant to feel like they came here for a physical vacation experience, but we all got a little, or a lot, lost.

We need to remember why we came and get back to the business at hand, creating heaven on earth. This begins with each of us feeling optimistic and alive. I can't urge you enough, as my friends, to take up this challenging path of uncovering the truth of who you are, so you can live the life you intended for yourself when you came here.

You are an eternal being, having a temporary physical experience. Don't you want to say you had a great time on earth when you go back home?

Here is a great perspective to start your new path forward: you're on an earthly vacation, and how you want to remember it is all in how you see, feel, and mentally map out your trip. You must first see it as you want it, and then hold onto that focus with detached optimism and full faith that it will come to pass. If you do this and you are determined, calm, confident and true to your new truth, you'll own your life for the first time.

CTA: Today, stay optimistic about your life. Focus on the good stuff. Literally count your blessings and take the reins of your thought life. My dear friend Dana Coletti was in my thoughts this morning and her dad was the president of The Upstate NY Chapter of The Optimists Club. She gave me a copy of their club credo, which I read on a regular basis. Google the Optimist Creed and print a copy for your bathroom mirror. Become it. You'll never look back.

Have a great day!

DECEMBER 6

The Gratitude Stone

I read about a man who lived a life of extreme poverty and tragedy when he was young. He grew up in South Africa and faced many of the horrors we see on the nightly horror show called the news. His entire family was killed in horrific ways by men who had sunken to the lowest depths of their earthly darkness. Atrocities that no one should ever know. He was the only one to survive.

He was saved by an international group of soldiers and he was allowed to move to the U.S. where he had an amazing family who took him in. Upon arriving, the only possession he carried was a stone. They asked him about this stone and why it was so important to carry such a benign object. He said his grandmother gave him this stone and he translated the meaning of it as his "Gratitude Stone."

His grandmother told him many times to be sure and always carry this in his pocket and every time he reached into it for anything, to feel this stone, grasp it for a moment, and give thanks for the many blessings he knows and will soon know. And no matter what happens, he must continue to be grateful rather than angry, bitter, or vengeful. No matter what!

He said that many times he wanted to throw this stone away for the things that happened. Many times he felt less than grateful for circumstances that occurred, but they he always heard the voice of his beloved grandmother to keep the faith despite the current circumstances, even horrible ones. He did this. He forgave those who killed his family, including the grandmother who was so steadfast in her belief. He would carry this torch for her and for himself. He knew that it was only in forgiveness that he could move on without the anger and vengeful demands of the very darkness that took the lives of his closest.

He would continue his new life in gratitude instead of a bitter mindset. This stone is still carried in his pocket to this day many years later, where he has seen amazing success, a loving new family with his own grandchildren, who now carry a stone in their pockets. He passed along love instead of hatred. He passed along forgiveness instead of being trapped and he passed along the blessing of wisdom and truth.

CTA: Today's practice is in being grateful despite your current struggle. Faith, patience, and gratitude lead to constant freedom and a beautiful, meaningful life. Give thanks often.

Have a great day!

DECEMBER 7

Sadness Offers Its Own Richness to the Soul

During times of grief we all come together to share our own, heal each other, and celebrate those who have gone home before us. This too is a time of growth for many. Our children get to see and process their own sadness.

Make sure to be an example of strength for them during these times. How you handle it will be their model. Make sure it's all about love. Let them see you cry and become vulnerable. But also show them that it's our ability to feel and identify the emotions as ok that offers the best message. It's in the healing process itself that we find the diamonds that are within the sadness.

Tears should be explained as coming from the heart, our rich storehouse of love and compassion. These are not tears to be labeled as pain forever, but as tears of loving memory and our temporary bastion of release.

Let it out. Let it all out. Feel the love and know that this temporary parting is but an illusion. That their true self, in another beautiful form, watches over all of us now as part of their continuing journey with God. You may not be able to see them with your Earthly eyes but they are indeed with you.

Talk to them and always show them that you will move onward and upward in their memory, for that is now what they want most, to see you happy and enjoying your own unique journey. Give that gift to them. Heal stronger and be more confident than you were before they left. They are now laying beauty in front of your path and wish you to keep following it. God bless.

CTA: Today, begin the shift to living in gratitude for the many gifts given and received each day. Your lesson is to see with new eyes. Your heart heals when you focus on the light. So *be* the light.

Have a great day!

DECEMBER 8

Dream Big

We all came here for a very special purpose and each of us has been given a particular talent or talents to create and live this purpose. I guarantee that it has everything to do with giving this world something it desperately needs. Your job is to move towards it if you're already not.

The practice of dreaming big and moving toward that dream is what creates happiness, purpose, and joy. It sharpens every one of our personal skills and it uncovers our talents. Ones you've known you've had and ones you never thought possible.

Your dream is a very personal desire. It is a gift from divinity and it has been given to you to build your life upon and unfold you in the process. This is the power of dreaming and doing big things. The bigger the dream, the more you'll realize that you cannot accomplish it without help from within and above (same thing). This puts you into the perfect place for co-creating your dream with spirit energy, the highest and fastest path to your goals and dreams.

Working as one, in alignment with the energy of creation will bring forth more great circumstances, people, travel, fun, and excitement than you ever thought you'd experience. This higher level of dream catching is what life is meant to be like. It says that your spirit is in the driver seat and the ego has no place in your life's path or your life's work.

Your dream is your purpose and your purpose is your dream. Moving toward this dream will bring new clarity and guidance to your life. Wisdom is gained and helping others realize their dreams will be part and parcel to this wonderful unfolding of creativity, love, and enthusiasm. Dream big, my friends. It's never too late to start.

CTA: Today, if you're not already on a path of purposeful creating, set some time aside to work on envisioning a new dream life. What would it look like? Who would be around you? If you could achieve anything, what would it be? Because you can achieve anything. Just start in the direction of that big vision and never look back. Never give up and keep the faith that you never create alone. Stay in the higher vibrations and watch it all come to pass. Just do it!

Have a great day!

DECEMBER 9

Selflessness

Selflessness is the art of humble service. It is the very energy of pure giving. Giving without expectations of any kind.

Selflessness is not giving your power away in negative servitude. Being selfless is a true power of your spirit. It comes from a place in the heart that says, we are all connected, how may I serve?

Selflessness comes from a confident inner knowing, not a fearful place that says you must serve in order to be accepted, approved of or under the thumb of another. That would be giving your power away.

The voice of selflessness gives deference to another just for the sheer joy of giving, lifting another, or playing a part in a larger vision of goodness in some way. This is true power. Being selfless means dropping your ego and putting others first, because you know how blessed *you* already are. You understand that it is in giving that you are also receiving. You know that great feeling you get when you've given from your heart. You immediately feel the reflective energy of this gift of love. It gets no better than that. You get a glimpse at your true nature and a taste of your real home.

The ego, on the other hand, knows nothing about being selfless. The ego wants to gain in some way by its actions. Your spirit only wishes to spread the wealth. The ego wants to be first, needs to win and conquer. The ego tells you you're separate from everyone and you'd better get yours first.

Let's continue this one tomorrow.

CTA: The spirit brings the very best to you when you give your best to others. Always remember that.

Have a great day!

DECEMBER 10

Selflessness *continued*

Loving yourself completely, with your supposed flaws and all, is the only way to know your true power. Once you own this power, you will always feel confident in giving it away freely, because it's eternal. You're eternal. This power never runs out.

Giving your very best to yourself certainly includes beautiful surroundings and quality things, but it's all about loving and accepting yourself just as you are right now. Yes, you are on the path to becoming your best self, but that will be a much faster process when you begin with self-love. Give yourself your best and it will overflow into your every relationship.

A big part of giving yourself your best is your ability to recognize yourself as a miraculous piece of the whole. You are an incredible being who can accomplish anything. Always treat yourself as such. Not arrogantly, but confident in this truth. Once you begin to really feel this as your truth, selflessness will just be a natural aspect of your everyday life.

CTA: Today, practice giving from the heart. No return favors are needed. Give just for the sake of giving. Feel the difference and say hello to your true self.

Have a great day!

DECEMBER 11

True Prosperity

If you want prosperity to enter your life you must help others prosper. How do you do this? There are many ways. We can give our time, our talents, our money, and our connections to others.

I love connecting friends with other friends with the intention of both parties prospering from their meeting. If you know two friends that would connect well, make a call to both and give them the scoop on each other. Tell them why you think they should meet. It could be romance, business, creation of something in a similar vein of passion, or to help a friend get hired for a new career. When we pay it forward for all the blessings that have been brought to us in a similar fashion, we all rise higher.

CTA: So today's practice is about giving for the sake of bringing prosperity into another's life. When this becomes your natural thought pattern, you too will see and feel prosperity fill your heart, mind, and life. This is how you become truly wealthy. The outside experience always shows up in accordance with what and who you are inside.

Have a great day my friends!

DECEMBER 12

Grooves

Since birth, we have all been sponges of this amazing journey we call, the human experience. We collect and download into our permanent vault, all of our thoughts, speech, actions, and outward experiences. Too many to remember, but they are *all* there in this vault. How we choose to sort and store our life's data will build many grooves in our minds. These grooves become our own unique perceptions about people, places, things, groups, and life as a whole.

So often in life we create a groove for each individual in our lives. They tend to be a mix of both positive and negative, but you have one for everyone. Too many times we have judged someone in our lives as less than us, more than us, worthy or unworthy of our love. We keep these people trapped in these grooves without ever giving our perceptions a second look. We also keep deep grooves about ourselves and hold these same negative judgments about ourselves in their own special grooves. Examining these grooves to see if it is indeed 100% true, or just an old, dug in judgment, is your path to freeing your mind, body, and soul from the negative grooves that destroy lives.

We shut ourselves off to infinite possibilities when we fail to constantly bear witness to our grooves and the judgments that lie within them. We live a very limiting life this way.

The only way to fill in these old grooves and clear out the storage house of negative thoughts and emotions is to shine the light of truth into each of our most challenging grooves.

I want you to think for a minute about that challenging person in your life. What is in your groove for them? Hatred, envy, inferiority, an old grudge or misperception? How do you describe the info held in their vault? Is it still true? Is it possible to be grateful for their role in any part of your life? Can you fill in that groove with a more understanding view? Forgive perhaps? My friends, the only way to release old hurts, traumas, judgments, and negative grooves is love.

Let's continue this one tomorrow.

CTA: I want you to think for a minute about that challenging person in your life. What is in your groove for them? Hatred, envy, inferiority, an old grudge or misperception? How do you describe the info held in their vault? Is it still true? Is it possible to be grateful for their role in any part of your life? Can you fill in that groove with a more understanding view? Forgive perhaps? My friends, the only way to release old hurts, traumas, judgments, and negative grooves is love.

Have a great day!

DECEMBER 13

Grooves *continued*

Love is the fastest and highest healing energy there is. When you decide to visit and indulge in your well-worn negative grooves, you betray yourself. Your job is not to constantly relive the stories contained in your grooves, but to examine them, forgive them, and release them. Give them up for the higher purpose of self-healing.

That story you're telling yourself right now about how unworthy you are to have a great life or seek your dream, or even have goodness constantly flowing into your life, is a lie. It's in a deep groove you've nurtured and grown, because you decided to believe the lies. Holding onto the past and constantly continuing to judge yourself in the present is the poison that feeds these grooves. Abandon this practice immediately. You have the choice in every moment as to which side of your dual nature you feed.

We also create grooves about those we've lost. Deciding to constantly fill their groove with pain and suffering instead of love and gratitude for their part in our lives. You must decide on love as your constant groove filler if you ever expect to create a life of inner peace and happiness. Always remember that your lost loved one wants love and happiness to be their only groove within you. They want you to know that they are a constant living presence in your life, even though we do not have the eyes to see them while we are here. They want only for your happiness. They are whispering to you to fill your suffering groove with a knowing. The knowing that you will be together again for certain and this is merely a temporary illusion of separation. This truth you must use to fill this groove.

Fill the suffering with meaning. Do them the honor of healing, instead of suffering in their memory. Talk to them. They hear you just fine. If you listen with a still soul, you will hear and feel them telling you it's ok to heal. Move forward and live your life. Be good to yourself and keep their memory in good stead by you rising from your old groove to a higher place of faith. Faith that we are all eternal in this universal dance. Healing comes from choosing light over darkness. Giving is your way out of this groove. Give love to yourself and others as your new life's practice and your heart will mend. You will then be a healer for others.

CTA: Today, begin to examine all your old grooves for validity. Release the unnecessary negative vault of all its belongings. Then fill it up intentionally with the good stuff. Forgive, apologize, release, and move forward. This is how you stay in the flow of who you really are, the loving, eternal traveler.

Have a great day!

DECEMBER 14

Acts of Kindness

We've all heard about and performed random acts of kindness. This practice is not only life-giving for both parties involved, but it brings your personal energy or vibration to a much higher level. This is your path to higher awareness and a great life experience.

Raising our personal energy field is done through daily practice. First in our thoughts, then in our speech, actions, and deeds. When you begin to awaken to your true self, acts of kindness will no longer be random in your life. In fact, kindness just becomes your way. Kindness is who you really are. You have the power to choose the energy of kindness as your daily calling card.

Intentionally choosing to be kind to yourself *first* is the bedrock on which you create this beautiful new path forward.

Being kind to yourself always involves forgiveness. Forgiveness for yourself and others for past transgressions is the first and highest priority. Letting go of these old, worn out stories, judgments, and grudges *frees you*! You need to be free of the garbage you hold into, in order to let in the light.

Clearing yourself of old poisonous thoughts and beliefs is like clearing the clouds to behold the sun. It's how you rise. Think of it like cutting heavy sandbags from your hot air balloon. The more you cut, the higher you rise. Only you can cut the sandbags. It's done by consciously choosing to forgive and let go.

Once you decide to let go in order to rise, you will need to fertilize this decision with daily acts.

Let's continue this one tomorrow.

CTA: In order to show kindness to others, you must first practice being kind to yourself.

Have a great day!

DECEMBER 15

Acts of Kindness *continued*

There are myriad positive acts you can choose from, but here are the big five:

1) Kindness: choosing to be kind over your need to be right.

2) Forgiveness: knowing that we all have internal battles with our own egos, we can understand our connectedness and need for forgiveness. We have all been asleep. Waking each other up takes constant forgiveness. For yourself as well.

3) Non-judgment: there are no accidents in life. Everyone and everything has a purpose and a meaning for us. If it shows up in your life, it's been attracted by you or given to you. There's a gift inside all your circumstances. It's always for your higher good, even if it comes in a crappy wrapper. Don't judge it. It's for you. Look for the deeper meaning and message. It's there.

4) Acceptance: accept everything as if you've chosen it. This keeps your energy clear to let in the hidden beauty or message. Acceptance is your tool for non-judgment. Acceptance keeps you free. You don't have to like what happens, but accepting it puts you into your higher power, in order to effectively deal with anything. Fighting against what is, only keeps you trapped in drama and suffering. Always choose to stay in your true power. Here is where answers come, meaning is found and inner peace is your natural home.

5) Gratitude: we all have been given a golden vacation ticket to the physical world. It's a very temporary vacation really. That's why it's so important to enjoy the ride and bring our best selves to this party. Being in a state of gratitude for all that we are able to freely choose to do and become while we are here, is the magic wand to staying in your most powerful, positive energy state. Say a consistent thank you during your day for things that you learn, people you meet, friendships, family, safety, and the constant flow of blessings that are bestowed upon you. You have much to be grateful for. We must make a daily practice of giving thanks. This keeps you in the

flow of all goodness. Health, wealth and happiness all come from being in this high energetic state.

CTA: Today, practice the Big Five. Choosing to live in this higher realm of energy will soon seem the most natural to you, because it is you. A daily diet of the Big Five will lead to a life of wonder. Go get it! You are it.

Have a great day!

DECEMBER 16

Being in Balance

Living in harmony with your true spiritual nature is what being balanced is all about.

We as humans are finely tuned instruments. We must think and treat ourselves this as such, or we become unbalanced.

We *all* know what it feels like to be out of balance. We call it things like depression, anxiety, constant sadness, or lethargy. Lack of drive, passion, will, determination, and all the other feelings of our darker, lower nature.

All this means, my friends, is that your energetic scale is tipped too much in one direction. The one most of us live in way too often.

We have the power to tip and balance our own scale. Yes, you will need to dig deep to do it, and it will be challenging, but it's the only way to take full charge of your own life. One you learn how to balance your own scale, you have found the key. The key to the inner peace you search for. The key to lasting happiness and fulfillment. The key to a great life.

Being in balance means that you now understand that the darkness in all of us is meant for contrast. It's not a path to keep following or get trapped within.

You've most likely become very familiar with your lower energies by now. You can easily recognize them. They are the ones that don't "feel" good. But within the "knowing " of these energies is the seed of change.

Let's continue this one tomorrow.

CTA: Your task is to practice what is called "transmutation." It is the re-shaping of the negative into its counterpart, or positive nature. For example, from fear to love, from self-conscious to self-confident. From anger to acceptance, forgiveness, and understanding. Get the picture? Knowing the darkness allows you to know the light. But now, it's your time to seek your light.

Have a great day!

DECEMBER 17

Being in Balance *continued*

Your light is where you want to live, full time. Your light guides you to all right paths. It shows you the way into the minds and hearts of all. Your light speaks and understands truth, because that's what light is and what light does.

Conversely, your darkness speaks lies to you and about you and others. Darkness is the inner and outer critic. It's the judge who loves to convict, compete, constrict, and control. It either dominates over others or it's fearful voice causes you to be dominated by others. You my friend are none of these in truth. You've decided (unwittingly) to become this side of your scale too often. Now it's just habits you must replace.

Picture yourself in a comfortable raft, peacefully floating down a beautiful stream. A sunny day, the sound of birds all around you. No one else around, just you. Now, on either side of this beautiful stream are rocky, jagged shores. These rocks can bust your raft up pretty good if you aren't aware of how you're steering your raft. You need to be very responsible with your rudder. You must pay attention and be a confident, peaceful captain. Self-assured, steady, and going with the natural flow of the stream.

Let's continue this one tomorrow.

CTA: Go with the flow and practice balancing your thoughts.

Have a great day!

DECEMBER 18

Being in Balance *continued*

You know when you are securely in the captain's seat. You're feeling your way through calm or treacherous waters, so as not to trash your raft on the rocks. You use the experiences of the rocks as a warning to keep using your light to steer.

In life, we tend to try to either over-control our raft, or we are fearful of taking control of our own raft. Both lead to hitting the rocks. You must relax more. You must steer more intentionally, but allow the flow of the stream to carry you, without interference.

Accepting the present moments as they are and letting your light guide you. You must steer with kindness. Steer with enthusiasm. Steer with love, joy, happiness, and conscious harmony.

When we have our hand on the steady rudder, we can expect a much more beautiful ride. And when we happen to experience the rocks, we know to continue doing our very best to use our light to get back to the middle of the stream. Back in balance.

CTA: Today, practice your balancing act. When the darkness wants to grab the rudder, toss those thoughts overboard and turn on your light. Be guided, stay in the flow of your true, peaceful, loving nature.

Have a great day!

DECEMBER 19

Being too Rigid

Recognizing your normal pattern of energy will always show you the reasons for your great results, or the less than desirable ones. It's all about your energy.

When we are rigid, self-conscious, judgmental, or fearful, we have constricted energy. We are pinching off the flow of natural goodness that is always attempting to enter our lives.

You are the very instrument that has control of this faucet. You have always possessed the free will to expand your instrument, or plug it up with the blockage of negative energy. It's a choice. You may not have known this.

If you were raised in a rigid household, you've inherited some of this energy as part of your makeup. Be brave enough to look inside. Feel and see your current patterns. Shed the light of love and truth upon them. Once you take this responsible step, the door to positive change has been opened. Never be afraid to walk through. It's the path to your freedom, inner peace, and prosperity.

Let's continue this one tomorrow.

CTA: Allow yourself to break free from negative patterns. Create new patterns using love and peace as your template.

Have a great day!

DECEMBER 20

Being too Rigid *continued*

Anger, self-judgment, judgment of others, creating fearful scenarios in your head or outwardly spoken, constant complaining, joining in on drama, jealousy, doubting yourself, greed, trying to control others, and all the other lower energy choices are blocking your flow. These you must replace. These are constricting your natural flow of the good stuff that is trying to get to you. Time to let go of being rigid.

When you begin the worthy journey of discovering your true power, the field of energy that emanates from you will shift. You feel better because you're thinking better, choosing better and releasing the old pattern. You'll begin to attract better people, better circumstances and amazing opportunities for continued growth. Go with it! If it makes you uncomfortable and challenges your old thinking, that must become your new signal to continue moving forward! Never go back! Positive change is always on the other side of these doors. Always choose to break through instead of retreating to your old negative cocoon of comfort! Your new flow will begin to guide you. Trust it. The new flow is truth, the real you. You can't get it wrong when you're in the flow.

CTA: Today, if you feel stuck, rigid, constricted, or trapped in some self-created negative scenario of the mind, do your best to look inside. Don't judge, just look. Ask yourself if this energy will serve you in any positive way. Chances are that you need to release it. Take a walk, have some fun, laugh with a friend on purpose. Break up the clouds by replacing them with the sun that is you. There's always a higher choice to being rigid. Be loose, be expansive and let in the flow.

Have a great day!

DECEMBER 21

That Challenging Person

That person who challenges you most is your best teacher. You have triggers that are easily pulled by them because they are somehow familiar to you. There's something you must let go of. Could be overreaction, bossiness, addiction to continuing a drama, or being easily offended. There's a knot that must be untied. You must do it.

You must choose to change your response in the very moment you are tempted to go into your usual role with this teacher. Breathe and say to yourself, "not this time. Today I will start my new way." "I no longer let others steal my joy."

This is a practice in releasing old patterns and drama from your life. You'll find that if you stop the low engagement and give up telling the story afterward, you'll bring more peace to your life. You must always become the change you wish to see in your life. Takes time and effort, but it's the noble path.

CTA: Today, become more like the reed rather than the oak when challenged. Bend instead of break. Give way to the bad behavior of others and let it go through you instead of absorbing it and becoming your own version of it. Stay free, my friend.

Have a great day!

DECEMBER 22

The Power of Writing Your Intentions

The power we have as humans to direct our own path and realize our goals and dreams is the very stuff that makes our temporary journey so worthwhile and fulfilling. This all starts by you being intentional about it.

Although the gift of hindsight tells me I was always intended to be right where I am in my journey, my intentional journey only really began in 2006, when I made the life-changing choice to write down what I wanted the rest of my life to look like.

At the time, my partners Jimmy, Gene, and I were going full steam, trying to build our business through the blood, sweat, and tears of perseverance, determination, and striving. It was a crucial part of all of our journeys, but then, we as a group took a turn. A great turn. The turn of higher knowledge and understanding.

I now know that it was more of a shift in our conscious understanding of how the flow of life really works to our advantage when we work with it and direct our own thoughts, intentions and energies in the correct way.

Part of this shift requires you to write down a list of your biggest life goals or intentions. I've decided to share my list from 2006. I imagine they would be very similar to many of your own desires, so feel free to use this as a model when you write your own down.

It went like this:

1) I intend to expand and grow continually, internally, and externally by uncovering my true, unlimited self and living from this higher energy.

2) I intend to create new and exciting relationships wherever I go. These will be quality relationships based on truth. These relationships will help me to expand and help others to expand. I will prosper others and it is sure to return to me.

3) I intend to live life to the fullest and give my best self in all my experiences.

4) I intend to increase the flow of wealth and prosperity into my life and the lives of those around me.

5) I intend to spread peace, love, joy, happiness, laughter, prosperity, praise, gratitude, and generosity as my personal energy.

6) I intend to spread wisdom and truth to help others realize their own true power.

So, there you have it. Six intentions that culminate as your personal mission. Once you write them down, put this list where you will see it every day. Live by it. Speak from it; give from it, every day. Your life course will have been charted and you are on your way to your best life possible.

So, eight years after writing these six simple, but powerful life intentions, I can gratefully report that this practice has given us an amazing life. We are living our dreams come true everyday and we are aware and truly grateful for all of it. Even the stuff that first came in an ugly wrapper.

CTA: Today, chart your own course. It is inside of your DNA. Bring it forth, write it down, and just follow your own path.

Have a great day!

DECEMBER 23

Too Serious?

Are you too serious or rigid in your energy? Is it your way or the highway? The more you attempt to control everything and everyone in your life, the more you will find yourself disappointed.

First, you'll judge others as less than you for not seeing it your way or living up to your high standards. Yes, you feel that you are giving useful information, tried and true methods, and all the rest of the good stuff. The issue is *how* you are doing it. Your energy is repelling and rigid rather than light and flowing. One says "do it or see it my way or you're stupid" and the other way says, "this is the best way I've found and take it for what it's worth. Hope it helps you."

Feel the difference in the energy of those two ways? Your lighter, higher energies are what always keep you on a smoother road. The lower, heavier ones are the ones that cause your suffering. Be open, give light. There's a very big difference in the results of these two approaches. Just keep using the high road in your thoughts, spoken word and your body language. Seek to raise others rather than judge them. You do this by raising them on the inside as they raise themselves from your kindness and truthful motive.

CTA: Today, try on a lighter approach in all things. Choose to use a lighter tone, a more cheerful countenance, and eye contact that says, "I come in peace." You'll find the world smiling back at you. You've found the new way.

Have a great day!

DECEMBER 24

More on Passion

Always know that if you love to do something, you'll always want to give it your all. You'd stay up later to do it and you'd get up earlier to go after it. You feel better, you give better, and your life naturally attracts more of what you're feeling. It's the Law of Attraction in action. You attract what you are, your vibe.

Having a vibe that is in harmony with your passion is the fastest, best and the long lasting way to real success. Your only limitation is your own imagination. There are people out there living extraordinary lives because they love giving their passion as their life's work. Everything they do has their love energy attached and embedded in it. It naturally attracts people to it and to you. Give your best and the best returns to you.

CTA: Today, if you are not passionate about much, no worries. Finding your passion is part of the journey. Try new things. Ask yourself the questions listed above and just *start*! Go take a class. Get on the computer and see what others are doing in your area of interest and just keep moving forward. Never stop.

Keep turning over stones until you feel great when you think of this new thing. That's your clue! Follow it and the rest will be shown to you as you keep making the decision to move forward. Never quit when a challenge arises! They are just growth hurdles you are meant to encounter and learn from. Go after life and never let life give you scraps. You are an adventurer here for a short trip! Make the most of it. Start today!

Have a great day!

DECEMBER 25

The Mirror

Life is a mirror, my friends. When you are in full-blown drama mode, go grab a mirror and see what this energy *looks* like on you. Is it what you think will bring you happiness? Better relationships? More prosperity? Laughter, joy, inner peace? *Never.* It ages you. It makes you sick and it lowers your quality of life by pinching off your true stream.

We all get stuck in the storm, but the storm and its energies are the opposite of what brings you the peaceful, happy life you say you long for. You need to use this dark energy simply as a truth detector, not as a means forward. You are the creator of your dream. You need to let go of your habit of creating your life with your lower energies.

CTA: Today begins your shift from the unnecessary choices you used to make, to the higher choices that are the real you. You've been handed a bill of goods that you've never questioned. Always question the validity of your thoughts and consistently ask yourself, "If I use this tone, or these words, or this assumption as absolute truth, will it bring a desired energy or result?" Or will it cause expansion of drama or suffering? This one question, given with some space, will change your life. Ask it consistently. Give love instead.

Have a great day!

DECEMBER 26

Going for It

You will be growing and learning many new things when you go for your dreams. You'll attain new talents that you never knew you had, and you will learn that kicking the butt of seeming obstacles is part of the fun. Never let anyone tell you that you can't. And never listen to your inner liar (which we all possess) tell you that you can't. It's a lie.

Chasing your dreams is the ultimate life experience. It's fun, it's exciting, it's challenging, it's expansive and it's the very pleasure of God to give you what you desire. As long as your path is one that aligns with the choices, thoughts, and actions of your best self. Not your ego.

CTA: Today, align yourself with inner truth. Kindness, compassion, generosity, faith, determination, and persistence are all examples of your inner truth and higher self. When you use these, you cannot fail. And remember to use your power phrases of "I can and I will" and "it will all come together." When you're in this flow, you can't get it wrong.

Have a great day!

DECEMBER 27

Let it Be

Too many times, we interfere with our own path. We try to control circumstances, people, and outcomes on our own, without ever knowing it can be a much easier and smoother process.

Another great thought to release your tight grip on how you think things should go, is to say to yourself, "it is what it is, and I trust that the best and highest good for me will arrive when I give up my need to control my outcome." I'm not saying you should just lie in bed while the world takes care of your problems. I'm saying to be your very best, calm, confident, trusting self through the process and allow everything to take shape without getting amped up, anxious or highly emotional.

Spiritual surrender is all about your belief that you are watched over, protected and lead to a better way. Trust, Faith, Hope. These are the rocks we hold onto during the seeming storms that come our way. Let go and let God. This is the gift of surrender.

CTA: Today, whatever the situation is that you've been pining over, let it be. Take a breath and give this problem the day off. Give God the entire load and ask for his solution. Let it come. It will. Be patient and trust in the soon to arrive path forward. It can come in many ways. Usually in ways such as an unexpected phone call, a new person entering the picture, information you've been needing, or the wisdom of someone close to you. It will come.

Let go, my friends, it will all come into view. Your job during this time will be to simply be still inside, as you look for the cues to move in a particular direction. This is called following your heart mind instead of your human mind. One brings healing, while the other keeps you in the dark. Just listen. Just surrender. The way forward will be made clear to you.

Have a great day!

DECEMBER 28

The Power of Faith

Faith must be verbalized within and without in order to be in harmony with its benevolent energy. Say "thank you for bringing me what's best for my highest good," instead of, "please make this particular outcome happen."

The divine source that brought you here and lives within us all, knows exactly what you like, but more importantly, what you need for your true mission here. Trust it.

When you don't continuously judge what comes, and you simply trust that it's there "for you , in order for you to bring your best "to it", the very best will come to you. Not always on your timeline, but you will recognize the many gifts as they come. These gifts will come forth as new wisdom and understanding, a deeper place of peace from your patience and presence, new and important people that are meant to bring you forward and upward. Because your heart has been cracked open, there is a sacred opportunity to let in new levels of light and faith itself.

In this new stillness, you will be able to see with higher eyes how blessed you truly are, and how God brings us healing through the love that converges around us in our time of need.

If you stay in fear, bitterness, anger, guilt and the rest of the ego's recipe for continued depression, you will miss these gifts. They will look dull to you, when in fact they are your light to follow. Be strong, move forward. Things will be different, but remember that we are in the dimension of constant change. You must rely on the light within you to guide you, for that light is your power to thrive and grow through every change.

CTA: Today, speak to your faith, that no matter what changes take place, you will make a new decision not to react like so many times before. Choose to stand taller as if all the answers you need are coming forth from your willingness to stay calm and listen for the right answer. The ego's voice is usually the first and the loudest. Move past that and listen. You will discover that a new power has entered your life. This power you must grow with daily, loving intention. It never lets you down, it only brings you up.

Have a great day!

DECEMBER 29

Becoming the Light

As you begin to shed more and more of the old you, you will naturally be adding more light to your life from within. You will begin to radiate a new vibe.

Yes, the circumstances of your life will improve. New and exciting relationships will appear. Prosperity, wealth, and health are also part and parcel. But the real treasure is the inner peace. Peace in knowing that you are finally in alignment with who you were meant to be. It's all good from this place. Even challenges and loss have a deeper and higher meaning. It's just a higher, more eternal view of it all. It is yours for the asking.

CTA: Today, begin or continue your intentional rise! Take your journey one day at a time. Then break it down to the moments of your day. It's about being aware and fully present in these moments that give meaning to our choices, and purposeful direction in our lives. *You* create your entire life with your moment-to-moment choices. Make sure it is *all* about choosing to give your very best. Love is your best.

Have a great day!

DECEMBER 30

What You Give

Give love, forgiveness, kindness, laughter, joy, and happiness and that is what you can expect to receive from others. It never fails. The key is to first give yourself these gifts, then work on becoming them. This will be your dominant energy field and it draws all goodness into your life. Always remember that life is like a mirror. Be brave enough to look into it and strong enough to wipe away the streaks that never serve you. You are of the highest order! Recognize it, believe it, and live it. It is truth.

CTA: Today be the light of truth and spread your beautiful vibe.

Have a great day!

DECEMBER 31

Thank You

It is with deep, heartfelt gratitude that I say thank you, my fellow awakening soul. By picking up this book every day and immersing yourself in truth, I know you have felt the loving expansion within. I hope these words have brought you comfort in turbulent times, love when you had none to give yourself, and a new light to follow forward. This is how I, too, was guided in my own awakening.

The truthful words of awakened souls is a language we all understand at the deepest levels, for it is the eternal language, the one that heals you and those you give it to. It is only through our intentional choice to be in the flow of all light that we will see and live our true, God-given potential.

I have been moved to give these words to you as part of my purpose. I love to share the treasure that I have been given, for it continues to be the vehicle for my own growth. This purpose is all of ours: to awaken to our inner light and power and then extend it outward in all we say and do. I ask that you pass along the gifts you have been given.

You my friend have much to offer, never doubt that. Let these 366 daily truths of life be part of you and how you now approach life. Do not attempt to use this as a how-to book but rather, read and re-read a page every day and simply use the uplifted energy it brings forth as your vehicle for that day. Give away this beautiful light in your own unique way.

This energy will take you farther than you can imagine, for it is who you really are under all the earthly disguises. You are love itself. Never give up, just keep growing and giving your very best. Beauty, love, and prosperity will land at your doorstep with little effort. With much love from a friend, thank you again for deciding to rise. May God bless your new path all the way back home to Him. More to come.

Your Friend,

Marty